The title says it all. Eric Weiss is going for the gold. I'm watching and believing.

—Michael Murphy
Cofounder of Esalen Institute
Author of *The Future of the Body*

In this bold work of philosophy, Eric Weiss offers a stunning and original vision of our universe, a vision rooted in the empirical and evolutionary sciences, but a vision that is free from the shackles of the reductionist, materialist worldview so pervasive among contemporary scientists. Beginning with the overall orientation of the mathematician-philosopher Alfred North Whitehead, Weiss expands and deepens the Whiteheadian framework until he arrives at a comprehensive metaphysics, one that encompasses matter, energy, time, space, life, death, life-after-death, reincarnation, mystical experience, and the interpenetration of the physical and transphysical worlds. For anyone interested in the enormously fertile synergy taking place between contemporary science and the esoteric and mystical traditions, there is no better place to begin than with *The Long Trajectory*.

—Brian Thomas Swimme, Ph.D.
Professor of Cosmology
California Institute of Integral Studies
Author of *The Universe Story* and *The Hidden Heart of the Cosmos*

As I read Eric Weiss' *The Long Trajectory*, I am often lifted beyond understanding into ecstasy. Weiss articulates with extraordinary clarity and sensitivity the cosmological vision of the universe as the involution and subsequent evolution of the Divine, bringing modern and postmodern science, the metaphysics of Alfred North Whitehead, and the cosmological vision of Sri Aurobindo into a new synthesis. Integrating the physical, transphysical, and spiritual dimensions, this is a metaphysical model that heals the past and opens the door to a new future for humanity.

—Christopher M. Bache, Ph.D.
Professor of Philosophy and Religious Studies
Youngstown State University
Author of *Dark Night, Early Dawn*

T0367538

The Long Trajectory is a compelling tour-de-force by a philosopher who has seen deeply into the nature of reality. Dr. Eric Weiss offers a rigorous and detailed metaphysical worldview that enables us to understand and explain "anomalous" phenomena—reported throughout history and across cultures—such as telepathy, remote viewing, out-of-body experiences, and, perhaps most important of all, the survival of consciousness after death. It has the hallmarks of a landmark book that could shift the axis of world thought—just as Copernicus, Darwin, and Freud did when they pushed the boundaries of contemporary knowledge and scholarship. *The Long Trajectory* could be the "next big thing"—a book so profound in perspective and persuasive in presentation that history will mark it as a turning point in humanity's perception of ourselves and our place in the grand scheme of the cosmos.

—Christian de Quincey, Ph.D.
Professor of Philosophy and Consciousness Studies
John F. Kennedy University
Author of *Radical Nature* and *Radical Knowing*

What a pleasure to follow the reflections of a deeply thoughtful philosopher as he combines science, philosophy, and parapsychology in the exploration of nothing less than the BIG picture of the human soul's place in the cosmos. Eric Weiss has given us a metaphysical page-turner.

—Allan Combs, Ph.D.
Professor of Transformative Studies
California Institute of Integral Studies
Author of *Consciousness Explained Better*

THE LONG TRAJECTORY

The Metaphysics of Reincarnation and Life after Death

Dr. Eric M. Weiss

iUniverse, Inc.
Bloomington

The Long Trajectory
The Metaphysics of Reincarnation and Life after Death

Copyright © 2012 by Dr. Eric M. Weiss

All rights reserved. No part of this book may be used or reproduced by any means, graphic, electronic, or mechanical, including photocopying, recording, taping or by any information storage retrieval system without the written permission of the publisher except in the case of brief quotations embodied in critical articles and reviews.

iUniverse books may be ordered through booksellers or by contacting:

iUniverse
1663 Liberty Drive
Bloomington, IN 47403
www.iuniverse.com
1-800-Authors (1-800-288-4677)

Because of the dynamic nature of the Internet, any web addresses or links contained in this book may have changed since publication and may no longer be valid. The views expressed in this work are solely those of the author and do not necessarily reflect the views of the publisher, and the publisher hereby disclaims any responsibility for them.

Any people depicted in stock imagery provided by Thinkstock are models, and such images are being used for illustrative purposes only.

Certain stock imagery © Thinkstock.

ISBN: 978-1-4620-6964-4 (sc)
ISBN: 978-1-4620-6963-7 (e)

Library of Congress Control Number: 2011962699

Printed in the United States of America

iUniverse rev. date: 9/4/2012

Dedication

This book is dedicated to the one infinite, eternal Divine Being that each of us is, and in whom all of us live, move, and have our being.

May the iron cage of the dark ages be dissolved.
May the light of the Divine shine on and through human beings.
May the biosphere on Earth, and all the realms of the universe,
be illuminated by that light.
May all beings find their way home.
May all beings enjoy eternal bliss.

Acknowledgments

I would like to acknowledge Michael Murphy; the Esalen Center for Theory and Research; John Cleese and Alice Cleese; and Sonia and Stuart Sapadin for the wonderful inspiration and the generous support that made this book possible. I also want to acknowledge the valuable editing that this book received from Dr. Christian de Quincey, whose help in clarifying both the ideas and their expression was invaluable. I also want to acknowledge Kat Snow for her invaluable help in preparing the manuscript. This book was influenced by many discussions, among which my conversations with Brian Swimme, Sean Kelly, Christian de Quincey, Paul Bogle, Victor Goulet, and Stuart Sapadin stand out as particularly significant.

Contents

Part One

Introduction

One of the most important questions we can talk about as scientists, philosophers, or laypeople is what happens to us after our bodies die. Who among us has not at some time wondered, *what happens to me when I die? What happens to the people I love when they die and cease to function in my waking life? Where do they go? Where do we go? What happens?*

Indeed, questions such as these, and the answers we provide, are immensely important to the structure of our civilization. It is clear to me that whatever we believe about what happens to our sense of self or personhood at the end of our days strongly affects our outlook on life. It determines our sense of ethics and profoundly affects our values.

For example, if we believe that at death everything about us is extinguished, we are likely to conclude that life is nothing but an opportunity to gratify our emotional, intellectual, and physical needs during the short span we are alive. That belief about life and the ethic it fosters feeds the tide of consumerism that dominates and afflicts modern civilization.

If, on the other hand, we do survive the death of our bodies, and further, if we return in a sequence of reincarnations that is somehow part of the evolution of the universe, then our whole attitude toward ourselves and life would be different. The question of our destiny, the meaning of our existence, and our ethical stance would take into account broad considerations about our place in the cosmos and the long-term impacts of how we choose to live.

Let me give some examples. Suppose, as a society, we were to confirm the fact that people's personalities survive bodily death, and suppose we were to find a way to regularly communicate with people who have died:

- How would that affect our sense of identity, our familial obligations, or our relationships with the living?
- What would that do to our secrecy laws? Could people be expected to keep state or financial secrets after they died?
- What would that do to our sense of privacy? What if we discovered that the deceased could eavesdrop on our conversations?
- What would this do to our large religious institutions with their conflicting ideas about the afterlife?
- What would that do to our property laws? Could dead people still own property? Who would have the rights to dispose of the estate?

From these few examples you can get a sense of how widespread the consequences would be if we came to know that the personality survives bodily death, and if we found a way to be in reliable contact with the deceased. Make no mistake: this is a profound issue.

This book began as a series of lectures organized and sponsored by the Esalen Center for Theory and Research, founded by independent scholar Michael Murphy, author of *The Future of the Body*. Mike likes to convene groups of passionate and competent scholars to discuss issues and themes that are not being addressed anywhere in academia. One of these ongoing conferences—begun in 1998—focuses on the topic of reincarnation and life after death.

The core members of this conference are a group of University of Virginia scientists who, since 1968, have been studying the evidence for reincarnation and the question of whether and in what way consciousness survives death. Their research continues a long scientific tradition going back to William James and Frederic Myers in the 19th century. Since that time, a vast body of hard scientific evidence has been collected that strongly suggests we do not die with the death of our bodies, and that makes a powerful case for reincarnation.

Nevertheless, the topic is not being formally considered, as far as we know, in any serious academic institution in the United States, or in any country of the world! It seems to us that our Esalen group is the only formal group in academia working to understand the "long trajectory" of human destiny—in other words, to fathom the profound nature of the human life cycle and the full facts of life and death.

Our team of scientists and other scholars began research nearly a decade ago with a commitment to evaluating, organizing, and documenting robust scientific evidence that supports the hypotheses of life after death and reincarnation. We regard the resulting book, *Irreducible Mind: Toward a Psychology for the Twenty-First Century*[1] as a landmark demonstration that the human personality is more than the body, and a powerful argument that the human personality survives bodily death.

Having assembled a formidable body of evidence, our next task is to ask, "If survival and reincarnation are actual facts, how can we make sense of this?"

In the absence of a theory of some kind, it is difficult to accept the facts. It is often the case that people will reject data that don't fit into the categories through which they customarily interpret the world. It is a source of frustration and bemusement among parapsychologists that many prominent scientists reject the data of parapsychology out of hand because they believe, on the basis of their usual way of understanding things, that those data are simply "impossible." Indeed, the picture of reality in the background of much scientific research is so mechanistic and reductionist that it is almost impossible to understand the existence of consciousness itself, let alone the survival of the personality after the death of its body.

Nonetheless, the data are there to be explained. As Galileo is reported to have said after his conviction by the Inquisition, "And yet, it moves." The problem we face in academia today is similar to that faced by Galileo in his day. Many of the learned doctors at Galileo's university felt no need to look through his telescope. After all, the idea that planet had moons was simply too preposterous to be entertained. It was not facts that finally awakened the world to the power of scientific reasoning—it was Newton's articulation of a general scheme of ideas that organized and made intelligible the scattered findings of known science.

---

[1] Edward F. Kelly and Emily Williams Kelly, *Irreducible Mind*.

So we need a theory to give coherent intelligibility to the data we are amassing. Such a theory will help make the data more acceptable to the scientific community, and will open up the field to more comprehensive investigation.

A good example of the power of theory in stimulating deeper research is the development of Mendeleev's Table of Elements. A first consequence of this theory was the discovery of new elements. A later consequence of this theory was the recognition of the possibility of elements that had never before existed and the subsequent creation of those elements in the laboratory. And these are only two of the developments in chemistry inspired by this theory.

If the study of the long trajectory of human existence is to open up to scientific investigation, if it is ever to become a topic upon which many investigators can focus their attention, it will only be when the data currently available concerning survival and reincarnation, along with the associated data of parapsychological investigation, are first organized into a general picture of reality.

Whatever theory we develop to illuminate the data we are about to present, that theory, to be credible at all, will also have to comport with the scientific understanding of reality that our civilization has pieced together over the last four hundred years of sustained social effort.

In this book, I will outline a way in which such a coordination may be achieved.

Since the beginning of the scientific revolution, work on the areas covered in this book has been rare. The ideas offered here sketch out a new way to approach the understanding of the actual world. While these ideas have a lineage—they are drawn from the works of Alfred North Whitehead, Sri Aurobindo, Jean Gebser, Ernst Cassirer, and many other thinkers—they nonetheless may be unfamiliar to many of my readers. Also, those readers who know some of these authors will find their ideas used in unfamiliar ways; it requires new ideas and new language to open up this new territory.

Finally, though this book was very much inspired by my work at the Esalen Center for Theory and Research, this work is my own, and does not reflect any consensus of our group.

Preliminary Definitions

This book focuses on two ideas. First, that the personality formed during life does, in fact, survive the death of the body; and, second, that we do incarnate more than once. I will explore these two challenging and provocative ideas in four steps:

- I begin with a series of definitions in this chapter that specify just what I mean by key terms like "survival of bodily death," "transphysical worlds," and "reincarnation." I will end this chapter with a set of five propositions that capture the essence of this book.
- I then present in Chapter 1 a brief summary of the scientific evidence for the truth of these five fundamental propositions.
- In the several chapters that follow, I will discuss what the reality of our world must be if these propositions are true. I will do this by outlining a metaphysical system capable of supporting the truths of modern and postmodern science *and* the truths of parapsychology.
- Finally, I will offer an expanded vision of the human life cycle and explore what it implies for the long trajectory of human evolution.

Let us start, then, with some fundamental definitions.

Dr. Eric M. Weiss

The Physical Body

By "physical body" I mean the living body as it is experienced in waking life. I am assuming that the living body contains inorganic entities such as atoms and molecules, and that these atoms and molecules are organized (in a manner to be explored) into cells, tissues, and organs.

This definition of "physical body" is unremarkable, but I do want to emphasize that I am most emphatically *not* making the assumption that the human body can be reduced to inorganic entities and their dynamic interactions. In other words, I am not suggesting that the body is already "dead" or insentient, even when it seems alive. In working to understand survival and reincarnation, the question of what makes the physical body a living body is one to which we will have to pay considerable attention. When I refer to survival, by the personality, of bodily death, I will always mean the "physical body" in this sense. Later, I will broaden the definition of "body" to include transphysical bodies as well.

Personality

I want to propose that we define personality in terms of five different characteristics. As you review these, I invite you to check them against your own experience.

Being an Individual among Other Individuals

It is certainly possible to refer to entities who transcend or pervade the entirety of the actual world. Such beings may be referred to as divine and may, perhaps, be reasonably called "gods," but such beings are not what I have in mind when referring to a personality. A personality is, first of all, finite. It is neither omniscient nor omnipotent. It is not a god.[1]

A personality is an individual and, as such, it is a finite being. It is

[1] We can, of course, suggest that we can experience ourselves *as* "God," and that our Divinity is the essential truth of our being. This is, for example, the position of Sri Aurobindo, and one I actually tend to agree with. However, the part of us that is God must be clearly distinguished, for most purposes, from the part of us that is a finite personality. It is that finite aspect of us I am concerned with when I discuss personality survival.

not coextensive with its environment, and it exists in the presence of others. To be finite is to be an individual existing in interaction with other individuals of some type. Further, individuals in causal interaction with one another must share some coherent context in which that interaction takes place. I will express this by saying that a personality is always contextualized by a world of some type. I am, therefore, assuming that personality is a finite being playing out its existence in a coherent world of others.

Throughout this work, when I use the term "world," it does not refer to a planet in a solar system but rather to a system of individuals causally interacting in a common space and time and serving as a context for the life of personalities.

Various arguments can be advanced in favor of this idea,[2] but I am going to introduce it here as a definition. I am using myself as a paradigm of what I mean by "personality." After all, one of my deep motivations for developing the ideas in this book is to discover the destiny of my own personality after the death of my physical body. As a personality, I am a finite being. I find myself in a world full of other beings—beings like myself who keep me company, and many other beings constituting the complex context of my existence. All of these beings exercise causal effects on one another, and all share a common system of spatial and temporal relations. These entities constitute the world in which I live, move, and have my being.

If I am going to survive the death of my body in a way that is truly interesting to me, I want to survive it as a finite being in a world I can explore.

Consciousness

The word "consciousness" has been used in so many different ways that each author is now obliged to define it for himself or herself.

In this work, I propose that we define consciousness as that factor of experience by virtue of which there is feeling and free choice.

---

[2] Sri Aurobindo, for example, works out an argument that shows how individual personalities can be derived, by a process that he calls "involution," from the existence of a non-dual Absolute he calls "Brahman." See Sri Aurobindo's *The Life Divine*.

Feeling

When I say consciousness is the factor of existence that brings feeling into the actual world, I am using the word "feeling" in a sense that includes all types of sensation. When we think of a cause (especially when we are being scientific about it), we mean an event that directly precipitates another event in its immediate future.[3] For example, suppose I throw a rock hard enough at a window that the window breaks. The movement of the rock *causes* the breaking of the window. When we think of cause in this way, we assume that the rock and the window are insentient and unaware of what is happening to them. If I were to suggest that the window "felt" the rock shattering it, I would probably be accused of naïve anthropomorphism. On the other hand, suppose the rock hit me instead. In that case, I would most certainly *feel* the impact.

Why is it that we think the window feels nothing as it shatters, while I feel pain when the rock hits me? I propose that I feel because I am a conscious being. To put this simply, there can be no feeling without consciousness and no personality without feeling.

A personality is necessarily conscious and, as such, a personality feels its environing world.

Free Choice

Consciousness is also the primary factor of experience by virtue of which there is choice. (Value or aim, a factor that is discussed below, is also needed for the operation of free choice.)

Classical science was entirely deterministic and made no room in its cosmology for choice. Scientific reductionists of the classical era thought of choice as a miraculous gift from God or as a mere illusion. Quantum mechanics has, however, pushed science beyond the narrow and excessively abstract position of earlier centuries. Our predictions about the outcome of events can only be probabilistic. We can never, in principle, generate perfectly accurate predictions of anything. Beyond

---

[3] Later on, I will equate *feeling* with the idea of *efficient cause* that our educated common sense imports from classical physics. In other words, I will suggest that feeling, and by extension, consciousness, is involved in all causal interactions. For now we will stay with the customary distinction.

blind computation, something else is involved in actuality. We might just label this "blind chance," but quantum physics goes still further.

Quantum theory recognizes that the consciousness of the "observer" not only enables us to observe the outcome of experiments, but is also a *causal factor* partially conditioning the outcome of experiments.[4] Quantum theory also opens up the possibility that the consciousness of the quantum event itself might be the factor responsible for the definite results that reduce quantum probabilities to definite actualities—i.e., that "collapse the wave function."[5] This factor of existence—*consciousness*—has real effects in the physical world, but its decisions are not determined by anything in the physical world at all.[6] Consciousness is that which feels and makes choices.

This interpretation of quantum theory is also consistent with various trends of Vedic thought. For example, in the yogic psychology of the *Bhagavad Gita, purusha* is the pole of pure consciousness around which individual experience is constellated and is also the ultimate origin of all free decisions.[7]

Finally, my waking consciousness is strongly flavored by my sense that I, the conscious being that I am, make the decisions that cause my behaviors in the world. My decisions are not mere echoes of randomness. They are conscious choices, made with awareness of possible outcomes. They are also made in the context of valuation: I decide which outcome to choose based on the values my decision will realize. It is only in a context of genuine free choice that moral responsibility makes any sense at all.

While consciousness is the factor of existence that makes those choices that we call free, it can do so only under the influence of value and purpose. In fact, the difference between randomness and choice is just the presence of values that give the choice meaning. As we will see

---

[4] This effect is related to the choice of which experiment to do.

[5] This effect is related to the outcome of the experiments. For an extended discussion of the idea that each quantum event is conscious (in a primitive sort of way), see Michael Epperson's *Quantum Mechanics and the Philosophy of Alfred North Whitehead.*

[6] This quantum consciousness is part of what is intended in the title *Irreducible Mind*—the first book to come out of the Survival Research conference at the Esalen Center for Theory and Research.

[7] See Sri Aurobindo's *Essays on the Gita*, Chapter VIII in particular.

later, this process of valuation is also a crucial factor in our definition of personality.

I define personality, then, as a locus of choice. As personalities, we make our decisions among the different options that open before us in the creative advance of the universe. Personality, among its other characteristics, is an ongoing sequence of conscious acts of decision.

Causal Power

The free decisions made by a personality exercise causal influence on the world inhabited by that personality. For example, it is I, the personality, who decides which way to turn at a crossroads. Also, it is I, the personality, who chooses which words to speak and write. In this book, I will take the position that all communication involves causal interaction. This is obvious in the case of any form of communication mediated by direct sensory experience in waking life. I will argue that it is true, also, of various forms of empathy (the direct communication of feeling states) and telepathy (the direct communication of thoughts).

To summarize: to know any finite fact is to be causally affected by the circumstances constituting that fact. To be a personality is to be a conscious, feeling entity who has causal effects in its environment.

Memory

Without my memories, I would not be a personality. Because I have memory, I discover time as a dimension that extends continuously into the causal past. Because I experience my extension into the past I can also anticipate my extension into the future. My anticipated existence in the future gives relevance to the range of possibilities I can embrace in any given moment.

Just as I assume that my past memories can be arranged in a linear sequence, so I assume that my future experiences will continue to be sequential. I anticipate that I will have one and only one experience at any moment of future time.[8] I also project my memories of causal sequences into anticipations of future causal sequences. By allowing

---

[8] The condition under which we experience only one instance of ourselves at a given time applies to our waking lives. Our existence in transphysical worlds is probably not governed by this condition. For a more detailed exposition of this idea see Eric Weiss's *The Doctrine of the Subtle Worlds*, Chapter 4.

me to recognize a difference between the past and the present, memory is implicated in my recognition of movement and thus memory is involved in the experience of spatial extension. (We will see in Chapter 9 that spatial extension cannot be understood apart from possibilities of movement.) Without memory, then, there is no experience of time, no experience of space, no experience of causality, no experience of a coherent world.

I remember the being I was a moment ago, the being I was on my last birthday, and so on. Although my memories are generally patchy and rather jumbled, I operate on the assumption that I could, given sufficient powers of discrimination and attention, order all of my waking memories (at least) into a linear sequence.

A personality, then, is a sequence of conscious experiences that stretch off, in memory, into the indistinct reaches of the past. A personality is always experiencing one moment as a present in which there are decisions to be made and always anticipating its ongoing existence in a similar sequence of future moments.

I want to emphasize here that memory is not "merely subjective"—it is a causal factor in the actual world. For example, suppose I am walking along a street in a particular direction, and suddenly I remember that I have an appointment with someone who lives off to the right. So I make a right turn at the next corner. My memory was a causal factor in the world, causing me to turn my body in a new direction. In this case, my behavior is influenced by a clear conscious memory. Memory also operates without my conscious awareness of it. My memories of past decisions and their consequences constantly impact the decisions I make in the present moment even when they do not become thematic in my current moment of experience. This causal continuity of personality, carrying the effects of past decisions into the present moment, is part of what is meant by the term "karma" in Buddhism and other Vedic traditions.

As we will see, the notion of the survival of bodily death involves a continuation of this sequence of memory and causation after the death of the physical body.

Continuity of Purpose

While some scientists imagine that the physical body is a system driven entirely by efficient causes, it is impossible to think adequately of the personality in these terms alone. Personality, as we live it, is always characterized by the operation of "purpose."

"Purpose" is a general term. It encompasses instinctive self-preservation, the desire for satisfaction, pleasure and joy, and the intention to achieve a consciously chosen goal. Every moment in the life of a personality enacts some purpose. In the realm of personality, nothing happens without a "reason why."

Every purpose expresses a value of some kind. I want to survive because I *value* my life. I want this job rather than that one because I *value* my free time. I will give to others because my moral *values* dictate that action.

Earlier, I defined consciousness as that factor in existence that makes free decisions possible. Clearly, one of the differences between a random event and a choice is the presence of consciousness, but consciousness, though necessary, is not in itself sufficient. A conscious choice made in the absence of any sort of criterion would still be random. Besides *value,* another key factor that distinguishes between randomness and choice is *purpose* (or *aim)*. When I make a choice, I am consciously choosing among a number of *meaningful* alternatives. And what gives the alternatives meaning is the value each option has for me.

However, personality is characterized by more than the mere presence of purpose. It is also characterized, in an essential way, by various types of *continuity* of purpose. All personalities pursue the value of continued existence for themselves, and they do so on an ongoing basis. As personalities become more developed, they also begin to hold specific purposes over time. Other animals, which are also covered by this definition of personality, display elaborate continuities of purpose. They demonstrate "instinctive" purpose when, for example, birds migrate over thousands of miles. But they also demonstrate the ability to hold a purpose through a complex series of operations designed to achieve a goal, as we see regularly in the domesticated animals with which we are most familiar.

Human personalities are differentiated from the personalities of other animals by factors such as the ability to speak and think in systematic languages,[9] and this allows us to consider significant ranges of the future when we make our decisions. Human personalities can hold conscious purposes for a significantly greater length of time—indeed, even spanning generations.

Continuity of Identity

Beyond the five characteristics already developed, we need to consider one other factor at this point. As a personality, I tend to assume there is an "I" that was earlier, is now, and will be later. In all three phases of time, this "I" seems, in some important sense, to be the same "I." The nature of this "I," however, is a hotly contested issue.

Many schools of thought take this "I" to be illusory. For example, materialistic reductionism denies the existence of personality altogether. Process philosophy (the intellectual context for the ideas in this book) has decisively rejected materialistic reductionism; among its problems are the following two serious difficulties. First, those advocating this position seem to be involved in a performative contradiction: in denying the existence of personality, they deny their own existence and the existence of their students and readers, thereby condemning their work to utter irrelevance. Second, they seem to be led to this conclusion by a classic instance of what Alfred North Whitehead calls "the fallacy of misplaced concreteness"—i.e., they try to describe all of reality in terms of abstractions that are relevant to only the part of reality explored in physics. I and many others have argued this point extensively.[10]

While acknowledging the existence of personality, Buddhists are well known for their denial of any permanent "I" that binds personality into an identity. But their rejection of the ongoing identity of personality is softened in two important ways. First, while Buddhists quite rightly point out that there is no single element of experience that remains constant in

---

[9] Language in humans seems to be differentiated from language in animals because humans have a word for everything. In other words, human language, in its internal structure, mimics the wholeness of the world in which we live. It is what Cassirer calls a "symbolic form." For an interesting analysis of human language versus animal language see Ernst Cassirer's *An Essay on Man*, especially Chapter III.

[10] Three examples are Alfred North Whitehead's *Science and the Modern World;* Christian de Quincey's *Radical Nature;* and Weiss, *Doctrine.*

the flow of experiences making up the personality, they do recognize the existence of a pattern of organization that does remain constant as long as the personality is functioning. This constant organizational pattern is spelled out in the "twelve links of interdependent origination."[11] In this way, the personality has at least the unity of an ongoing system.[12] In addition to this unity, Buddhists also have a doctrine of karma, which provides for the causes generated in one lifetime to affect a subsequent reincarnation of that same personality. This allows the unity of the system to survive a change of bodies.

Other schools of thought posit a permanent identity in the form of a soul. (Each school tends to define "soul" in its own way.) Arguments for the existence of the soul, while they can be quite compelling, are not, generally, rooted in empirical observations of the kind usually characteristic of scientific work.

When we come to discuss reincarnation near the end of this book, complex issues surrounding the idea of soul will emerge and will be explored more deeply. Meanwhile, for our current purposes, we will adopt something similar to the Buddhist position—that the unity of the personality is guaranteed by its unity as a system and by its significant (though hardly complete) continuity of memory and purpose.

Transphysical Worlds

If the personality is to survive bodily death while still remaining a personality in the sense just defined, it must continue to exist after death in some world other than the "regular world" of our everyday waking experience. (The precise nature of this world will be explored more fully in Chapter 7.) Therefore, a central idea of this book is the notion of "transphysical worlds." The doctrine of the transphysical worlds can be summarized as follows:

---

[11] See Bhadantacariya Buddhaghosa, *The Path of Purification (Visuddhimagga)*, translated by Bhikku Nanamoli, p. 696.
[12] Joanna Macy, *Mutual Causality in Buddhism and General Systems Theory: The Dharma of Natural Systems*.

- The physical world is part of a larger system of interlocking worlds.
- These other worlds are not physical (hence, "transphysical") and they operate according to laws different from those that govern the physical world. They are, nonetheless, objectively real.
- Processes taking place in those other worlds directly impact what takes place in the physical world—whether or not human beings are aware of them.
- Human beings can consciously experience those other worlds and can operate in those other worlds in ways that significantly affect the unfolding of events here in the waking world.[13]
- The idea that the personalities of the deceased inhabit the same world in which we live our daily lives belies the evidence. If we are surrounded by disincarnate personalities during our waking lives, then it is remarkable that they have such minor causal effects. Also, as we will see, the descriptions of the afterlife received from deceased personalities by mediums generally describe a world quite different from the one we share in our waking lives.

Because the definition of survival I am using in this book requires the existence of transphysical worlds (other than physical worlds), one of the prime tasks of this book is to make these worlds intelligible.

Reincarnation

While many people profess a belief in multiple incarnations, we will see in Chapter 11 that "reincarnation" has a variety of meanings. In the strongest sense of the term, we can understand it as a situation in which the personality survives the death of its body, and then, without losing continuity, embodies itself in another physical body. In the weakest sense, we can understand it to mean that every individual is a reincarnation of all past individuals. Reincarnation may, as in some Buddhist teachings, involve no continuity of identity, or, as in soul-

---

[13] This definition appears in Weiss, *Doctrine*, p. 3.

15

theories of reincarnation, it may involve a strong sense of enduring identity between successive lives. We will leave the term "reincarnation" somewhat vague until we tackle these issues in Chapter 11.

Summary

In this chapter I have defined what I mean by "physical body," "personality," "transphysical worlds," and "reincarnation." The definition of "body" is unremarkable, though we have left for later consideration an analysis of the difference between a living body and a dead one.

The definition of "personality" is descriptive of what we mean by that term in everyday life—*a personality is an individual sharing a world with other individuals.* It is conscious, which is to say (at least) that it feels its surrounding world and makes free decisions that have effects in that world. It is endowed with some significant measure of continuity in terms of memory and purpose.

The definitions of "transphysical worlds" and of "reincarnation" given in this chapter are necessarily preliminary, and will be expanded in following chapters.

Five Fundamental Propositions

Our exploration of survival and reincarnation will be organized around the following five propositions:

I. The personality exercises causal agency in its actual world.
II. Transphysical worlds are part of our actual world.
- This proposition is sufficiently questioned by scientific thought that it needs to be established separately in order for a conversation about personality survival to be intelligible.
III. The personality can function in transphysical worlds, independently from the physical body, even during the life of that body.
- While this is not implicit in the definition of personality, establishing this will make the personality's survival of bodily death plausible.

IV. The personality survives the death of its physical body, and it does so in transphysical worlds.

- Materialists might think of survival in terms of the survival of the matter that makes up the body. The thought of that matter returning to the general store of matter making up the world and participating in many generations of future life may give materialists some feeling of continuity after death, but this is in no sense a continuity of individual *identity* after death, and that is what I mean by personality survival in this book.

- Some more spiritually oriented philosophies may imagine survival in terms of the individual personality as a drop, dissolving into the ocean of Divine Unity. There, its essence lives on, even though its individuality is no more. Again, in this approach, there is no continuity of personal identity.

- Alfred North Whitehead seemed to have imagined survival in terms of one's own experience living eternally, in the perfect memory of God. Here there is some sense of a preservation of personal identity, but it is preserved as a special and complete memory and not as an ongoing personality.[14]

- Each of these ideas of personality survival is built around some important truth and deserves respect in its own right. However, in this book, when I say that the personality survives the death of its physical body, I have in mind a strong definition of survival—one in which the very personality I have formed in the course of my lifetime wakes up after the death of the physical body to find itself in a different world, while retaining consciousness, causal efficacy (including, under some circumstances at least, the possibility of communicating with beings who are still alive), and at least as much continuity of memory and purpose as I share with myself in earlier phases of my life.

---

[14] Alfred North Whitehead, *Process and Reality*, pp. 337–51.

V. Reincarnation is part of the human life cycle.

- Reincarnation and personality survival are, logically speaking, two entirely different phenomena. Personality survival, as we have seen, involves the continuation after death of the personality formed during bodily life. This survival is not the same thing as immortality, since the personality that survives may, and indeed probably does, die after a time in its own world. There may be personality survival without reincarnation.[15] On the other hand, certain Buddhist accounts of reincarnation suggest reincarnation without personality survival.[16]

In general, we are born without accessible memory of previous lives, and our personalities are formed by the experiences and decisions made during this current lifetime. Many traditions suggest that the personality formed in this life, whether or not it survives the death of its body, does eventually die, and then there is a new lifetime—somehow connected to the old one yet enjoying an entirely new personality that forms in the future.

Later, when I discuss reincarnation, I will examine more fully the nature of the continuity between personalities that is implied in reincarnation.

In the next chapter, I will examine the evidence supporting these propositions.

---

[15] While the evidence documented by Ian Stevenson (see next chapter) can be said to prove that the personality sometimes does survive bodily death and then reincarnate in a new body, it does not prove this is the general case.

[16] Buddhaghosa, *Path of Purification*, p. 451.

Chapter 1: Challenging Evidence

In the last chapter, I introduced five propositions that form the essential content of this book. They are as follows:

- The personality exercises causal agency.
- The transphysical worlds are part of the actual world.
- The personality can function independently of its body, even during the life of the body.
- The personality survives the death of its physical body, and has its ongoing existence in transphysical worlds.
- Reincarnation is part of the human life cycle.

In this chapter, I will review the evidence that supports these propositions. This chapter is a very brief summary of evidence. Those seeking a more exhaustive enumeration of evidence should consult *Irreducible Mind*.

While some of this evidence has been produced in scientific laboratories under strict experimental controls, much of the evidence relevant to personality survival and reincarnation consists of carefully researched case studies. For example, evidence for near-death experiences can be produced in conversation only with those who claim to have had the experience. This forces us to rely on the perspicacity and truthfulness of the participants and the witnesses whose stories constitute the core of anecdotal accounts. Can we take such evidence seriously?

In considering this issue, I want to begin by acknowledging that the experimental method has brought to science a degree of objectivity, accuracy, and an ability to be replicated unmatched by any other means of establishing evidence. And I want to point out that methods of experimental science, while perfectly suited to the investigation of inorganic and, to a lesser extent, biological systems in nature, fail us entirely when we are dealing with the richness, diversity, and complexity of our ongoing personalities. In the study of personality, we cannot achieve anything like scientific objectivity, and we do not have the power to replicate any single moment in the life of a personality. We simply cannot expect to investigate the long trajectory of human life by means of experimental science.[1]

This brings us back to the issue of the anecdotal evidence that I will summarize in this chapter. Anecdotal evidence is the only kind of data we can share with each other regarding the nature and prospects of the personality as it is lived.

Scientists often dismiss such evidence with a catchphrase: "The plural of anecdote is not evidence." This sounds clever, but it sweeps under the rug the key function of anecdotes, which are found even in the strictest of scientific research. By and large, unless we actually repeat the experiments, the only way we can know their results is from anecdotal reports—for instance, in journals or at conferences. These anecdotes, like all reports, are liable to distortion, particularly when the emotional (and funding) stakes are high. In order to minimize the danger, the scientific community insists on independent verification. Once that is achieved, everyone but the original researcher and the scientists who replicated the experiment has only more anecdotes. It is then assumed that multiple anecdotes about the same experiment are more evidential than just one. The entire edifice of worldwide scientific cooperation is based on simple (and usually well warranted) faith in anecdotes about experiments.

So, rather than taking seriously the dismissive quip, scientists would do well to realize that, when it comes down to it, most of what they know about science is inevitably anecdotal.

In this book, therefore, I do accept as evidential the reports of instances of unusual human capacities when witnessed and investigated by researchers with reputations for high intelligence, high competence, and high integrity. And here, too, the more instances of an anecdote

---

[1] I have developed these ideas in more depth in *Doctrine*, Chapter 1.

I hear, the more credibility I give it. For example, if I hear about a single case of a near-death experience, I might dismiss it as an aberrant dreamlike wish fulfillment produced by a stressed brain. But when various individual stories begin to show remarkable similarities, when they begin to appear more and more frequently in my readings and conversations and, finally, when I myself can speak to people and hear their own personal experiences about a near-death experience, the anecdotes become evidential.

The various types of evidence presented here have met the tests outlined in the previous paragraph. These are instances of extraordinary human capabilities that are regularly reported in ancient spiritual texts, that are repeatedly described by primal peoples, that have been witnessed by multiple reliable witnesses on many separate occasions, and that (in a number of cases) I have personally verified by speaking with people who have had these experiences. All of these capacities are extensions of powers of personality we already exercise in the course of daily life.[2]

One important application of the metaphysical system I develop in this book is to take these disparate data and organize them into a coherent cosmology that exhibits our actual world as one in which

- The phenomena so exhaustively documented by centuries of parapsychological work are all understood in their actuality
- Human beings do, in fact, enjoy a life cycle that comprises much more than just bodily life
- Four hundred years of scientific work would produce exactly the body of evidence that we now have available to us

Before we begin to address that larger concern, and before we consider the evidence for each of the five propositions, let us pause to consider the historical evidence for survival and reincarnation in general.

---

[2] For the decisive development of this idea see Michael Murphy, *The Future of the Body*.

Historical Evidence for Survival and Reincarnation

First, every civilization we know of in history and prehistory believed in some form of afterlife and reincarnation. Only in the modern world do we espouse a material ontology that makes this seem impossible. Of course many civilizations, particularly those of primal peoples, held an understanding of individual identity very different from that which we hold today.[3] Nonetheless, they all experienced the boundary between life and death as fluid and believed in some kind of contact with deceased persons. Most assumed a kind of recycling of personalities through family and tribe.

Many cultures recognized that honoring and dealing with their ancestors was a priority. They built special shrines and rewarded members of their communities who could communicate with the dead. It would be arrogant for us today to assume that these people were unenlightened or primitive. They were genetically identical to us and were at least as smart as we are. Throughout history, they experienced communication with ancestors as not only possible but as effective and valuable.

Furthermore, no pre-modern society made the strict distinction between "inner" and "outer" in quite the same way we do. The idea that reality might somehow exist "out there," beyond experience, never occurred to them. Earlier civilizations assumed, rather reasonably, that they experienced reality as it actually is. The contents of dreams and apparitions were just as real for them as the contents of sensory perception—just in a different way. All pre-modern historical civilizations also understood the physical world to be accompanied by worlds of divine and demonic beings of various sorts and understood human beings as possessing bodies that could function in those worlds. These beliefs have been exhaustively documented in J. J. Poortman's *Vehicles of Consciousness*. These transphysical worlds appear in my fundamental propositions (Proposition II) and are necessary for the existence of personality survival as defined in this book. I will offer arguments for the existence of these worlds independent of the historical evidence, but it is nice to have the support of my ancestors.

Only modern industrial civilization—rooted in a metaphysics of

---

[3] For a fuller development of this point, see, for example, Jean Gebser, *The Ever-Present Origin*, translated by Noel Barstad and Algis Mickunas; and Ernst Cassirer, *The Philosophy of Symbolic Forms, Volume 2: Mythical Thought.*

reductionistic materialism and, therefore, imagining that personality is a product of dead matter or brute energy—has conceived the idea that the physical world is the whole of reality and has held the idea that personality terminates with the death of its body.

Modern materialistic reductionism not only makes survival and reincarnation seem impossible, it makes consciousness *per se* seem impossible. After all, how could any collection or system of insentient things ever produce consciousness? As an idea, materialistic reductionism has outlived its utility. The theoretical framework that I will be introducing here not only allows us to preserve all of the findings of modern science but also makes room for the wisdom of our magical, mythical, and classical ancestors.

Let us now turn to an examination of the evidence for the plausibility of our five fundamental propositions.

Proposition I:
Evidence that Personality Has Causal Agency

Common Sense

Before we move on to more exotic forms of evidence, let's look at the evidence for this proposition that surrounds us daily. While classical scientific reductionism tries to tell us that our personalities are merely epiphenomenal and have no actual effects in the causally closed domain of the physical world,[4] our entire lives are based on quite a contrary belief. While we are willing to accept reflexes, instincts, habits, and various sorts of unconscious motives as determinants of our actions, nonetheless, we know in general that it is we ourselves, as personalities, that make all the major and many of the minor decisions of our lives. I decide how I will dress, where I will go, what I will say, and so forth.

It is impossible to read a news story, a history, or a biography that does not make innumerable references to choices made by personalities. It is also impossible to imagine any of the everyday feats of engineering

---

[4] I am calling this "classical scientific reductionism" because it is a Newtonian reduction. Quantum mechanics opens this issue up in a new way. The metaphysical perspective being developed in this book can be understood as a metaphysical generalization of quantum mechanical ideas.

we witness—construction of buildings and ships, for example—without recognizing the conscious purposes and decisions that lie behind their realization. Indeed, our entire legal system, which assigns responsibility to people for the decisions they make, would be unintelligible if we did not credit personalities with causal effects in the actual world.

Only when our attention is directed by the very abstract ideas of modern science can we imagine personality to be void of causal efficacy. Indeed, the very real and significant act of judgment that condemns the personality to a non-causal status is itself a causal act performed by a personality. To put it simply, any personality that judges the personality to be epiphenomenal, and that strives to convince other personalities of this point of view, is engaged in a blatant performative contradiction.

We all live and act on the assumption that our personalities are causal agencies in the actual world.

Beyond the essential evidence from our own everyday experiences, however, other evidence suggests that the causal power of the personality is much greater than it appears in the normal course of our lives.

Instances of Unusual Causal Impacts of Personality on Its Own Body

A great deal of evidence suggesting that the mind has unusual causal influence on the body is presented in Chapter 3 of *Irreducible Mind*. Emily Kelly, the author of that chapter, drawing from published research as well as from her own investigations, meticulously documents the following:

- Cases in which purely psychological factors trigger symptoms of full-blown diseases (such as mass hysteria in closely associated groups)[5]
- Studies correlating chronic negative emotions (such as depression or helplessness) and physiological illness[6]
- Cases where people died suddenly, usually from cardiac arrest, after receiving an abrupt emotional shock or (more rarely) swift unusual joy[7]

---

[5] Kelly and Kelly, *Irreducible Mind*, p. 123.
[6] Ibid.
[7] Ibid., p. 124.

- Cases of "voodoo" death in which a person who has been cursed or otherwise led to believe "by another, usually authoritarian, person ... that he or she is going to die at a particular time does in fact die [at that time]."[8] Some of these occur entirely outside religious or "magical" contexts. J. L. Mathis in 1964 described a case[9] in which a man who had first developed asthma at the age of 53 died nine months later of an asthma attack. A closer examination of his history revealed that he had suffered his first attack two days after his mother had cursed him for going against her wishes, saying that as a result, "something dire will happen to you." The man had several more attacks over the next several months, always after encounters with his mother. Finally he was found semi-comatose an hour after a conversation with his mother in which she repeated her warning, and he died twenty minutes later.
- Many cases in which people "postpone their death until after some meaningful occasion, such as the arrival of a loved one or a significant day"[10]
- Cases documenting the power of placebo effects—even a case in which patients given a placebo surgery did better than those who received the real thing[11]
- Cases of sudden whitening of the hair or skin[12]
- Cases of false pregnancy, in which the signs are so convincing that even doctors are often fooled[13]
- Stigmata and related phenomena in which people see another person get injured and develop corresponding wounds on their own bodies; or in which people reliving traumatic experiences reproduce the wounds from the original incident; or in which people make geometrical

---

[8] Ibid., p. 125.

[9] J. L. Mathis, (1964). A sophisticated version of voodoo death. *Psychosomatic Medicine, 26*, 104–7. As quoted in *Irreducible Mind*, p. 126.

[10] Ibid., p. 129.

[11] Ibid, p. 143.

[12] Ibid., p. 148.

[13] Ibid., p. 149–52.

blisters or writing appear on their skin merely by willing or imagining it[14]

- Cases in which different personalities all belonging to one person with dissociative identity disorder require different prescriptions for their eyeglasses and have different allergies[15]

In all of these cases, the personality seems quite clearly to be exercising unusual influence on the body with its own independent, causal power. But we can go one step further and also produce cases in which the personality has a *direct* causal effect on the bodies *of other* individuals.

Causal Impact of Personality on Other Living Bodies

Here is a sampling of the evidence that suggests a personality can, without the mediation of its own physical body, have causal impact on other living physical bodies:

- First, in daily life, considerable evidence exists for "empathy," or direct communication of feeling states between personalities, unmediated by physical causes. Many of us have the experience of "feeling vibes" when, for example, we walk into a room where people are fighting and sense the anger thickening the air. While these experiences can usually be "explained away" by references to elaborate processing of subtle sensory cues, many of us experience this sort of empathy as a regular phenomenon and make extensive use of it in daily life. In the metaphysical system I will present and explore here, it is natural to think of this sort of empathy as a direct causal connection among personalities.
- Daily life and parapsychological research also provide evidence for various forms of "telepathy," or direct sharing of thoughts among individuals.[16] Sigmund Freud, though

---

[14] Ibid., p. 156–59.
[15] Ibid., p. 167–74.
[16] Rene Warcollier, *Mind to Mind*.

generally a materialist, was nonetheless convinced of the reality of telepathy by his exploration of dreams.[17]

- Numerous cases have also been documented in which one person takes on the symptoms of another—for example "couvade syndrome," in which a man takes on many of the symptoms of his pregnant wife.[18]

- More striking are cases of "maternal impression," in which a fetus manifests characteristics that can be attributed only to the experiences of the mother while the fetus is developing. One case documents a woman who, during her pregnancy, was shocked and impressed by seeing someone on the street with a birthmark covering half her face. Her child was born with a nearly identical birthmark.[19]

- Other cases include a woman who could "reproduce on her skin [by entirely subjective means] target pictures or writing." Not only could she "somehow translate an image presented to her normally into corresponding marks on her skin," in some instances the target information had not been conveyed to her in any normal sensory way. In other words, it was communicated via some kind of extra-sensory modality, such as telepathy.[20]

- Many cases have been documented in which a hypnotist could put a subject into a trance without being in any way physically present to the subject. L. L. Vasiliev of the University of Leningrad, over a period extending between 1933 and 1934, conducted over 260 trials in which hypnotists could successfully induce trance without being physically present to the hypnotists. These experiments were successful 90 percent of the time.

- Finally, there is evidence, though it is not entirely conclusive which strongly suggest the efficacy of the power of distant

[17] Roger Luckhurst, *The Invention of Telepathy*.
[18] Kelly and Kelly, *Irreducible Mind*, pp. 219–21.
[19] Ibid., pp. 221–24.
[20] Ibid., p. 225.

prayer. The specific cases, and also the doubts concerning them, are discussed extensively in *Irreducible Mind*.[21]

These cases show not only that the personality of one person can exercise causal influence on his or her own body but also that a personality can exercise, without physical mediation, causal influence *on the bodies of others*. In addition, as we will see when discussing the Ian Stevenson evidence below, cases exist in which it appears that a recently deceased personality produced marks on the body of a subsequent incarnation.

Causal Influence of Personality on Inorganic Systems

In considering the causal power of the personality, we must also look at the considerable evidence demonstrating that personalities can influence the behaviors of inorganic systems. These studies usually involve the ability of individuals to influence the outcome of random events through the simple act of intending to do so.

Robust results, obtained in rigorous experiments, are documented in Robert Jahn and Brenda Dunne's *Margins of Reality* and Dean Radin's *The Conscious Universe*. For years, scientists have experimented with digital random number generators (RNGs) in which people wish, will, or intend that either zeroes or ones show up with a frequency greater than chance. Because these machines operate via quantum effects and are shielded from any physical influence by humans, the results should turn out to be statistically random. Nevertheless, when human subjects are tested to see if they can influence the behavior of the RNGs using only their minds, the results reveal patterns significantly greater than chance. The experimental system is electronic, operating close to the speed of light, so scientists have been able to perform millions of trials. Meta-analysis reveals highly significant statistical results demonstrating some kind of psychokinetic (PK) effect.

Besides these cases in which personalities influenced the results of random number generators, Stephen Braude has documented numerous cases of so-called "macro PK," in which skilled subjects, ostensibly using

---

[21] Ibid., pp. 227–30.

only the power of their minds, have levitated tables, bent spoons, and made clocks run backward.[22]

Finally, it is important to mention "remote viewing"—the ability to tune into, and to see, situations that are distant in space and possibly in time, without the mediation of the bodily senses, and without any sort of out of body experience.[23]

Summary

Consider that:

- We all live with the assumption that our personalities exercise causal power over our own bodies.
- The entire moral and legal foundation of our civilization rests on the assumption that the personality generally controls, and is therefore responsible for, the behaviors of its body.
- We have strong anecdotal evidence for the power of the personality to create sickness and health, to postpone death, and even to produce voluntary stigmata.
- We have strong anecdotal evidence for direct, unmediated causal influence by one personality on another.
- We have strong anecdotal evidence for the ability of the personality to perceive physical events that are remote in space and, possibly, in time.
- We have extensive evidence for the direct, unmediated influence by the personality on inorganic systems (such as random number generators).

It seems clear that we have more than ample reason to believe my first proposition: that the personality has the power within itself to create effects in the actual world.

Bottom line: whatever a human personality is, it appears to have the ability to affect the waking world in meaningful and significant ways

---

[22] Stephen Braude, *The Limits of Influence: Psychokinesis and the Philosophy of Science.*

[23] Russell Targ, *Limitless Mind: A Guide to Remote Viewing and Transformation of Consciousness.*

directly, without working through the body. We do not know yet where the outer limits of this ability lies.

Given the impressive weight of all the parapsychological data, plus our own commonplace direct experiences of influencing our bodies through choices generated in our minds, the worldview of modern science is seriously called into question. I present this work with a clear understanding that the standard metaphysics of materialism—the view that nothing ultimately exists but physical matter or energy—is not only incomplete, but inadequate. We need a comprehensive set of metaphysical assumptions if we are to account for indisputable realities such as consciousness itself and our thinking, feeling personalities, and if we are to explain "anomalous" data indicating that the human personality has the capacity to survive physical death and even to reincarnate through multiple lives.

Proposition II: Evidence for Existence of Transphysical Worlds

In the chapters that follow, I aim to establish the plausibility of the existence of the transphysical worlds. Such worlds are alien to the sensibilities of modern, scientifically informed common sense. Consequently, it is difficult to find works that discuss the existence of these worlds. Nevertheless, I take it that the evidence in support of propositions III (functioning of personality independently of its physical body) and IV (personality survival) below also count as evidence for the existence of the transphysical worlds. Furthermore, much that is difficult to understand about our waking lives can also be illuminated by the doctrine of the transphysical worlds.

Proposition III: Evidence for Independent Functioning of Personality

The idea that the personality can survive the death of its body will be credible if it can be shown that the personality can function independently from its body while the body is alive. Evidence for this idea falls under several headings:

Dreams

In modern times, we have come to think of dreams as entirely private shows put on for us by our brains when they are unoccupied with the processing of external sensory data. This idea, however, is not without its difficulties.

If it is indeed possible for our brains to generate what appear to be entire worlds for us to explore, and to populate those worlds with various objects and the expressions of other seemingly human and non-human personalities, then how can we know whether or not our waking worlds are merely unusually coherent dreams? And if we can't tell the difference between waking and dreaming, how can we know whether other people are merely figments of our brains? In other words, the idea that dreams are entirely private productions raises a serious problem of solipsism—it makes it plausible to imagine that we are the only actual personalities in existence and that everyone else is merely a projection of our own brains.[24]

Other difficulties exist with the idea that dreams are entirely private. (I have explored this elsewhere, particularly in *The Doctrine of the Subtle Worlds*.[25]) For now, I simply invite you to consider not the differences but the *similarities* between waking life and dreaming life. In both, we are dealing with process and the flow of time (of course, time may behave very differently in dreams than it does in waking life; nevertheless, events in dreams can be sorted, more or less, into before and after). In both experiences, we are dealing with some form of space in which various objects are arrayed. In both we are a subject at the center of a situation involving multiple objects and with various sorts of causal relations among ourselves and those objects.

Even though dreams are often confused, confusing, and difficult to remember, I would like you to at least consider that dreams are glimpses into transphysical worlds. To the extent that we are willing to accept this, we can interpret our ordinary dreams as evidence for the independent functioning of the personality in transphysical worlds.[26]

---

[24] See Weiss, *Doctrine*, Chapter 1.

[25] Ibid.

[26] The well-established fact that dreams have personal meaning does not mean that they are not objective experiences of an actual world. Our waking lives also have meaning that can be interpreted by the same tools that we use to interpret dreams.

Near-Death Experiences

Near-death experiences (NDEs) are "generally understood to be the unusual, often vivid and realistic, and sometimes profoundly life-changing experiences occurring to people who have been either physiologically close to death, as in cardiac arrest or other life-threatening conditions, or psychologically close to death, as in accidents or illnesses in which they feared they would die."[27] These experiences often include the sense of floating outside the body and/or of seeing events transpiring around the body while it is unconscious (sometimes in ways that can be clearly verified afterward). They frequently include the feeling of moving through a tunnel with a bright light at the end. People experiencing NDEs regularly report clarity of perception and thought greater than that enjoyed during normal waking life, even though "according to conventional psycho-physiological theory, such activity should be diminishing or even not possible."[28] Many people who have NDEs come away with the conviction that they have functioned independently from their physical bodies and that they will do so after they die. There are a large number of studies suggesting these experiences are relatively common, and happen to 10–20 percent of patients who are close to death.[29]

After a thorough analysis of the data, and of the various explanations that have been proposed, the authors of *Irreducible Mind* conclude, "We should not rule out categorically that NDEs are essentially what many of those who experience them think they are—namely, evidence that they have temporarily separated from their body and, moreover, may survive the permanent separation that occurs at death."[30]

Out-of-Body Experiences

NDEs are closely associated with out-of-body experiences (OBEs). In fact, many NDEs are reported to begin with OBEs and then move into more elaborate scenarios. "In an OBE, a person experiences his or her consciousness as having separated from the body, but also as continuing

---

[27] Kelly and Kelly, *Irreducible Mind,* p. 369.
[28] Ibid., p. 386.
[29] Ibid., p. 371.
[30] Ibid., p. 391.

to function normally."[31] It is estimated in a significant number of studies that as many as 10 percent of the general population has had one or more OBEs[32]

A large body of literature exists on the subject of OBEs, most prominently the extensive personal records compiled by Monroe, Bruce, and Vijera.[33] Reports include veridical perceptions of events that could not have been sensed by the body, communication with other individuals who are, at the time of the contact, asleep and/or in a dreamlike condition, and communication with deceased individuals.

Some OBEs include "reciprocal apparitions" in which one person either deliberately tries to "project" his or her personality, or is having a spontaneous OBE, or is having a dream in which he or she seems to go to a distant location. At the same time, a second person—unaware of the first person's experience but being present at the location being visited by the first person—sees an apparition of that first person. One famous case from 1863 involves a Mrs. Wilmot, whose husband was onboard a ship on a storm-tossed Atlantic crossing. She "had an experience, while she was awake during the middle of the night, in which she seemed to go to her husband's stateroom on the ship, where she saw him asleep in the lower berth and another man in the upper berth looking at her. She hesitated, kissed her husband, and left. The next morning, Mr. Wilmot's roommate asked him, apparently somewhat indignantly, about the woman who had come into their room during the night."[34] Kelly and Kelly, in *Irreducible Mind*, discuss a large number of more recent cases of the same type that have been reported.[35]

Lucid Dreams

Lucid dreams are closely related to OBEs and NDEs. A lucid dream is a dream in which we are mentally awake and aware that we are dreaming. I have had lucid dreams several times, and thinking about this experience brought my attention to the kind of taking-for-granted that pervades my

---

[31] Ibid., p. 394.
[32] Ibid., p. 396.
[33] Robert Monroe, *Far Journeys*; Robert Bruce, *Astral Dynamics*; Waldo Vieira, *Projections of the Consciousness*.
[34] Kelly and Kelly, *Irreducible Mind*, p. 396.
[35] Ibid.

ordinary dream experiences. I may have a very strange dream in which I am doing strange things in strange places, but while I am dreaming it always seems perfectly normal. It's as if I've always been there, in that dream space, and the dream experience is entirely undisturbed by memories of waking life. In lucid dreams, that taking-for-granted is interrupted. Suddenly, it is "I"—my waking self, the person I am in my everyday, waking life—who is there in the dream. I remember having been awake, and I'm appreciating the uncanny strangeness of the dream space and anticipating waking up. The waking "I" brought with it to dream space whatever lucidity and clarity of purpose it can muster in waking life. Alfred North Whitehead himself described a lucid dream that he had. In an essay called "Uniformity and Contingency," Whitehead says: "I remember once having the dream of hovering, and in my dream, taking the most careful notes. I remembered that I had had the experienced before, and I had subsequently decided that it was a dream. Accordingly, I decided to observe all the circumstances with great exactness . . ."[36] Lucid dreams can merge into OBEs, and vice versa. Extensive literature on lucid dreams also exists.[37]

Summary

People who have had out-of-body or near-death experiences and lucid dreams feel them to be clear instances of the functioning of the personality outside the physical body. These people are often convinced they will survive bodily death. Near-death experiences and lucid dreams not infrequently lead to out–of-body experiences. Near-death experiences are particularly evidential in that they happen under the conditions of intense medical monitoring that are normal in surgical operations, and it can be shown that while they are happening, the electrical activity of the brain is entirely flatlined. Thus they seem to show clear instances of personality functioning in the absence of the normal bodily support. Given that dreams can turn into lucid dreams, which closely resemble certain aspects of out-of-body experiences, we may also choose to take

---

[36] See Whitehead's essay, "Uniformity and Contingency" in *The Interpretation of Science: Selected Essays.*
[37] See footnote 39. See also Stephen Laberge, *Exploring the World of Lucid Dreaming*, and Robert Waggoner, *Lucid Dreaming: Gateway to the Inner Self.*

our ordinary dreams as further evidence of our ability to function independently of the physical body.

By a show of hands in my own classes over the last ten years, as many as 60–70 percent of my students have had or are regularly having lucid dreams and out-of-body experiences. My classes are composed, of course, of people who are open to and curious about these matters, so this says nothing about the general population. However, these experiences are probably more widespread than the available research suggests, since cultural suspicion may make people reluctant to speak of them. This summarizes the evidence for Proposition III.

Proposition IV: Evidence for Personality Survival after Death in Transphysical Worlds

Ian Stevenson's evidence, which I will present shortly when I discuss reincarnation (Proposition V), is also relevant to the issue of "personality survival." Stevenson's evidence is extensive and consists of careful documentation, over a period of 40 years, of "Cases of the Reincarnation Type (CORT)." Stevenson presents over 3000 cases of young children who have vivid and demonstrably accurate recollections of previous lives—usually of lives that were recent in time and close in space to the life they are now living. I introduce this evidence here because 20 percent of his cases include reports of what the personality was doing during its sojourn out of the body and between incarnations. This particular part of the Stevenson data will be discussed more extensively in Chapter 11.

Evidence from Mediums

The most interesting and informative evidence we have for personality survival comes from mediums. Mediumship, also known as "channeling," involves special individuals who claim to be able to communicate directly with various sorts of disembodied entities—spirits, demons, and disincarnate people—and to relay messages from those entities to the living. Awareness of mediumship has grown so broad and mainstream that some more commercially minded mediums now practice their art on television. I will not attempt to review the vast literature on this subject, other than to note that the descriptions of the afterlife communicated by mediums often seem to be corroborated by the descriptions of afterlife conditions given by individuals who report on these matters in terms of their out-of-body experiences. These descriptions include the ability of individuals in the afterlife to change their form depending on their mood and to transport instantaneously from place to place. Also, the laws that operate in the world of out-of-body experiences and life after death are more fluid and flexible than are the physical laws that largely govern waking life. These issues will be further discussed in Chapter 8.

Reports of Extra-Bodily Activities of Personality

Some evidence, particularly among reports of out-of-body experiences, supports the idea that the personality may travel about in the space of our waking lives.[38] The vast majority of these reports, however, attest to the existence of strange and wondrous worlds that transcend the physical world in their variety of form and function, and in the freedom and profound adequacy of self-expression that the personality can find in them.[39]

Once we take our own experiences of these worlds (at least in dreams), and the documented stories of these worlds as evidence for the ability of the personality to function independently of its body, then it makes sense for us to take the contents of these stories as evidential as well.

Without going into a detailed analysis of the many stories that can be found throughout literature, I point out that popular fiction alone has explored extensively the type of world these stories imply.

Here are a few examples, distinguished only because of their vividness in my own memory:

- The environments explored by Dr. Strange, a longtime character in comics of that name published by Marvel Comics

---

[38] Some authors, however, suggest that even in out-of body-experiences that appear to take place inside the space and time structures of waking life, there are always details out of place—which suggests that such experiences happen in those portions of the transphysical worlds that most closely approximate that of our daily lives.
[39] What is probably the most exquisitely evocative description of these worlds in all of English literature is to be found in Book II of Part I of Sri Aurobindo's *Savitri*.

- Movies such as *Roger Rabbit*[40] and *What Dreams May Come*[41]
- The environment inhabited by the wormhole aliens who serve as religious prophets in the television series *Star Trek: Deep Space Nine*
- William Gibson's *Neuromancer* and the cyberpunk tradition to which it belongs, which imagine cyberspace as one in which beings can change forms and transport themselves instantly, very much as the astral world is depicted in the theosophical literature[42]

These are all descriptions, under the safety of science fiction, of the types of transphysical worlds people enter when they are functioning in a mentally conscious way, and, with some continuity of memory, outside their physical bodies. These fictional explorations are far from the sort of aesthetically, ethically, and intellectually coherent cosmology that we need for deeper investigation of these issues, but it is evidence that awareness of these experiences and a willingness to entertain them— even if only "in fiction"—is growing.

The need to weld these early imaginings into a new cosmology is not, however, being heard in the halls of mainstream academia. Indeed, the very issue of transphysical worlds has been anathema to mainstream academics during the last four hundred years.[43] However, as we have already seen, we have no need to start from scratch in such an undertaking. A multi-world cosmology of some sort has been held by all cultures, with the notable exception of the modern industrial West. Particularly relevant to the model developed in this book, a multi-world cosmology was developed by the Vedic tradition in India and Tibet and has been tested and refined by many generations of yogis.

This Vedic cosmology has also been expressed, with increasing clarity and vigor, by a number of prominent—if extra-academic—writers over the past 150 years. A sampling of these authors include Emanuel

---

[40] *Who Framed Roger Rabbit*, Disney Home Video, 2003.
[41] *What Dreams May Come*. Polygram Filmed Entertainment, 2003.
[42] A. E. Powell has admirably summarized the theosophical cannon in *The Astral Body*. See also Powell's other works, cited in the bibliography.
[43] J. J. Poortman, *Vehicles of Consciousness*.

Swedenborg, Madame Blavatsky, Annie Besant, C. W. Leadbeater, and other, more recent theosophists such as Alice Bailey, Rudolf Steiner, and Sri Aurobindo.

These various authors agree on a cosmology that supports the existence of the physical world and a variety of transphysical worlds. All agree that personality survives the death of its physical body and enjoys further experiences after that death in transphysical worlds. And each provides a coherent interpretation for the various stories that are told by modern explorers concerning the adventures of the personality while out of its body.

All of this together amounts to what we might term a "circumstantial" case for personality survival. There is no particular phenomenon that we can isolate and replicate scientifically that somehow would prove the existence of personality survival. In fact, it is difficult to imagine what such a phenomenon might be. But what we do have is the following:

- Evidence supporting the proposition that the personality can function independently of its body in dreams, lucid dreams, out-of-body experiences, and near-death experiences, even when the electrical activity of the brain flatlines
- Evidence that the personality has causal effects in the physical world—by deciding on the behaviors of its physical body, by directly influencing the feelings and thoughts of others without the mediation of the physical body, and by impacting the behaviors of inorganic systems (for example, in remote viewing and psychokinesis)
- Ian Stevenson's CORT data, including stories which gain strength from their association with the verified cases of reincarnation that they accompany
- An extensive body of literature on dreams, lucid dreams, out-of-body experiences, near-death experiences, and the activities of mediums
- The corroboration of these stories by people of all civilizations prior to the modern West

- The ordering of these stories into a general multi-world cosmology—some version of which appears in Vedic thought, Buddhist thought, and Neoplatonic thought[44]

As this book progresses, I hope to strengthen this evidence still further by showing how not only is it compatible with modern science but it can actually help explain certain phenomena with which postmodern science is struggling.

Proposition V: Evidence that Reincarnation is an Intrinsic Part of the Human Life Cycle

The Stevenson Data

Probably the most conclusive body of evidence for survival and reincarnation is the research done by Dr. Ian Stevenson, a psychiatrist and University of Virginia professor. During fieldwork in India, Sri Lanka, Africa, and Europe, from 1957–2007 he discovered and thousands of cases of young children who had vivid and detailed memories of previous lives.[45] At three or four years of age, they said such things as, "I really don't belong here, I belong in another house," or "My sister is named _____ and my brother is named _____. My cat is named _____. But in that lifetime I was killed in _____way."[46] When Stevenson interviewed these children, he found that almost all of them claimed to have lived a previous life in the recent past and in geographical proximity to the location of their current life. Typically, they reported detailed stories about prior family lives, often in other villages they had never visited in this life, and, when checked out, the details of their stories were confirmed. In many cases, the people involved had died at a young age and usually had suffered a violent death—circumstances that were confirmed by local records. Frequently,

---

[44] Gregory Shaw, *Theurgy and the Soul.*
[45] Ian Stevenson's research was published in *Twenty Cases Suggestive of Reincarnation*; and *Cases of the Reincarnation Type,* Volumes I-IV.
[46] Ian Stevenson, *Children Who Remember Previous Lives: A Question of Reincarnation.*

Stevenson found birthmarks on the children's bodies corresponding to the wounds that had killed the person in a previous life.

For example, one person had been shot through the throat with a shotgun, and the bullet had gone right through and out the back. In this life, the ostensibly reincarnated man has a matching birthmark on his neck. Even more curious, when Stevenson and his team looked closely at the subject's skull they found he had birthmarks where the exit wounds would have been as well.

Since the late 1950s, Stevenson has investigated and meticulously documented such cases. Often he would arrive at the site of the previous-life incident before news of the case of a reincarnated child had traveled from town to town, and was able to confirm the name of the dead person and the location and other details the child had reported to him about the circumstances of the death. To an objective, unbiased reader, Stevenson's work, based on robust data, constitutes powerful evidence for reincarnation. In fact, I consider this evidence to be scientific confirmation that at least some people, under certain circumstances, die and are reborn in another body. This is indeed momentous and has not received anything like the attention it deserves.

I regard Stevenson's data as substantial proof that at least one type of reincarnation—the type that occurs when a personality leaves a physical body that has died and then, after some interval, reincarnates directly in a new body—is regularly taking place.

Evidence for Other Modes of Reincarnation

It is important to note, however, that this type of reincarnation does not seem, on the surface at least, to be the general rule. Overall, very few young children speak about their previous lives. Nevertheless, the vast literature on the subject suggests that reincarnation is a worldwide phenomenon.

Accounts drawn from Sri Aurobindo and other theosophically inspired sources suggest that a more frequent type of reincarnation involves first the survival of the personality for some unspecified but finite duration in transphysical worlds, then a death of the personality, and then some period of time that can be characterized as a "soul" existence.

I will return to this subject and explore it in more depth in Chapter

11. The point I want to make now is that reincarnation of this type does not involve the ongoing existence of the personality per se. Rather, it suggests a model in which each personality is unique and mortal, but that each personality is in some sense an expression of a soul, and that it is the soul, not the personality, that reincarnates.

Buddhists, who reject the existence of the soul but still maintain a doctrine of reincarnation, have suggested at least one model in which there is no survival of bodily death in the sense that we are discussing here, but there is still a form of reincarnation that establishes a causal (karmic) connection between two successive personalities.[47]

Arguments made for reincarnation on philosophical grounds go back as far as Plato. Sri Aurobindo makes a particularly sophisticated argument of this type in his book, *The Problem of Rebirth*. Anecdotal evidence for rebirth comes from "past-life memories," supported somewhat by data obtained by psychics in "past-life readings."

Past-life memories are, at least in some circles, far from uncommon, but many are difficult to credit. Some seem almost mechanical, as, for example, when someone with healing talent discovers a past life as a great healer; and some seem entirely too flattering, as when an otherwise unremarkable person remembers himself as having been Napoleon or Genghis Khan. But past-life memories are sometimes quite surprising and can have a profound impact on the person having them. I have had some personal vivid experiences that I am tempted to interpret as past-life memories. These consisted of sudden and very vivid first-person recollections of scenes from other times and other places, as lived through other bodies with different personalities than mine. These memories were far from flattering, though they were related to psychological issues I was working with at the time the memories occurred. I am undecided as to the evidential value of such experiences.

I take Stevenson's evidence for at least one type of reincarnation as valid, and later I will give the benefit of the doubt to the scant scientific evidence for other types of reincarnation. I will explore how the metaphysical ideas in this book can support the existence of reincarnation in ways that might suggest other ideas for gathering evidence on this important issue.

---

[47] Buddhaghosa, *The Path of Purification*, p. 451.

Summary

This, then, is a survey of the evidence that supports my five propositions. At this point, I will turn attention to more theoretical issues and begin the task of developing a metaphysical and cosmological framework within which we can understand these propositions, and their relation to the truths of modern and postmodern science.

Chapter 2: Science and Metaphysics

I began this exploration into the nature of *personality*—and the question of its survival beyond death by offering definitions for "personality" and "body." I also articulated five fundamental propositions that the new metaphysical framework developed in this book is meant to support:

I. The personality exercises causal agency in its actual world;

II. Transphysical worlds are part of the actual world;

III. Personality can function separately from its body, even while the body is alive;

IV. The personality survives the death of its physical body, and has its ongoing existence in transphysical worlds; and

V. Reincarnation is part of the human life cycle.

In the previous chapter I reviewed some of the evidence that supports these propositions.

However, even if the evidence is persuasive, for many people something much more compelling is required before the propositions or the supporting evidence will be accepted. Evidence, by itself, is not enough. It needs to be accompanied by a theory that makes sense of it. This is understandable. From the perspective of modern science, and even from the perspective of everyday common sense, the kind of reality suggested by the propositions and revealed by the evidence amounts to a major break with widely accepted assumptions and beliefs about the nature of reality.

Because I will be criticizing beliefs that are often thought of as "scientific," I need to say a few words about what I mean by "science." The word has several common meanings:

- Science can be defined by referring to its Latin root *scientia*, which means knowledge. In this sense, "science" just means knowing, in general.
- Science can be defined in a more limited way, as rational knowledge. In this sense of the term, any knowledge about the actual world that can be reduced to a set of coherent propositions is considered to be science.
- Science can be defined still more narrowly by specifying that it is knowledge gained by a special method—the scientific method—which proceeds by means of hypothesis and testing.
- Finally, science is sometimes restricted only to those knowledge activities, like physics, that analyze phenomena through mathematical modeling.

In general, it is assumed that science is empirical, in the sense that it restricts its data to evidence that can be gathered through the bodily senses.

When I use the word "science," I will be referring to a particular knowledge tradition that has existed in the West since the time of Plato and Aristotle. I will divide scientific knowledge into three phases:

- "Natural history science," or "classification science," which began with the Greeks and is still strong today through sciences such as biology.
- "Modern science," which began around the time of the Renaissance, crystallized with Newton, and was dominant up until the beginning of the 20th century.
- "Postmodern science," which includes relativity, quantum mechanics, chaos theory, non-equilibrium thermodynamics, and the theory of self-organization.

I will also make a distinction between science in general and something I will call "reductionistic" or "materialistic" science. In general, science is ontologically neutral—it either classifies entities or analyzes functional relations among entities, but it minimizes its assumptions as to what those entities really "are." On the other hand, there is a certain scientific culture, still based in modern science (as opposed to postmodern science), which takes the ontological position that only physical matter—dead, insentient stuff with nothing but mathematical properties—is the ultimate reality. I will have considerable reason to criticize this sort of reductionistic science, but I want to be clear that in doing so I am not criticizing science in general.

Most of us are aware that our everyday, scientifically conditioned common sense, as well as the fundamental assumptions at the foundations of *materialist* science are inadequate, to say the least, when we are dealing with phenomena that involve mind, consciousness, or any form of subjective experience. Consequently, if we are to expand science to include not only the objective physical world but also the domain of subjective experience, we will have to move science well beyond the bounds of strict materialism.

As things stand today, scientific materialism provides no way to illuminate the mystery of consciousness. As a result, the worldview handed to us by modern science tells us that we—conscious, living beings—are accidental products of automatic forces destined for inevitable universal decay (entropy). It is a bleak and absurd vision, offering no meaning or purpose to life.

We are, as Thomas Berry[1] and Brian Swimme[2] have said, in need of a new story. The metaphysical system that I will present in this book provides the foundation for a new story of the universe—for a world where consciousness, mind, soul, and spirit are just as real and obvious as the matter and energy that currently occupy the restricted gaze of materialistic science. In short, I am offering a new way of thinking about consciousness, matter, life and death, evolution, and the human role in the evolutionary process. In particular, I am proposing a new vision of our actual world that not only allows us to accept the truth of my five propositions, but also accounts for the kinds of results that scientists actually get in their experiments.

As is immediately evident from my opening propositions, and as will become clearer as we proceed, I am identifying a major gap between the

---

[1] Thomas Berry, *The Great Work: Our Way into the Future.*
[2] Brian Swimme and Thomas Berry, *The Universe Story.*

world of modern reductionistic science and the new approach outlined in this book. But it is a gap that can be bridged. Our essential tool for building this bridge is *metaphysics*—in particular, the rigorous ontology and cosmology developed by the great twentieth-century philosopher Alfred North Whitehead.

As Whitehead did, we'll begin our metaphysical quest by "taking it down to earth"—in other words, by grounding it in our own familiar experience. While some of the key concepts and terminology may be initially unfamiliar, and therefore may require some extra care and attention, my aim is to use the tool of metaphysics to help make philosophical and scientific abstractions more concrete by connecting them to our familiar experience of the world.

We'll start by looking at different forms of explanation that we use to make sense of our lives and the world around us. For example, we use ethical explanations to account for why we take one course of action rather than some other as we attempt to balance self-interest with the interests of others and the good of the whole. We also use aesthetic explanations to justify choices based on perceived values that determine or influence actions intended to create beautiful objects and environments. In addition to modes of explanation focused on the "good" and the "beautiful," we also seek to explain what we understand to be "true." Scientific explanations are of this type. Modern and postmodern science is a body of knowledge based on an experimental method and designed to tentatively confirm or decisively refute assumptions, hypotheses, or theories about some aspect of physical reality. Specifically, modern and postmodern science seek to demonstrate how some particular phenomenon fits into a general scheme of efficient causes that unite the waking world into a single mathematical system.

Each of these forms of explanation takes certain basic ideas as given and then uses those ideas in its explanatory work. Ethical explanations hinge on motives, ideals, and knowledge available at the time of the moral act being explained. Artistic explanations hinge on sensitive descriptions of sensory patterns and felt relationships, for example, between parts of a composition and the whole, and so forth. Scientific explanations hinge on observing and classifying the sensory characteristics of the entities found in the natural world, or on reliably measuring qualitative variations in those characteristics and producing mathematical statements of the relations among the results of those measurements. All scientific work assembles its explanatory ideas into logical structures. Classification science tends to use Aristotelian logic, while mathematical science requires some form of propositional logic.[3] To explain something within a particular explanatory discipline, then, is to account for it in terms of the ideas appropriate to that discipline.

Metaphysics is yet another form of explanation. It is generally similar to science in a number of ways:

- It is rooted in logic.
- It attempts to describe the actual world in its totality.
- It proceeds by means of hypothesis and testing.
- It seeks to bind the entirety of its domain into a single system of logical relations—in other words, it seeks explanations with terms that hold their meanings in different contexts and where contradictions among terms and statements are avoided.

Metaphysics is unlike science, however, in the object of its study. Science restricts its domain to actualities disclosed through the bodily senses. It attempts to bind these actualities into a unified system in two ways: first, in the "natural history" phase, science aims to order the natural entities that it observes with the bodily senses into a hierarchy of logical categories. Then, in the more modern "experimental phase," science aims to represent those entities by measurements and to reduce those measurements to the unity of a single, all-embracing mathematical theory (a "grand unified theory").

In contrast, metaphysics takes for its domain the *entirety* of experience, not just experiences mediated by the bodily senses. It

---

[3] Aristotelian logic is a logic of classification and is generally associated with substance ontologies. Modern propositional logic is a logic of functions. It describes relations among entities in a general way. Modern propositional logic is much more general than Aristotelian logic. In fact, Aristotelian logic is a subset of propositional logic that analyzes the particular functions involved in assigning characteristics to entities and classes, and assigning entities to classes. Mathematics can be derived from propositional logic, but it cannot be derived from Aristotelian logic. For a deeper consideration of these issues, see Ernst Cassirer's *Substance and Function and Einstein's Theory of Relativity*, pp. 3–26.

includes not only the domain of physical events but also the domain of consciousness and all its operations—such as free association of thoughts, rational thinking, emotional and poetic musing, aesthetic and cognitive judgments, and so forth.

Metaphysics also differs from science (and other modes of knowledge such as ethics and aesthetics) in an additional fundamental and important way. Whereas, for example, science takes as its foundation a set of (often unquestioned) metaphysical assumptions, metaphysics *begins by questioning its own assumptions* as well as the assumptions of other disciplines such as science, ethics, and aesthetics. The attention that metaphysics brings to the issue of fundamental assumptions sets it apart from other knowledge disciplines. Other disciplines tend to start with a set of ideas that seem self-evident and then use those ideas to form explanations. Metaphysics, by contrast, looks *at* explanatory ideas themselves and critiques them in terms of their coherence and usefulness.

The *methods* of metaphysics are also quite different from those of other modes of knowing. It does not restrict itself either to hierarchical categorization or to mathematical analysis. Rather, metaphysics encompasses all of the different ways in which the field of experience can be coherently unified—in terms of story, in terms of aesthetic composition, in terms of various sorts of logic—and attempts to appreciate the values and the limits of each of the disciplines that it examines.

The method of metaphysics begins with the study of explanatory disciplines per se. Metaphysics takes on this task in order to identify and clarify key ideas that are used within a particular discipline—including the discipline of metaphysics itself. In doing so, it aims to see how far the ideas and connections used within any one discipline can be generalized and coherently applied to other disciplines and, ideally, to the whole range of experience.

Each individual discipline provides a set of conceptual tools applicable within its own domain. Examining those conceptual tools, metaphysics searches for ideas that can be generalized and shown to be *adequate* over the entirety of experience. For example, from quantum mechanics we get the idea that actuality is composed of discrete, causally interacting events. We know that this idea is applicable to the analysis of the subatomic realm. The metaphysical system we will be exploring here attempts to generalize this idea to cover all of actuality—from the exotic realm of the subatomic to the unfolding experience of human beings—which, as we will see, can also be understood as a system of causally interconnected discrete events.

As a kind of preview or foreshadowing of what is to come, you can essentially consider this book an exercise in metaphysics that generalizes the revolutionary insights of quantum mechanics to the entire spectrum of experience—including consciousness itself and, in particular, human personality. However, I want to make it clear that I am not suggesting we can turn to quantum physics to *explain* consciousness or personality. Rather, I am saying that we can use the tools of metaphysics to show a fundamental coherence between certain ideas in quantum physics and a more comprehensive cosmology inspired by the metaphysics of Whitehead.

Testing Metaphysics

Having assembled a set of applicable ideas,[4] metaphysics then proceeds to a kind of phenomenological testing. That is, a metaphysician will see whether or not a description of experience based on these ideas actually serves to illuminate experience in interesting and useful ways. Does this description actually correspond to experience? Does this description open up new possibilities that experience can explore?

Metaphysics, as we will understand it, does not start with dogmatic axioms as, for example, mathematics does. Rather, it starts with what Whitehead calls "tentative formulations of the ultimate generalities"[5] of experience, which it then tests against experience itself. But then, like science, it proceeds to make deductions from those tentative generalizations to see how successful they are at illuminating our experience. Some metaphysical generalizations pass this test, and others do not. When the deductions from the generalizations are unsuccessful, the metaphysician, like the scientist, goes "back to the drawing board" and examines his or her assumptions to see where they were wrong and how they can be revised.

---

[4] For a discussion of the assemblage of applicable ideas, see Alfred North Whitehead's *Modes of Thought*, Chapter 1.
[5] Whitehead, *Process and Reality*.

Finally, metaphysical activity is a search for ideas and forms of connection among ideas that can be generalized over the totality of experience so as to exhibit it in its orderly wholeness, and to find a place within that whole for all of the truths revealed by the various specific disciplines.

Newton's astounding success in explaining the motions of moving bodies lulled our dominant academic institutions into the belief that modern science had uncovered the literal truth about the nature of the actual world, and that it had no need whatsoever for the discipline of philosophy in general, and for the discipline of metaphysics in particular. However, as science developed, its very successes forced it into a series of metaphysical revolutions. Since Thomas Kuhn's groundbreaking work in the philosophy of science, we now think of these metaphysical revolutions as "paradigm shifts."[6] A paradigm shift is, among other things, a change in the basic set of explanatory concepts of a science. It is a testament to the vitality and integrity of the scientific tradition that it has embraced these paradigm shifts. Unfortunately, scientists tend to think of themselves as dealing merely with facts and measurements and not with the total activity of explaining the actual world. So the paradigm shifts within science have led us into a terrible philosophical muddle and have left quantum physicists and other advanced scientists out of harmony with the general ideas of scientifically informed common sense.

In other words: science-inspired common sense (the general worldview of educated laypeople and most practicing scientists) is out of step with the great twentieth-century revolutions in the physics of relativity and quantum mechanics. Contemporary "scientific common sense" is anachronistic—still stuck in the seventeenth-century mechanics of Isaac Newton or the eighteenth-century electromagnetism of James Clerk Maxwell.

My objective, then, is to outline a framework of ideas that will allow us to make sense of postmodern science and of the five propositions at the core of this book. It is my hope that this general metaphysical system will allow us to be comfortable in holding the well-proven facts of science and the facts that point toward a more complex and interesting life cycle for human personalities—the prime concern of this book.

---

[6] Thomas Kuhn, *The Structure of Scientific Revolutions*.

I am sure some of my readers will question the need for such a radical move and would prefer to find some way to extend current modes of scientific explanation to accommodate the anomalous data we are considering. However, I will show why a major shift in our mode of thought is indeed required, and why metaphysical ideas assumed by pre-quantum science cannot be stretched to account for the data of parapsychology, personality survival, or reincarnation.

A Brief History of Scientific Ideas

In order to appreciate why we need this shift, let's briefly review how the metaphysical ideas of modern science developed.[7] We can pick up the story of the development of these ideas with Copernicus and Kepler in the sixteenth and seventeenth centuries. Both men were members of a kind of Platonic underground—a long line of scholars who kept alive certain of Plato's ideas in the face of the dominant Aristotelian tenor of the times. One of the Platonic ideas that inspired the work of Copernicus and Kepler was the belief that mathematics is the key to understanding nature. In particular, both were attempting to justify Plato's conjecture that the mysterious movements of the planets against the fixed stars must be governed by some elegant mathematical function. The fact that they could simplify their calculations of planetary movements by placing the Sun in the center of the system of planets was enough to convince them of the truth of the heliocentric view.

The successes of Copernicus and Kepler later influenced Galileo, who expanded their work by mathematically analyzing the movements of not only celestial objects but objects on Earth.

If we view the ideas of Copernicus, Kepler, and Galileo from the cosmological perspective current at that time, we can clearly see the absurdity of the heliocentric theory. Nothing, after all, is more obvious than the stillness of the Earth and the movements of the sun, moon, and the other planets around it. Also, as anyone who has ridden a horse would clearly realize, moving through space at high velocity is a dramatic and risky business. If the Earth were actually moving, we'd

---

[7] For an excellent treatment of this history going back to Aristotle, see Ivor Leclerc's *The Nature of Physical Existence*. For an excellent and highly readable history going back to Copernicus and Kepler, see A. E. Burtt's *The Metaphysical Foundations of Modern Science*.

all be thrown off. Furthermore, if the Earth were not at the center of the created world, all objects on its surface would naturally fall toward the real center. Logic, backed by observation, was clear: if the sun really was at the center of things, everything would fall off the Earth and tumble into the sun's burning furnace. With the benefit of hindsight it might not be so obvious, but in fact the medieval scholars who rejected Copernicus' heliocentric view did so with reasons that were entirely valid at the time. Of course, in time, science found ways to neutralize those objections within its own framework.

The core lesson we learn from paradigm shifts is that obviousness is no guarantee of truth. Perceptions can be deceiving and beliefs can be profoundly mistaken. For example, in Galileo's time, accepting the heliocentric theory was just about as difficult as accepting my five central propositions and the new metaphysics they imply might be today. But greater comprehensiveness, coherence, and adequacy of a worldview sooner or later trumps more limited ideas and beliefs.

Despite the evidence of daily observation, scientists found a way to overturn the obviousness of Earth-centered cosmology. They began by developing a theory of gravitation in which each body attracts all other bodies to itself. They could then show that the Earth moves around the sun and that falling objects released in proximity to the Earth would still hit the Earth, and that the Earth could move at high velocities without people and things spinning off into space. By demonstrating how it could *seem as if* the sun revolves around the Earth, even when the Earth is really revolving around the sun, the new science began to win converts and initiated a new industrial civilization.

We are in a similar position today. The world must be very different from what we were taught to believe based on the ideas of scientific materialism. The data of parapsychology, evidence in support of survival of consciousness beyond death and reincarnation—not to mention the simple fact of consciousness itself—compel a latter-day paradigm shift comparable to the Copernican revolution. The dimensions of this metaphysical shift are suggested by the five propositions I have offered as a way to begin making sense of all the data. Make no mistake: neither these propositions nor the supporting data can be accommodated within the dominant worldview of modern reductionistic science. We need a new metaphysics, a new world system, that not only shows why science gets the results it does but explains these results in the context of a universe where the revolutionary five propositions are true.

The importance of Galileo's breakthrough, and its significance for our times, can hardly be overstated. Nearly two millennia earlier, Plato had believed that the incorruptible, sacred heavens moved in a perfect mathematical order. Earth, the realm of mere appearance, could not be intelligible in terms of the perfection of number. Yet that is precisely what Galileo believed he had demonstrated: Earth is guided, or ruled, by an intricate perfection of mathematical order. Over time, it came to seem as if God had ordered all things by number, and that the ability of humans to discern mathematical order in nature was a unique communion between man[8] and the Divine creative intelligence. From the beginning there was a shadow side to this inspiration: if reality is ultimately intelligible through mathematics, then we gain an extraordinary ability to turn facts about the present into precise and accurate predictions about the future. All of modern technology with its consequences for good and for ill is a testament to the power of that realization.

When Galileo and others began to articulate a new metaphysical cosmology, their foundational premise was that mathematics is the language of creation and that mathematical analysis reveals nature's most intimate secrets. In one form or another, the question echoing through the new science was: What must nature be like, given that she is ultimately mathematical in nature? For a century or so following Galileo, scientists debated the relationship between numbers and reality—for example, whether matter is anything other than extension itself, whether there are individual atoms, and whether or not atoms have extension or mass. Finally, late in the seventeenth century, Newton stunned the scientific world by producing a masterful mathematical description of the laws of motion that accounted, in great detail, for everything from the movements of planets in the heavens to the falling of leaves. The Copernican–Galilean cosmology had vindicated the power of numbers to a range of application and degree of precision Plato could hardly have imagined. Henceforth, following Newton, the

---

[8] I use the masculine pronoun here deliberately as it is characteristic of the mode of thought I am describing. To see only numbers in nature is to miss "the Mother" entirely, and to fall into dismal patriarchy.

philosophical basis for the mathematical analysis of nature was secured. Nature was now understood to be a collection of changeless, minuscule, massy particles occupying, at any given instant, a volume of Euclidean space and, through God's perfect calculations,[9] influencing each other as if through mathematically described gravitational forces that fall off in intensity as a function of distance. If reality were truly as Newton's equations suggested, then mathematical analysis would be the Holy Grail that unlocks the deepest secrets of nature, giving humanity access to and mastery over her latent powers.

If reality truly is as the Newtonians believed, then mathematical physicists are the ultimate oracles—using numbers to predict nature's every move. Coupling religion with science, the corollary naturally follows: If all of reality is mere movement of insentient mechanical matter, and humans alone possess the gift of intellect, then God has surely given "man" dominion over the Earth. With our "divine intellect" and the ability to discern mathematical patterns, we have direct insight into the mind of God, guaranteeing our right to do exactly as we please with the material world. This is the shadow side of science and technology.

On the other hand, if we agree with the scientists that nature is nothing more than a very complex mechanical device, how are we to account for our own personalities—for *consciousness*? Should we grant ourselves the status of divine spirits who miraculously inhabit high-tech biological machines? Or, taking the other view, should we relegate ourselves to the status of epiphenomena, observing nature but having no real effect on it? More extremely, should we regard ourselves as entirely delusory, being confused about the unreality of our own merely *seeming* existence?

---

[9] Newton's synthesis was entirely dependent on God's ability to calculate. Since Newton still believed in a mechanical philosophy, he appreciated that his atoms were inert and could only be moved externally, by God. Thus, Newton imagined his work as powerful proof of the existence of God. Immediately after Newton, scientists dropped God out of the system and began to act as if the atoms themselves "possessed" gravitational fields. But gravity, understood in this way, is action at a distance—something in complete contradiction to mechanism. Without realizing it, scientists here slipped into a profound metaphysical shift that eventually led to Einstein's relativity theory and to Whitehead's rethinking of the very nature of space and time (see Chapter 8).

These disturbing ontological questions follow, unavoidably, if we take Newton's cosmology as ultimate truth. And, as mentioned earlier, we also need to deal with a decisive epistemological conundrum lurking in the heart of materialistic science itself. Science is based on experiments that depend on sensory observations, and these, in turn, require conscious experience. However, there is no way to derive conscious sensation, let alone the interpretive activity that necessarily accompanies it, from the mere hurrying about of insentient atoms. These problems are well known and have been an outstanding scandal in Western thought for many generations.

The problem, when viewed from a metaphysical perspective, is not difficult to understand. It is a simple confusion of a conceptual model with the actual world. Let me explain.

Newton succeeded in creating an abstract model that is exceptionally useful for studying the motions of macrocosmic entities of all sorts—from peanuts to planets. If we represent space as a Cartesian grid, and each entity as a point (or a set of points) in that grid, and if we represent gravitational interaction as a vector field[10] on that grid, then we can use calculus to compute how those points will move over time under the influence of gravity. Remarkably enough, the movements of the points on the grid will more or less approximate the movements of actual entities in space over time. That is brilliant modeling.

But given the complexity of the actual world, there is always some margin of error in applying the calculations back to the actual world. Actuality is more complex than any model can capture—the model is an *abstraction* from the *fully concrete actual world*. Ignoring the difference between the actual world and the model, scientists assumed that the *model* depicted the *real* world, while our perceptions of the world, where they differed from the model, were illusory. This move—confusing a model of the world for the actual world—was what Whitehead called the "fallacy of misplaced concreteness."[11]

---

[10] To turn a grid into a vector field, we place a little conceptual arrow at each point, representing the forces operating on that point that will tend to cause an object in one moment to move in a particular direction and velocity at the next moment.

[11] To fully understand the meaning of the "fallacy of misplaced concreteness," we must keep in mind that Whitehead uses the word "concrete" to refer to the opposite of the abstract. In other words, that which is concrete is that which is fully actual. The concrete is infinitely complex. Scientific and philosophical abstractions are

Since the time of Newton and Descartes, this fallacy has more or less gone unchecked because it seemed to confirm the scientific idea that mathematical form alone determines the processes of nature. But under critical philosophical analysis, the difficulties quickly become evident.

- First, the Cartesian–Newtonian view requires the separation of perceptions into those that reveal *primary qualities* and *secondary qualities*. Smell, taste, hearing, and the perception of color were all held to be secondary because they did not reveal qualities that could be quantified, whereas touch and the visual perception of form were held to be primary because they figured prominently in measurement and revealed qualities that could be quantified. Of course touch and the visual perception of form are, as soon became apparent, also subjective and open to interpretation and error. And thus the epistemological morass of modernity came into being.

- A second consequence of mistaking the model for actuality was the notion that the physical world is a causally closed domain. After all, if the model discloses the actual world behind appearances, and if the model is complete, then no factors other than those represented by the model can affect the macroscopic movements of actual entities. Furthermore, because the mathematical structure of the model is entirely deterministic, there is no room left in the real world for freedom, value, and genuine choice. Thus, the physical world is causally closed. Add to this the fact that Newton's model could not represent consciousness or personality at all, and the very fact of conscious experience becomes a "hard problem"[12] indeed. The task of trying to derive consciousness from a model designed only to analyze fully determinate macrocosmic motions of inanimate objects is quite impossible.

---

simplified models of the concrete. To confuse a simplified abstraction with the concrete actuality from which it has been abstracted is to commit the fallacy of misplaced concreteness.

[12] Chalmers, David. (1995). Facing up to the problem of consciousness. *Journal of Consciousness Studies 2*(3), 200–19.

The point here is that classical science, which is based on techniques that respond to a narrow interest (the interest in measuring and predicting macrocosmic movements), is entirely too narrow in its scope to be applied to consciousness and personality and thus hopeless when it comes to parapsychology, personality survival, and reincarnation.

Now science—unlike scientifically shaped common sense—has not remained wedded to the simple Newtonian model. In fact, science has gone through several paradigm shifts, or metaphysical changes, in which its basic ideas have been modified.

In particular:

- Science has come to accept the actual existence of "fields" and has supplemented gravitational fields with electromagnetic fields and strong and weak nuclear fields.
- With the theory of relativity, science was able to embrace a fusion of space with time, a fusion of energy with matter, and, finally, a fusion of energy with time-space itself.
- Through the use of computers, which permit the deep exploration of recursive functions, science has developed "chaos theory," which illuminates the tendency of natural systems to self-organize into stable, macroscopic structures; and it has developed the theory of fractal geometry, which illuminates nature's habit of reproducing similar structures at various scales of organization.
- Through Prigogine's "non-equilibrium thermodynamics," science has succeeded in showing how living organisms can function without violating the second law of thermodynamics, thus bringing the phenomena of life more into harmony with the principles of physics.
- Finally, at the frontier of classical science, Maturana and Varela[13] have proposed a theory of self-organizing systems that suggest life is defined by a particular *organization* of otherwise insentient matter, bringing life even more solidly into the purview of a modified classical physics.

---

[13] Humberto R. Maturana and Francisco J. Varela, *Autopoiesis and Cognition: The Realization of the Living.*

These developments in scientific metaphysics have given us a deeper understanding of the behaviors of the physical world. They have also allowed us to include within the purview of science some of the patterns expressed by living matter. But, for our purposes, they remain excessively narrow and abstract. While chaos theory, non-equilibrium thermodynamics, and autopoiesis can model certain external *behaviors* of living system, they cannot say anything about consciousness and personality and so cannot help us in our attempt to understand our five fundamental propositions.

Quantum mechanics, however, the most recent and most far-reaching metaphysical revolution to develop within the scientific tradition, has finally developed a scientific model sufficiently rich to make room for consciousness and personality. Quantum theory revises our conception of the physical world in these fundamental ways:

- First, it gives up the idea of substantial atoms—of finite entities that endure unchanging through time—and replaces it with the idea of causally interacting *events*, each of which takes place over a finite interval of time. Also, these events are *not* fully determined in advance. There is a certain irreducible uncertainty involved in predicting how they will behave. Further, this uncertainty can be, and often is, interpreted so as to suggest the existence of objective probabilities as part of the real world.

- Second, in at least some of its interpretations, quantum theory implies the existence of consciousness that is causal, and not determined in any way by anything in the physical world. An observer, for example is a source of the decisions among alternatives that collapse the wave function. Thus quantum theory not only makes room for the *existence* of consciousness, it breaks the causal closure of the physical by making consciousness a significant factor that actually determines how events play out in the physical world.[14]

---

[14] See, for example, Henry Stapp's, *Mind, Matter, and Quantum Mechanics*, and *The Mindful Universe: Quantum Mechanics and the Participating Observer*; and Epperson, *Quantum Mechanics*.

- Third, quantum theory thoroughly rehabilitates those qualities that classical science had tended to dismiss as "secondary." In the quantum world, any quality that has a determinable probability of being detected by an emerging event can be represented in the model[15] and thus is held to be fully actual.

With quantum mechanics, science has, at last, advanced to a set of metaphysical ideas that open it to the presence of consciousness and personality and so bring it within range of helping to explain our five propositions. But quantum mechanics is still primarily a theory concerning the behavior of inorganic events. It is not yet a full metaphysical system, capable of dealing with the phenomenology of the personality, and with the ideas with which we are concerned.

The Current State of Metaphysics

Newton's staggering success in predicting the motions of macrocosmic bodies so impressed the educated West that metaphysics as a discipline began to fall on hard times. The German philosopher Hegel was the last of the famous metaphysicians, and his synthesis fell apart—partly because it could not keep up with advances in science, partly because it painted eighteenth-century Prussian society as the ultimate achievement of cosmic evolution, and partly because the shock of two world wars resulted in a great cynicism toward any form of systematic thought.

During the first half of the 20th century, metaphysics was an academic backwater. During the second half, it became practically nonexistent. Nonetheless, the need for a comprehensive understanding of the actual world continued to be felt, particularly after relativity theory and quantum mechanics swept the rug out from under the classical sciences that inform so much of modern common sense. Certain scientists[16] tried to fill the gap, but their ignorance of the larger philosophical tradition kept their work focused on narrow issues. Nonetheless, a few philosophers continued to work in this area, among them Alfred North Whitehead, Ernst Cassirer, and Sri Aurobindo. These writers

---

[15] It will be represented in "Hilbert space" as a dimension.
[16] For example, Schrödinger, Von Neumann, Heisenberg, and Bohr.

are truly remarkable for the depth of their insights and perhaps equally remarkable for the lack of attention their ideas have received. I believe, for example, that Alfred North Whitehead entirely solved the mind-body problem back in the 1930s, and yet that issue is still debated as if he had never published his masterpiece *Process and Reality*. The ideas of these three philosophers form the central inspiration for the system I will shortly outline.

The fact is that our civilization is in desperate need of a comprehensive metaphysical framework that can integrate spiritual inspirations, moral and aesthetic aspirations, parapsychological investigations, exploration of the "long trajectory" of human existence, our ongoing investigations of the physical and biological sciences, and our technological manipulations of the world. We need some way of understanding how it is that all of these diverse explorations take place in the context of a single, unified world.

That is the task of the new metaphysical framework presented in this book—drawing heavily on the process metaphysics of Whitehead and the metaphysical and cosmological ideas of Sri Aurobindo. I call it "transphysical process metaphysics."

Chapter 3: Actual Occasions: As Above, So Below

Articulating a new set of metaphysical ideas that can ground mainstream science and parapsychology is a bold undertaking. I am proposing the foundations for a new way of understanding reality itself. This is a necessary step if we are going to understand a world where we must take into account not only the data of science but the vast body of evidence—scientific and anecdotal—that reveals parapsychological phenomena in general and that points to the personality's survival after bodily death and to reincarnation. We need a new "story," a comprehensive metaphysics large enough to hold the vision of a world that is more than mere insentient matter whirling about in a blind and "dead" universe—a world rich with sentient beings who inhabit a far more complex time-space than what science and our bodily senses have so far detected. I believe that our science, our philosophy, and, indeed, our civilization itself are in need of a new story like this if we are going to surmount the enormous challenges posed by the evolutionary crisis unfolding itself on our planet today.

This enormous task, however, is made easier because, to echo Newton, I stand on the shoulders of giants. Much of the essential groundwork has already been laid, and my contribution is to gather, recombine, and develop the fundamental insights of metaphysical revolutionaries such as Alfred North Whitehead, Sri Aurobindo, Jean Gebser, and Ernst Cassirer.

Beyond Substance

I start with Whitehead's idea of "actual occasions." This is Whitehead's metaphysical generalization of "events," which form the building blocks of quantum mechanics. This idea is central in his attempt to develop a metaphysics that would account for science in general, and the theories of relativity and quantum mechanics in particular, as well as the rich experience of everyday life. As we will come to discover, a slight extension of Whitehead's notion will allow us also to account for my five fundamental propositions and bring our understanding of the long trajectory of human life into harmony with today's scientific knowledge.

Before Einstein's theory of relativity and the advent of quantum mechanics, scientists took for granted the idea of "substance" as the metaphysical background for how to think about reality. Substance, they believed (following Descartes) was that which needs nothing other than itself to exist. It is stuff, things, atoms. Little bits of hard matter that endure in time and occupy space.

Relativity modified the notion of substance by interpreting matter as nothing but temporary configurations of energy or, even more radically, as twists in the curvature of space-time. In the context of relativity, energy just *is*. In special relativity, it is a tenuous, fluid-like substance that flows through time and occupies space. In general relativity, it exists as local distortions in the space-time continuum—which is itself, as the permanent basis of things, also a sort of substance. But quantum mechanics does away with the idea of substance altogether, describing reality as a system of abrupt, short-lived, discontinuous energetic *events* that, while having a spatial center, endure in time only briefly. Furthermore, as many writers have pointed out (a fact highly relevant to the ideas explored in this book), quantum mechanics cannot be understood apart from some reference to consciousness as an independent, causal factor in the actual world.[1]

Whitehead was intimately familiar with the theory of relativity[2] and early quantum theory. As a metaphysician, Whitehead was critiquing the dominant conceptual toolkit of science and suggested science could be

---

[1] Stapp, *Mindful Universe*; and Epperson, *Quantum Mechanics*.
[2] Whitehead wrote a book in which he reworked Einstein's entire theory because he felt that Einstein's definition of simultaneity was inadequate. See Whitehead's essay, "The Principle of Relativity with Applications to Physical Science" in *Alfred North Whitehead: An Anthology*.

liberated from many of its current conceptual confusions by interpreting quanta as instances of a new scientific idea: "actual occasions."

The Idea of Actual Occasions

My body, and the things I interact with in the world around me, are clearly decomposable. I have the sense that somewhere at the bottom of that decomposition process there must be some final level, some primitive *stuff* out of which everything else is made. What is that stuff like?

The answer we get from materialists, the guardians of scientific orthodoxy, dominates the imagination of modern civilization. As we saw in the last chapter, the basic explanatory concepts of materialism have evolved considerably over the past few centuries. They began with the idea of "atoms" as finite, self-existent, fully actual, endlessly enduring, ontologically independent *things* existing in a Euclidean space and enduring in an independent, uniformly flowing time. Later, the concept of simple enduring atoms was expanded to include new metaphysical categories (for instance, energetic fields, probability fields, variable interactions between space, time and mass, complementary sets of properties for physical entities, and even non-local interactions among such entities). The original metaphysical simplicity of the Newtonian vision had subsequently elaborated itself into a vast and baroque complexity. But no matter how elaborate their notions became, scientific materialists were and still are unified in their conviction that the ultimate stuff is "dead," or insentient.

The five propositions I outlined in the previous chapters are alternatives to a set of propositions that underlie the metaphysics of scientific materialism—namely, that the ultimate stuff

- Is *not* conscious or aware
- Is governed by laws that are automatically administered and can be mathematically expressed
- May act randomly but never purposefully
- Is not aware of itself or of others and thus has no value for itself

For some of us at least, this is a stark and terrifying view of reality. It leaves us with the sense that we are epiphenomenal, accidental, and unimportant byproducts of vast, indifferent processes. Others, however, find in this view a kind of austere beauty. It brings a sense of freedom from the meddling of a parental God. It confers on its adherents a hugely pragmatic view of life and an awesome power over local configurations of physical events. Whatever the aesthetic merits of this view, however, and in spite of its practical power, it does not do a good job of explaining the ultimate nature of reality.

No materialist has ever explained just how it is that dead stuff could manage to configure itself to become aware, to feel—to be alive, imaginative, and conscious. More to the point, since materialists must interpret personality as somehow a function of the physical operations of the biological body, they can provide no coherent explanation for the facts of personality survival and reincarnation.

The failure of materialism makes room for philosophical idealism, in which both things, and questions about those things, are always experiences *in consciousness.* Philosophical idealists approach the question "what are things made of" *through* the question "how are things experienced." Every truth to which you or I have access is a truth that we experience. The sensual, the vital, the emotional, and the cognitive are so many ranges in the spectrum of experience. Experience is, by definition, conscious.[3] All knowledge is knowledge of the contents of consciousness. Philosophical idealists, then, see consciousness, or perhaps mind, as the basic *"stuff"* out of which things arise.

The problem with idealism, though, is that it has a tendency to degenerate into solipsism; it leaves us with a sense that the world around us ought to be dreamlike and unsubstantial. Idealists have a hard time

---

[3] Whitehead uses the word "conscious" in a technical sense to mean *intellectually* conscious—i.e., conscious of perceiving actualities against a background of possibility. He thus distinguishes between "experience," which is a kind of bare awareness, and "consciousness," which is a more complex operation. In this book, I will use the word "consciousness" to mean what Whitehead means by "experience"—the intrinsic subjectivity of all actual occasions. This use of "consciousness" is closer to the way that word is currently employed in discussions of the philosophy of mind. Note, however, that in the philosophy of mind, consciousness is usually understood as something "extra" that is somehow added on to the dead and automatic functioning of the physical world. In transpersonal process metaphysics, consciousness is understood as, among other things, the capacity to feel (to be causally affected), and to decide (to generate causal conditions for the future).

accounting for the stubborn, indifferent, alien facticity of the material world.

Idealism also fails us in our quest for an understanding of personality survival and reincarnation in another way. If we posit that all manifestation is the expression of one featureless, undifferentiated consciousness (as, for example, in Advaita Vedanta), it becomes difficult to account for the multiplicity of *individual* consciousnesses that are prominent in our experience. Indeed, Advaita Vedanta itself relegates the individualization of consciousness (along with all of the other specific and changing characteristics of differing personalities and of the worlds they experience) to the status of an illusion. A framework that provides no way of intelligibly accounting for the individualization of consciousness is unlikely to be a fruitful context in which to discuss the survival and reincarnation of the individual personality.[4]

When we see that neither a monism of matter nor a monism of mind or consciousness is entirely satisfying, we may then be tempted to posit some kind of dualism—for example, in the modern era, we may assume that the results of the hard sciences are valid within the domain of physical matter, but that there is also another kind of reality, a kind of conscious substance, that is ontologically distinct and separable from physical substance. On the face of it, this approach seems appealing because it allows us to imagine that consciousness, rather than the body, survives death and ultimately reincarnates in a new physical body.

This dualistic approach was most famously pioneered in the early modern period by René Descartes, who proposed that there were two kinds of substance: *res extensa* (extended things) and *res cogitans* (thinking things). The difficulty with this idea and, indeed, with all forms of ontological substance dualism, is that they provide no necessary or intelligible relationship between the two kinds of substance. In the context of Cartesian dualism, all of the causal interactions we can measure and that, therefore, we credit as real, take place within the closed domain of the *res extensa*. Thus, while a dualistic perspective

---

[4] In fairness to idealism, there are other versions that do find ways of accounting for the existence of separate individuals. The "absolute idealism" of Hegel comes to mind. I would argue, however, that once there are separate individuals in any kind of causal interaction, we are dealing not with idealism but with a form of panpsychism. I have chosen Advaita Vedanta as the example to critique because of its popularity in popular New Age culture.

allows us to imagine that a consciousness, as an independent substance, survives the death of its body, we are hard-pressed to understand the relevance of that consciousness to the body that it inhabits in the first place. After all, there is nothing about the body—a substantial entity that needs nothing other than itself to exist—that requires it to be conscious, and nothing about consciousness, another independent substance that also needs nothing other than itself to exist, that requires it to have a body.

The doctrine of metaphysical dualism is unstable. It may, as we can see in our modern intellectual tradition, quickly reduce the *res cogitans* to the status of an epiphenomenon, thus rendering it essentially irrelevant and banishing it from respectable discourse. Or, as we can see in some significant strands of Western idealism and in some significant strands of Vedic thought, it may fall back into a monism of consciousness by relegating matter, and all other differentiations, to the status of an illusion. In either case, like materialism and idealism, dualism does not provide a satisfactory resolution to the hard problem of explaining how mind and body, or consciousness and the physical world, are related.

Materialism claims that mind emerges from brain. Idealism claims that either the material world emanates from pure consciousness or that it's illusory. Dualism claims that both mind and matter are real but exist in separate ontological domains. The hard problem for materialists is to explain the *emergence* of consciousness from dead matter; for idealists, it is to explain the *emanation* of a world of discrete individuals from an undifferentiated unity; and for dualists, it is to explain *interaction* between two radically different and separate substances. The stubborn persistence of this hard problem, or "world knot" as Schopenhauer called it, indicates that something is profoundly mistaken about the basic metaphysical terms used to figure out the mind-body relation. Whitehead's great contribution to this issue was to identify the notion of "substance" as a prime source of the error. Instead of substance, Whitehead famously reconceived the mind-matter relationship in terms of "conscious process."

Philosophical debate over the past few centuries in the West has constellated into arguments between idealists, materialists, and dualists.[5]

---

[5] For a deeper and more elaborate consideration of these basic ontological issues, see de Quincey's *Radical Nature*.

Either the basic stuff out of which things are made is dead matter, or it is the conscious mind, or it is some awkward combination of two kinds of ontological ultimate. Each of these positions is compelling and represents some important element of the truth of things. But none is entirely satisfactory.

Recognizing this impasse, Whitehead opened up a new and useful way of re-conceptualizing the basic nature of reality. First, he pointed out—in perfect accord with our experience of the world and with scientific understanding—that the actual world is made up not of self-existent things that endure unchanging through time but of *happenings* or *events*.

When we look to science, we find that the early modern atomists had a difficult time accounting for the richness of the world and, in particular, for the richness of interactions among atoms, in terms of the simple "billiard ball" idea of atoms. In attempts to account for chemical and electrical interactions among atoms, scientists first resolved them into moving systems of particles, each of which carries an electrical and a gravitational field. Later, quantum mechanics, further resolved these smaller particles into dynamic fields of probability that occasionally collapse and manifest themselves as short-lived, causally efficacious, energetic blips. Scientists have now discovered that describing ultimate reality in terms of enduring, self-existent, independent things is not tenable. Instead, they have been forced to describe objective reality as a field of causally interacting, temporally extended events.

Because we are familiar with scientific reasoning, it is not too surprising for us to follow this line of thought, and to see, with Whitehead, that we can conceptualize outer, objective reality in terms of interacting events rather than in terms of substantial, self-existent things.

But what happens if we turn around and look at the texture of our own everyday experience? Suppose we ask, "What unit of analysis best serves for producing an interesting and useful description of our own experience?" Whitehead suggests that the most interesting way to describe the fine grain of our own existence is in terms of "drops of experience."[6]

If I ask myself what I am experiencing, I begin to notice meaningful

---

[6] Whitehead borrowed this phrase from William James.

67

"chunks," such as "I am experiencing this room," or "I am experiencing that table." These chunks are not, of course, entirely separate from one another. They are causally interconnected, and they do run into one another in our experience. Nonetheless, if we play back our experience in memory, we can notice that we are not consciously aware of any process in the formation of the objects that we perceive. For example, I see the lamp on my desk. The "lamp experience" comes to me all at once, without any awareness that I am composing that experience out of smaller parts. I may, under certain circumstances, be confused and not know just what it is I am perceiving. Perhaps, for example, I am looking into a room through a narrow crack, and am not quite able to make out the lines and shapes that I am inspecting. In that case, I am experiencing, let us say, a grey blob and a black line. The experience of the grey blob comes to me all at once, as does the experience of the black line. And, if and when I do recognize those shapes as belonging to a chair, that recognition comes to me all at once, as a discrete drop of experience.

I want to be clear that neither Whitehead nor I are denying the obvious continuity of our experience. But I am pointing out that there is a certain grain, or texture, to experience that allows it to be analyzed into distinct (though not separate) drops or "occasions" of experience.

The point here is that the actual drops of experience I find when I inspect my own consciousness are full, complex, internally structured events that exhibit, in spite of their particularity, intrinsic relations with other events in the larger field in which they are situated.

If we look more closely at these drops of experience, we see that they are always composed of other, simpler, drops of experience. If I look at my experience of that chair, across from me in my office, and I try, retroactively, to further decompose it, I notice smaller drops such as the experience of an arm rest, the experience of the back, and so on. Each of these elements is itself encapsulated in a whole drop of experience. Each is intrinsically interrelated with other drops in my field of experience. Each may be further decomposable. Whitehead calls the drops of experience, out of which more complex drops of experience are composed, "prehensions."

We can leave for later the question of whether or not this decomposition has a unique bottom. We are not entirely certain that subatomic particles (such as quanta, quarks, or superstrings) are the ultimate constituents of physical reality. Similarly, we need not know, for our current purposes, whether the process of analytically decomposing our experience has a unique bottom. The point is that no matter how far we take the analysis, we find not independent, self-existent, enduring things, but rather dynamically interacting, whole, temporally extended, distinct drops of experience. We notice, in fact, a striking resemblance between the wholeness, discreteness, and interrelatedness of quanta and the wholeness, discreteness, and interrelatedness of our drops of experience. It seems that the physical world and the world of experience both take place one drop at a time and are, thus, "quantized."

We see, then, that we can describe outer objective reality in terms of causally interacting events and inner subjective experience in terms of dynamically interconnected drops of experience.

We are now in a position to dissolve the bewildering gap between mind and matter played out in debates between materialists, idealists, and dualists. Whitehead invites us to consider the possibility that all of actuality, whether objective or subjective, is composed of just one kind of entity: "actual occasions." Experienced from the outside, actual occasions are objective events; experienced from the inside, they are drops of experience. Each moment of my experience is an actual occasion in the outer world. Everything I experience outside me is some configuration of other actual occasions. The process of manifesting as an energetic event on one hand, and of coming into consciousness as a drop of experience on the other, are the same process seen from two points of view.

This way of conceptualizing reality frees us at a stroke from the ontological divide between mind and matter that has haunted the modern psyche for centuries.

The ontological notion of actual occasions carries with it an interesting epistemological implication; it provides a compelling philosophical justification for the old Hermetic principle of correspondence: "As above, so below" can be reformulated now to read "As without, so within." This principle, supported by an analysis of reality into "actual occasions," is radically at odds with a fundamental assumption of modernity. Since the beginning of the scientific revolution, the split between the outer reality of matter and the inner reality of mind has been thorough and complete. It has been a given that any attempt to reason about outer reality by reference to inner experience is both inadmissible and erroneous, and can be dismissed as projection or anthropomorphism.

However, this rejection of the Hermetic principle involves a performative contradiction. No matter what our epistemological claims, we reason from inner experience. Our fundamental notions of space, time, energy, and causality are drawn from experience, as idealists, at least, have recognized. As long as we imagine consciousness and physical stuff to be entirely different orders of being, however, our reasoning from inner experience has to be, at least in scientific discussions, bracketed out and ignored. As a result, the explicit use of the Hermetic principle has been relegated to the philosophical hinterlands of psychology and occultism.

By contrast, in a world of actual occasions, the Hermetic principle is rehabilitated. For example, my ongoing experience is an ordered sequence of actual occasions occurring from moment to moment. Each occasion is partially constituted by its experience of past events. And each of those past events was itself an actual occasion. In turn, the actual occasion constituting this moment of my experience will be an event for all future occasions.

If I am brought into being by the same kind of process that brings all other events that I experience into being, then I am entirely justified in reasoning about the nature of those events by reference to my own experience.

Now let us see what happens if we apply the Hermetic principle to an analysis of events. First, we know that every drop of experience that constitutes *us* has a dipolar structure. That is, our experiences are experiences *of* and experiences *by*. Every drop of experience is, thus, a relationship between a subject and a field of objects. The subject of an experience—Whitehead calls this the "mental pole" of the actual occasion—is an *active, purposeful, deciding awareness.*

In every conscious moment, I am (however dimly) aware. I notice that my awareness is the centralizing pole around which the experience of diverse objects is organized into some kind of unity. I notice that my awareness is my capacity to be affected by external events and that what I am aware of is precisely those external events that are affecting me.

Whitehead invites us to generalize this characteristic of our own experience to all events constituting the universe. In other words, he suggests that every experience I have of some entity in the objective world—whether a human being or a billiard ball—is the experience of the outside of drops of experience that occurred in my past. And, he suggests, every drop of experience—including, for example, the one I am having right now as I write this word—is an event that can and will be experienced by actual occasions in the future.

To those of us educated in modern times, this is a shocking assertion. In general, we are willing to grant awareness to humans. We are usually willing to grant awareness even to domestic animals. But many of us think it's going too far to suggest that there might be awareness in jellyfish, plants, cells, atoms, or in subatomic events.

It is important to realize, however, that Whitehead is not suggesting that atoms are self-aware, thinking beings. He is also not suggesting that a billiard ball is conscious of itself as such. (I will return shortly to the important subject of differences among events and between events and the systems they form.) What Whitehead *is* suggesting is that all events—from those constituting human awareness to those that make up subatomic particles—have the same general structure involving some degree of matter and mind. He is suggesting that each and every event is ordered around a pole of awareness and that the capacity *to be causally affected and to respond* on one hand, and the capacity *to experience and to respond* on the other are two sides of the same coin.

Let's pause for a moment to admire the formal elegance of this suggestion. In our modern, materialistic way of thinking, we imagine a closed domain of non-conscious things—we call it the physical world—among which causal interactions take place. Causal interactions are thus imagined as entirely automatic. Consciousness, if there is such a thing, is a transparent, ineffective double, a ghost in the machine. Once we have banished consciousness from the workings of nature, we are hard-pressed to see how it could have any actual effect on the world in which it appears. And yet, in all of our practical dealings, and especially in our ethical dealings, we have no option but to act as if conscious choice (at least in human beings) *is* of decisive importance.

Whitehead's notion of actual occasions structured around a core of awareness resituates consciousness *within* the natural world. Every event, as we know from our study of physics, arises out of a field of possibility.

It emerges into manifestation as it resolves the partial indeterminacy inherent in that field. Whitehead suggests that the factor in every event that allows it to register possibilities and to resolve their indeterminacy is consciousness or awareness.

The awareness of a subatomic particle and the awareness of a human being are evidently very different in *degree*, but we need not imagine that they are entirely different in *kind*. Once we realize that "to be aware of something and to respond" and "'to be causally affected by something and to respond" are, in a deep sense synonymous and complementary phrases, many of the philosophical conundrums of modernity disappear. Consciousness presents itself no longer as an extra-cosmic mystery but as the crucial factor that, by making choices, resolves possibility into actuality and gives to the universe its discrete determinations. I am conscious *not* because I am miraculously different from all other material entities; rather, I am conscious precisely *because* I am, in my process of coming into being, structurally similar to all other material entities. *Sentience goes all the way down.*

The first result, then, of applying the Hermetic principle to the analysis of events is the realization that *all* discrete events are structured around a mental pole, a "drop" or "quantum" of conscious, deciding awareness.

Let us continue the investigation and see what other results we might derive.

The Internal Structure of Every Actual Occasion

We will now see that the arising of every actual occasion, or "drop of experience," involves the same dynamic structure that includes *experience, imaginative interpretation,* and *choice.*

For example, when I deconstruct a moment of my own waking life, I perceive that it grows out of an experience of the past. As I begin each new moment of my existence, I *feel* the last moment of my existence, and I *feel* the immediate past of the present situation around me. But my experience is more than that original rush of feeling.

Not only do I feel the immediate past—in each moment I *interpret* the immediate past. This process of generating a coherent interpretation is quite complex. Whitehead has analyzed this in great detail, particularly in *Process and Reality*.[7] For our purposes, we can be satisfied with a general description: the process of interpretation arranges all of the diverse data of the past into a coherent pattern, ordered around the mental pole of the "concrescence" occasion. ("Concrescence" is Whitehead's technical term for the process whereby a new actual occasion arises out of the diverse occasions of the past and then becomes one of those diverse occasions for future occasions.) The process of interpretation is not uniquely determined by the past. It sometimes happens that in the process of interpreting the data of my experience, I have a new idea, a new way of organizing my perceptions. This capacity to introduce novelty into the interpretation of the past is part of what we mean by "imagination."

Finally, in order to close out, as it were, the interpretive process in any given moment, I must make a *decision*, a choice among many incompatible possibilities that my imaginative interpretations present. Say I am walking down a path that splits in two. I have a moment of awareness, an actual occasion, in which I must decide which of the two paths to take. I draw the situation into my awareness by a process of feeling the sensory inputs; I interpret the situation (possibly in some novel way); then I make a decision.

Thus, we see that, in ourselves at least, every actual occasion of experience involves *feeling, imaginative interpretation,* and *decision*. First, an *experience* of the past out of which we are arising; then an *interpretation* of that past; sometimes followed by an *imaginative* grasp of new *possibilities;* and finally, a *choice* that selects from the field of possibilities. This whole process of feeling, interpreting, and deciding is what Whitehead calls the concrescence of an actual occasion.

Can we fruitfully generalize this internal observation to the understanding of events in the outer world? Are all events the outcome of a process of concrescence?

Certainly other human beings seem to operate in this way. Again, it is plausible that domestic animals do so as well. But with domestic animals, the function of *decision* seems to be less developed. Other animals make

---

[7] See Whitehead's *Process and Reality*, Part 3, Chapter 2. For a less technical presentation of these ideas, see Thomas Hosinski, *Stubborn Fact and Creative Advance: An Introduction to the Metaphysics of Alfred North Whitehead*, Chapters 3, 4, and 5.

decisions—when confronted with a split in the road they do go left or right—but the range of options they consider seems to be smaller, and their process of decision making seems less elaborate than it is in humans. But clearly other animals *feel* their own past and the immediate past of the surrounding world; they *interpret* that world into an ordered and sometimes novel whole; and they make *decisions*. As we examine less and less complex forms of life, we see that all exhibit this same trio of functions: *feeling, interpretation,* and *decision*. However, the simpler the form, the more simplified and abstract its feeling of the past is, the less elaborate its imaginative interpretation of that past, and the fewer the number of possibilities it considers in its decision making process.

There is nothing to prevent us from applying this same analysis even to atoms of hydrogen. Every hydrogen event elaborates its past into a probability matrix and responds with some decision that collapses the wave function to bring about a new hydrogen event. Thus it feels, interprets, and decides.

This use of the term "imagination" needs some elaboration. As a quantum event, the behavior of a hydrogen atom in any given moment is not entirely predictable. In fact, given a particular hydrogen atom at a certain time, there is some uncertainty regarding the position and momentum of its next appearance. The way in which the hydrogen atom interprets its world presents it with a field of possibilities among which it must choose as it comes into actuality. Generally speaking, a hydrogen atom considers only those possibilities that will lead to its reappearance as hydrogen. However, for example, under the extreme pressure and temperature obtaining in a star, two different hydrogen atoms might each interpret the world in a new way—a way that registers (or prehends) the possibility of becoming helium. This registering of a new possibility is what I am calling "imagination."

Finally, subatomic particles, which emerge out of the collapse of a field of probability, are particularly easy to understand in terms of actual occasions.[8] It is important to note that none of these ideas contradicts any of the findings of physics. If subatomic particles were, as I am suggesting, actual occasions structured around a pole of deciding and

---

[8] See Abner Shimony's chapter "Quantum Physics and the Philosophy of Whitehead," in *Philosophy in America*; also Shimon Malin's *Nature Loves to Hide: Quantum Physics and the Nature of Reality, a Western Perspective.*

appreciating awareness, they would still behave the same way physicists say they do. The range of options surveyed by these occasions is very small. Nonetheless, the indeterminacy attending their behaviors could not, by the methods of physics, be distinguished from the results of a limited free choice.

The second result of our use of the Hermetic principle is the idea that the occasions making up our stream of conscious thought differ from the other occasions in nature not in fundamental kind, but only in emphasis on one or another of their constituting processes. By drawing analogies to our own ongoing experience, we can validly extrapolate to the experiences of animals, vegetables, minerals, and subatomic particles. We are all alike—either actual occasions or complex groupings of actual occasions. And every occasion making up all of these groupings is constellated around a pole of awareness.

To express the continuum of differentiations among occasions, Whitehead suggests we group occasions into "grades."

- *Low-grade* actual occasions, which correspond to inorganic events, experience the initial rush of feeling (by means of which they are causally affected by the past) in a simplified and abstract way. An electron, for example, interprets the entirety of its past as an electrical field. It interprets the initial rush of feeling with a bare minimum of imaginative variation. By and large, it simply decides to perpetuate the past it has experienced without considering other possibilities.

- *Medium-grade* occasions, which correspond to living events, experience the initial rush of feeling in a full and complex way. In their process of interpreting the past, they regularly introduce novelty. As often as not they decide to perpetuate what they have imagined rather than what they have received. In other words, they respond to circumstances with novel adaptations. In fact, medium-grade occasions regularly introduce novelty into the creative advance of occasions. Change is built into their nature and manifests as growth, decay, and adaptation.

- *High-grade* occasions, which correspond to thinking events, not only have a rich feeling of the past they interpret it with imaginative freedom and they apprehend a variety of alternatives for the future and then consciously choose among them.

As we proceed, we will consider in some detail the modes of interaction among actual occasions of various grades. In fact, I will define the human personality as "a society of high-grade occasions embodied in a society of medium-grade occasions, that are, in turn, embodied in a society of low-grade, inorganic occasions."

In the third application of the Hermetic principle, we arrive at the insight that all causal transmission between events may, in fact, be understood as a transmission of feeling, or a kind of impersonal memory.

Whenever any event is causally affected by another event, the affected event *feels* the determinate qualities of the affecting event. Say, for example, at this moment I prehend a past actual occasion (or some group of such occasions) that was characterized by the property of redness. I see a red flash. I receive it into myself as a felt experience. How did a past actual occasion come to express itself (to "objectify itself" in Whitehead's language) as red? Only by receiving redness into itself from some actual occasion in *its* past and passing that redness on unchanged; or by receiving the objectification of some non-red past, imagining red as a response to that experience, and then *deciding* to pass on redness into the future.

Now, if we define memory as an experience of past experience, then we realize that any causal transmission is an experience of a past experience, and so it is a kind of memory.[9] This identification of causal transmission with memory will be a useful component of our understanding of personality survival and reincarnation.

Whitehead suggests that all entities in the universe, including us, are composed of actual occasions. If so, and we apply the Hermetic principle one final time, then it follows that *all discrete events in the universe are, on the inside, drops of experience.*

---

[9] What we usually mean by "my memory" is just a particularly rich transmission of causes that takes place through what I will define as a "personally ordered society."

To summarize:

- When we, as observers, see an event being causally affected, that event feels those effects in its own subjective immediacy: To be causally affected is to feel.
- When we, as observers, see the emergence of an event with novel qualities, then some actual occasion has, in its own subjective immediacy, engaged in an act of imagination: to improvise is to bring new feelings into being through imagination.
- When we, on the outside, see the indeterminacy of a situation resolved by a particular event, on the inside of that event a decision has been made: to become definite is to decide among possibilities.
- All actual occasions come to have their determinate characteristics by a process of feeling, imagining, and deciding. All occasions in the future will experience past actualities by feeling some portion of the experiences that constituted those actualities. *All transmission of causes through time is a transmission of experiences, or a flow of memory.*
- Actual occasions differ among themselves to the extent that they emphasize one or another of their three primary stages of functioning, and thus fall roughly into three grades— inorganic, living, and thinking.

In this chapter, we saw that one of the key stumbling blocks to an adequate metaphysics is the notion of substance. Reality cannot be merely a collection of atoms in space because that could never produce sentient, experiencing beings like us. We saw, too, that Alfred North Whitehead has provided an opening to a radically new way of understanding the world by substituting "events" and "process" for the old ideas of substance and quality. Instead of atoms in the void, Whitehead tells us, reality is fundamentally constituted by causally interacting drops of experience, or actual occasions.

With this idea, we can now define reality in a way that includes not only everything we know about the world through the lens of science but also what we know from our own direct experience. Nothing need be left out.

In the next chapter, as I push deeper into an exploration of what it means to be "real," I will focus on an important distinction between *the abstract* and the *concrete*—between those aspects of reality that are *possible* and those that *actually exist*.

This may seem an unexpected place to focus our inquiry into reality. However, I am suggesting that the distinction between the abstract and concrete—the possible and the actual—is at the root of all philosophy and science—and, in fact, ultimately of all human endeavor. Confusion about what is actual and what is possible is a kind of psoriasis of the mind. It leaves us scratching our heads trying to figure out how we could ever have gotten our civilization mired in so many serious problems that, together, leave our very future in question.

Let's now turn attention to this very basic and crucial distinction between the *abstract* and the *concrete*.

Chapter 4: From Possible to Actual

Whitehead famously said that all of Western philosophy can be viewed as a series of footnotes to Plato.[1] Among other things, he meant that Socrates and Plato were the first philosophers in our tradition to clearly articulate the distinction between abstract and concrete, between ideas and reality. They were, in fact, the first to focus attention on ideas per se. The relationship of ideas to actuality has preoccupied philosophy ever since. Classical science tended to ignore this question (I explain why below), but quantum mechanics, which must contend with the existence of objective possibilities, has been forced to deal with it once again. In this chapter, I demonstrate why this distinction between *ideas* (possibilities) and *actualities* (entities existing in the actual world) is crucial in forming an understanding of the five fundamental propositions at the core of the new metaphysical model I am proposing.

Forms and Events

If we want to know *anything*, we have no option but to pay attention to our experience, which is the foundation of all philosophical and scientific knowledge (indeed, of *any* knowledge). This is what we mean by empiricism: knowledge grounded in experience.

Philosophy and science always begin with descriptions of experience. Of course, we cannot *describe* experience without resorting to the use of abstractions and the words in which they are expressed. Metaphysics helps us identify and clarify the concepts that describe the most

---

[1] Whitehead, *Process and Reality*, p. 39.

general aspects of experience, to see if the set of concepts we are using is coherent,[2] to see what other assumptions may be implied by those basic concepts, and to examine what consequences logically follow from holding those ideas. In short, metaphysics rigorously questions and investigates the *assumptions* behind our words, thoughts, and beliefs, and in doing so empowers us with greater clarity and insight into what we take to be knowledge or truth. In Whitehead's hands, metaphysics goes one step further and helps us realign our conceptual abstractions with our actual experience.

In this book, I invite you to examine your experience and begin a phenomenological description of your experience using "form" and "event" as your most general ideas.

Events Are in Time

For example, I am looking at—*experiencing*—a cup on the desk beside me. In this moment it is an event, a happening, an actual part of the world. If we stop to think about it, we know that objects such as cups are always changing. At one moment (sometime in the past), this cup hadn't yet been created; at another moment it will be gone (either into the dishwasher or, if it breaks, into the trash). And even though we can't perceive it directly, we know the cup is undergoing subtle changes at every moment, because of its molecular and atomic structure.

Not only is it changing in response to changing temperature, illumination, and pressure, it is gradually decomposing as molecules fly off. Even if the molecules stay relatively constant, the event that makes up this cup is, ultimately, an expression of the whole universe. The cup is a causal outcome of the entire evolutionary process, from the primordial flaring forth (the Big Bang[3]) to the present. The whole fourteen-billion-year evolution of the universe is, in some important sense, expressed in this cup. Again, whether we are aware of it or not, this cup is responsive even to the movements of distant galaxies in their ever-changing dance. The event that is this cup at this moment will, therefore, never be repeated. The event that is this cup at *this* moment

---

[2] A set of concepts is coherent when what is unique about each cannot be articulated apart from reference to the others. See *Process and Reality*, p. 3.
[3] Mainstream scientific cosmology currently takes the Big Bang as the beginning of the physical world.

and the event that is this cup at the very *next* moment are not the same. If it is to endure in time, the cup must do so as a sequence of subtly different events.

Of course, not only is the cup constantly changing, everything in the universe is in constant process. However, if *everything* is changing all the time, how can I *recognize* that the cup I am holding now is the same cup I was holding before? Throughout all the changes, *something* remains the same. What is it then about this cup that remains the same if there is a new "cup event" every moment?

Forms Are Unchanging

Well, the *form* of the cup hasn't changed even though there is another cup event being characterized by that form every moment. In his native language of ancient Greek, Plato referred to form as *eidos,* which is the root of the word "idea." Form and idea are essentially the same. At every moment, we have form and event, or idea and event. The cup idea is the form, and it is an ingredient in a series of events. Think of a waterspout or a tornado: the spiraling twister is the form, and it is an ingredient of a dynamic, ever-changing system of events consisting of air currents, water droplets, and dust particles.

Now let's look more closely at the distinction between forms and events and how scientific thought lost sight of it.

In daily life, we don't typically make this distinction between form and event with any clarity, but if we take time to do so, it opens the way to a philosophical understanding of the ever-changing world of experience. Modern philosophy and science have lost track of this distinction, and the story of this loss is instructive. Very briefly, it happened like this:

- First, early scientists, like Copernicus and Kepler, following a suggestion by Plato, searched for and found mathematical regularity—unchanging mathematical *forms*—in the movements of the planets.
- Then Galileo and his followers found mathematical regularity in the movements of terrestrial objects. The movement of pendulums and falling bodies, and the trajectories of cannonballs can all be described and predicted

81

by mathematical equations analogous to those that predict the movements of the heavenly bodies.

- Newton synthesized the ideas and the research of his predecessors into his magnum opus *Principia Mathematica*— and effectively established invariant *mathematical* forms (articulating universal "laws" of nature) as the ultimate expression of scientific knowledge.

From that time forward, the *only* forms considered relevant to the unfolding of actual events were mathematical. Mathematical equations, therefore, were believed to describe actuality better than the fuller, more concrete abstractions from experience that had been used by earlier philosophers. This meant that abstractions such as purpose, value, truth, beauty and goodness were no longer held to be relevant to the real world "out there." The mathematical abstractions were assumed not only to describe the natural world, but in a very real sense were erroneously assumed to *be* the essence of nature itself. The task of science, then, was to progressively experiment with nature in order to reveal her mathematical essence, expressed as invariant, universal, mathematical *laws.*

The Fallacy of Misplaced Concreteness

In this way, scientific thought fell into what I described earlier as "the fallacy of misplaced concreteness"—that is, mistaking a model or representation of reality as reality itself. Newton had discovered that a mathematical abstraction, called "point-mass," enabled him to use calculus to analyze all the motions in nature observed by the science of his day. However, he and his followers then confused the useful mathematical abstraction "point-mass" for an actual thing: an "atom." But the Newtonian atom is not an *actual* entity; it is an *idea* (a form), a mathematical abstraction that describes certain regularities in the field of experience that we, as high-grade actual occasions, can abstract from experience and use in scientific descriptions and predictions.

This is not to say that nothing actually corresponds to what we call atoms. Clearly, some atom-like processes do exist, contextualized by time and space, and have measurable effects on other such processes. Indeed, I have seen pictures that claim to be pictures of atoms, and I have found them to be quite convincing. But none of the evidence can convince me that those atoms are *nothing but* insentient patterns of energy described mathematically as point-masses. To be sure, I cannot explain my experience of the world without positing something *like* atoms, but if I assume that those atoms are just what Newton imagined them to be, then I will fall into the fallacy of misplaced concreteness, and my explanations will not get me very far if I'm interested in understanding phenomena such as life and consciousness.

The form "atom" is an abstraction from *something*, but the actuality is more than the form, and the form itself can be more or less adequate to what it describes.

In order to move beyond the muddle of modern thought that prevents us from understanding the nature of consciousness and matter, and how mind and body relate to each other—the infamous hard problem in contemporary philosophy of mind—we must break out of the fallacy of misplaced concreteness. Failing to do so, we will not be able to understand or explain the anomalous parapsychological phenomena detailed in *Irreducible Mind,* or know what to make of the documented evidence for reincarnation in the works of Ian Stevenson, or what these phenomena imply about the nature of reality, or about the nature of the human personality and how it can survive bodily death. If we want to address these issues and make progress in our scientific understanding of them, we need to radically revise our assumptions about the nature of mind and matter, or consciousness and energy. In short, we need a radical revision of the metaphysics underlying modern science.

Let's summarize: from the standpoint of process metaphysics, what we usually call a "thing" consists of a form, or idea, and a series of events that are characterized by that form. In Whitehead's useful terminology, we say that ideas or forms are "ingredients" of events or that ideas or forms are "ingressed" into events. Events occur in time and space, and each is unique. Events happen only once, but forms happen again and again. For example, this particular cup that I am holding happens again and again and again as I watch the cup endure, even though the events keep changing. What is the same in each occurrence is just the form itself. The events never repeat.

Forms and Events in Time and Space

It is important to realize that ideas or forms are *not* related to time and space in the same way events are. If you could see my cup at this moment, you would perceive a particular shade of bluish-green. You might see it from a different angle, and maybe your blue-green experience is different from my blue-green experience. Nevertheless, each of us sees *that* particular color, the one we do, in fact, see.[4] At this moment, something else in your field of experience might disclose itself with the same color; you might also have seen that color thirty years ago, and you might see it again tomorrow. Every time you see it, it is the *same* color; the color itself doesn't change in time. A particular shade of blue-green is always just that particular shade of blue-green, and so on. The point is that when you perceive a specific color, wherever or whenever you perceive it, it is *always* just that same color. That particular color doesn't change from moment to moment or from place to place. You can see the same shade of blue-green tomorrow, next year, and 50 years from now, and you can see it just as easily in California as in New York, or in Sydney or Timbuktu. A color (or any form) can have more than one location in space at a time (multiple objects may be bluish-green), and it may occur at any time, whereas events (actualities) are just where they are and just when they are, never to be repeated.[5]

Feeling the Difference

Once it is pointed out, this distinction between forms and events may seem obvious, even trivial. But it is neither obvious nor trivial. So before we proceed, let me ask: Do you *feel* that distinction? I'm aware it is not easy because it is not something we think about very much. If you

---

[4] The particular color I see is, of course, a product of many factors including the lighting, the context in which the object bearing the color occurs, the physiology of my perceptual apparatus, and so forth. In the current context, however, none of that is relevant. I'm just pointing to the color itself *as it is experienced.*

[5] This does not mean that the event could exist just where it is, without the participation of the rest of the universe. Whitehead points out that space does not just separate things, it also connects them. Each position in space-time is intrinsically related to all other positions in the same space-time. Each position is unique, and part of its uniqueness is its particular relationship to all other positions. For a deeper discussion of this point, see Whitehead's *Science and the Modern World*, Chapter 3.

pick up a cup, what are you holding in your hand? Is it the dynamic causal activity (an event) or is it the form of the cup? Or, more likely, is the cup a particular relationship between the event and the form? Can you imagine the cup as a society of actual occasions, each one of which *decides* to incorporate the form of the cup into its momentary flash of being? If, *in our experience*, we actually begin to differentiate events from objects, ideas, or form, we can bring about a change in the way we see reality.

Notice that I am emphasizing the importance of beginning our new approach to philosophy by paying attention to *experience*. *The only way we can access and know reality is through our own experience.* And our first task, then, is to focus attention on our experience to reveal the fundamental distinction between forms and events and the different ways they show up in time and space. This will lead us to an understanding of the difference between the abstract and the concrete, or between the possible and the actual.

You might already be aware that modern science is a discipline in search of its own justification. Quite simply, science doesn't know why its methods work. The philosophy of science, practiced for the last half-century or so, has ended up with the ridiculous idea that scientific truth is essentially a function of laboratory politics.[6] Given its starting premise—that reality is essentially a pattern of mathematical abstractions—there is no way to make sense of science. To put it plainly, neither modern nor postmodern science can account for its own knowledge or ideas in terms of the forms (atoms, electrons, quarks, probability fields) that it studies. All scientific knowledge begins in the subjective experience of individual scientists. But neither science nor the modern philosophy of science has developed a satisfactory account for the relationship between subjective experience and the presupposed objective reality of atoms, geometrical space-time, and energy fields "out there" beyond experience.

If we start with events and objects, however, we can make sense of science in terms of our own experience. Whitehead has shown that we can start with our own experience and then abstract from it all the

---

[6] Peter Godfrey-Smith, *Theory and Reality: An Introduction to the Philosophy of Science.*

forms and data of science, as long as we perform our original analysis of experience in terms of events and objects.[7]

Ideas (or Forms) Are Possibilities

It will be helpful at this point to note key characteristics that distinguish forms from events.

All ideas or forms (Whitehead calls them "eternal objects") are, in themselves, *possibilities*. In other words, an idea, or form, is a characteristic that an event might have. For example, redness is an idea; it is a characteristic certain events have or may come to have. Similarly, roundness, curiosity, anger, sorrow, squareness, and hardness are characteristics that might become ingredients of events.

Ideas, then, are possibilities—specific potentials for the determination of fact. If I look at someone's shirt and I see it is blue, the idea "blue" has characterized my perception of that shirt. The form or possibility has been actualized. Then, if I think I will make a painting of that shirt, the blueness now characterizes a future possibility as well as a past fact.

Just to be clear, I am suggesting that the distinction between the concrete and the abstract can be mapped on to the distinction between the actual and the possible. An abstraction is a possibility; it is a possible form of definiteness. For example, when we think, we are working with abstractions, entertaining possibilities. The objects of thought are possibilities—previously actualized or potentially actualizable.

Events Are Actual Occasions

Up until this point I have been speaking about events and forms as we find them in the field of our experience. The notion of actual occasions, discussed in the last chapter, develops from this analysis. It then adds a crucial observation: *we* are present in the actual world *as* events. Thus, the event that is my experience in this moment includes, in an important sense, all the events in my past and will, in turn, be an event in the experiences of all occasions that follow it.

Because in most cases macrocosmic entities in our environments can be resolved into interrelated multiplicities of actual occasions, we have to redefine the word "event" (as used in this chapter) so that it now

---

[7] For a summary of this derivation, see Weiss, *Doctrine of the Subtle Worlds*, Chapters 3 and 4.

refers *either* to a single actual occasion, or to some interrelated group or network of actual occasions.

Actual Occasions Actualize by Making Decisions

Actual occasions, as we have seen, move toward actualization by making decisions among mutually incompatible possibilities. Actual occasions *choose*, within limits, the objects that will come to be ingredients in them.

There is no actualization without thinking and deciding.

Moments in the personalities of human beings, like all actual occasions, entertain possibilities (that's what thinking is), and by deciding among them, collapse the field of probabilities into actuality (I will elaborate on this shortly). It follows, then, that thinking conditions reality. *Thinking is causally implicated in the ongoing flow of actual events.* This is a crucial point to grasp because the implications are far reaching, not only for philosophy and science but also for how we live our day-to-day lives. Yet this relationship between thinking and reality is largely overlooked in modern science. In fact, given the basic metaphysical premises of most scientists, any such causal role for thought is automatically ruled out.

I am making a very different claim here, based on a radically different metaphysical assumption which, in turn, is rooted in my experience: *thinking is not separate from reality; rather, it is a crucial factor in the process of actualization.* Quantum mechanics has taught us that we do not live in a predetermined world. Every new event in the actual world emerges out of a probability-weighted set of possibilities. Something decides among those probabilities every time a definite event occurs. That factor is the mental pole of actual occasions—or thinking—the ability to consider possibilities and decide among them.

What Have We Learned So Far?

I am presenting a way of making sense of experience that begins by distinguishing between the concrete and the abstract. I have pointed out that abstractions are characteristics that events have, or might have. For example, I look at a cup and I can ask, "What color is it?" I can then abstract whiteness and blue-greenness. Next I look at the cup from the top and say, "What shape is this?" I then abstract roundness and so on.

Abstractions are specific characteristics of events that we can bring to our attention by selective focus responsive to our interests. We abstract "possibilities for definiteness" that have been realized previously and/or possibilities that may be realized in the future. We have abstractions, characteristics, forms, or ideas (e.g., red, electrical, good—any quality you can name) and then we have actual events, or actual occasions, that are defined by some selection of those possibilities, forms, or ideas. In short, reality consists of possibilities (eternal objects) and actualities (actual occasions or events).

Possibilities per se are not in time or space the way events are. As noted above, possibilities can recur and can be in more than one place at a time. Events, by contrast, are specifically located in time and space, and are unique.

Let's now identify some more important properties of abstractions and events.

Events can have a character that is more or less complex. Events vary in complexity depending on the number of ideas included in their character and the intricacy of relations among them. To give an obvious example: the event that is my cup in any given moment is not as complex as the event that is me in any given moment.

Abstractions are always beheld by actualities. You are an actuality; I am an actuality. We behold or "prehend" other actualities, and from those actualities we abstract ideas or forms. We also on occasion prehend forms that are relevant to our current situation, but have never before been realized. This is how transphysical process metaphysics accounts for the emergence of new forms in the evolutionary advance. The forms we abstract open up possibilities for us, and we then decide among them and contribute to the determination of future actualities. Understanding this is fundamental to the new approach to science and philosophy I am unfolding here. We are continually actualizing possibilities, and consequently each one of us is a prime example of an actual entity—as actual as anything ever could be. Note, then, that in our own case, actuality includes consciousness. In the model I develop here, I make the case that the nature of human actuality is essentially no different from the actuality of all other events—from apes to atoms, bees to beryllium, cats to carbon.

Abstracting is an activity performed by countless beings like us. Only actual occasions abstract characteristics or possibilities from actuality and decide among them, and thus partially determine the future.

Abstractions can be more or less adequate to the objects they represent. For example, when I behold or look at someone I know intimately, my impression of that person—the way I represent him or her to myself or, as Whitehead would say, the way he or she "objectifies in me" (becomes an object for me)—is very full and rich. I abstract much more of their form or possibilities than I would those of a stranger. Their whole history with me is there before me, along with their familiar interests and presence. Although I never fully abstract the complete set of possibilities embodied or actualized in that person, if I am appropriately attentive and present, what I do abstract is, to a greater or lesser degree, adequate to who they are. We could say that although I still necessarily objectify them, I do so in a way that is much closer to their own subjective sense of who they are.

When I look at a close friend, my objectification of him is complete. On the other hand, I could regard a person serving my table as simply a "waiter," in which case my sense of that person would be abstract by comparison. If I abstracted only the single characteristic "waiter," it would not be an adequate representation of that person as a human being. Or, take another example: if I were an economist, I might treat all people as "rational consumers." That would be an abstract and inadequate beholding of them, ignoring the full richness and complexity of who they really are.

The point to get here is that the abstractions we pull from the events in our life can be, to a greater or lesser degree, adequate. Likewise, as philosophers, scientists, or lay people, our descriptions of the real world can be, to a greater or lesser degree, adequate.

No set of abstractions can ever encompass the whole actuality it describes. Once we recognize that at any moment, in any circumstance, our experiences always involve abstractions, and these are conditioned by our interests and goals, we can be aware that these abstractions are not absolute. No philosophical system or truth will be an absolute truth.

Nevertheless, we should also keep in mind that the abstractions we use can be, to a greater or lesser degree, adequate to what we want them to do.

The Inadequacy of Reductionism

The central claim of this book is that the reductionist scientific abstractions that have been used for the past few centuries by modern Western civilization to explain reality are not adequate to the full spectrum of human experience. The set of abstractions I will present here is more adequate, though I am not claiming that these new abstractions are in any way ultimate.

The basic metaphysical ideas of science are too abstract and too simple—they aren't full or concrete enough to represent much of what is important in human experience.

Take, for example, Newtonian mechanics. Standing on the shoulders of the giants who preceded him, Newton crystallized a set of metaphysical ideas that justified the mathematical analysis of the motions of macroscopic bodies. This works fine as long as what we're interested in are macroscopic objects moving through time and space. But why would anyone think that the set of abstractions adequate to describing the movements of bodies with mass would also be good for the analysis of chemical interactions, or living systems, or psychology, or ethics, or aesthetics? To assume you can represent all of reality in terms of abstractions suited to moving masses is simply not good philosophy or good science. Nor is it good sociology, good economics, good psychology, or good medicine. It violates good old common sense.

The abstractions of physics are great for describing what happens to low-grade inorganic systems, but they are vastly inadequate for describing the reality of human, animal, or even plant experience and behavior.

Making the mistake of assuming that a set of simple abstractions can fully describe a complex reality is the fatal flaw of scientific or any other kind of reductionism. We short-circuit thought when we try to explain the richness of our psychological, social, or spiritual actuality in terms of a set of abstractions appropriate to moving bodies—because those abstractions respond to and represent far too narrow a range of interests. In other words, if we ignore all vitality, emotion, thought, volition, and the important characteristics of life that cannot be measured, we can describe the macroscopic properties of what's left in terms of changes of position in a four-dimensional Cartesian grid dotted with tiny blips of matter interacting according to the laws of gravity and a few other physical forces. This is valid, and for technological purposes at least, quite useful. But many high school science teachers, and, indeed, many reductionist scientists take another step. They assume Newton's set of abstractions (or the abstractions of relativity and quantum physics that came later) describes the *real* world objectively "out there," while our subjective experiences "in here" are dismissed as merely epiphenomenal. Such a view commits the fallacy of misplaced concreteness.

It's important to see this: modern science, in its reductionistic mode, has got it backward. It treats mathematical abstractions as if *they* are actual, while treating *our* actual experience as "merely" subjective. It's topsy-turvy metaphysics. If we were to take modern science at its word, then we should believe that what we actually behold or experience is just some sort of confused subjective appearance "in here;" but "out there," on the other side of the appearance, the real world consists of four-dimensional space-time sprinkled with tiny, insentient blips.

Whitehead decried this separation of the domain of experience from the domain of actuality as the "bifurcation of nature."[8] Once we say that reality is "out there," outside of experience, and once we imagine that our abstractions from experience tell us what the outer world is like, all our knowledge becomes deeply problematical. By adopting this split between concrete subject and abstract object, between experience and "external" reality, we make our actual experience into an unreal and unreliable witness. How could what is unreal ever know anything about what is supposed to be real? In fact, if reality were truly "out there" beyond experience, knowledge of reality itself would be *impossible.*

To put it bluntly, modern science finds itself like Wile E. Coyote, running off a metaphysical cliff into metaphysical thin air, saved from falling only so long as he forgets to look down into the metaphysical abyss over which he is suspended.

The Buddha describes ignorance as one of the fundamental causes of suffering. Many Buddhist schools interpret ignorance in line with Whitehead's fallacy of misplaced concreteness. We have an idea, an

---

[8] Whitehead, *Concept of Nature.*

abstraction, that we call our "ego"—the "I" or "me." We confuse this idea-ego with our actual, true identity and then act as if the idea is more real and more important than our own infinite depths.

That is yet one more way we bifurcate reality—with profound consequences for our personal and collective lives. We should recognize abstractions for what they are. Abstractions are not actualities. They are mere possibilities, becoming actual only as they are realized in actual events.

My starting point, then, following Whitehead, is to declare the commonsense position that what is actual is concrete, complex, causal, communal and involved in process. The abstract is not and cannot be the actual. Sentient beings like you and me are actual; every moment of experience is an actual fact. We need to recognize that three-dimensional space, four-dimensional space-time, atoms, energy, probability waves and their collapse—all of these are mere abstractions.

The Nature of Explanation

When we begin to differentiate abstractions from concrete actuality, we can begin to understand what any explanation is, including, of course, all scientific explanations: they are ways to account for what is concrete in terms of what is abstract.

All philosophical and scientific explanations are logical stories told in terms of some particular set of abstractions. And we have seen that the fallacy of misplaced concreteness consists in confusing the elements of the explanation for the actuality being explained. I have spoken about this in terms of imagining that the abstraction is a reality outside experience. But there is another way of speaking about this that is also psychologically valid.

Certain ideas—for example, our preferences for which political party ought to be in power—are recognized as choices among *thinkable* alternatives. But other ideas, in the background of consciousness, are so taken for granted that *we never even imagine the possibility of alternative ideas*. These ideas may be inherited from society, imbibed with language itself, or inculcated at such a primitive level that they might almost be felt as instinctual. They tend to be rooted in regions of our psyche that are highly charged with emotional resonances and are often shielded behind various psychological defenses. Ideas we take for granted have, by definition, never been consciously scrutinized. They have not been seen against a background of other possibilities that might, instead, be actualized. They are felt as just "the way things are," and any attempt to suggest otherwise takes on an air of the ridiculous.

Most of us frame our explanations in terms of such abstractions— first without realizing they are abstractions, and second without realizing that other abstractions might also serve to describe the actualities under investigation. We each take for granted a slightly different set of ideas, making for endless strife in personal, business, political, and international relations. When we learn to listen for the abstractions by which other people are framing their explanations, these others begin to seem saner, and new depths of communication can open up.

I want to be clear that I am not suggesting we dispense with abstractions—scientific or otherwise. Besides being impossible, it wouldn't serve us. We need our abstractions because the finite human mind, as it is now functioning,[9] cannot possibly embrace the infinite complexity of the actual world at any particular moment. We need to interact with actuality in manageable chunks. Remember, abstractions are possibilities, and one of the greatest gifts we have as sentient beings is the capacity to apprehend possibilities and select among them. So abstractions are necessary and useful.

Problems arise only when we mistake our abstractions for actuality— the fallacy of misplaced concreteness. The possible and the actual: both are real, but different.

In fact, like many quantum physicists, I am suggesting that possibilities are *real* (though not *actual*). Possibilities are apprehended in thought, and we recognize them as ingredients in what is actual. Every actuality comes into being surrounded by a cloud or halo of possibilities that it then makes available to future concrescences. In the concrescences of future occasions, some of these possibilities are selected or "collapsed" into definiteness and become part of a new actual event.

A moment ago I mentioned that possibilities and actualities are real and that they are different. One important difference is that while every actual event is always in process, possibilities or potentialities (the

---

[9] Sri Aurobindo argues extensively for the possibility that through deliberate self-cultivation we can open our minds to the infinite, thus transforming ourselves utterly.

forms) are not. They exist timelessly, which is why Whitehead referred to them as "eternal objects."

Now we can clarify key factors involved in the occurrence of each actual occasion.

The Characteristics of Actuality

Actuality requires consciousness. Consciousness functions as an agency of actualization. Without the presence of consciousness (and specifically the action of choice or decision) to select among the range of probabilities, nothing would ever collapse into actuality. In this, Whitehead's metaphysics squares with the evidence of quantum physics.

Actuality is temporal. Every moment of actualization is an activity. The present moment of experience is the cutting edge of the cosmic creative advance. Settled actualities of the past are the raw materials for the present and (with the addition of new possibilities) for the future. Actuality cannot be imagined apart from its temporal dimension.

Actuality is communal. Another consequence of the constant coming-into-being of every actual entity (including you and me right now) is the fact that actuality is necessarily communal—involving the contributions of all ancestral actualities or events. To be actual is to emerge out of the past, where the past consists of a multiplicity of prior actualities. We always have to have a past to be actual. Each moment of actualization is a convergence or communion of all the actualities of the past.

Actuality is causal. Because of the inevitable influence of the past flowing into the present, every event or actual occasion is always involved in networks of efficient causation. One actuality causes another in a universal interconnected matrix. Right now, as you read these words, I am effectively, if indirectly, causing something to happen in you. And while it might not be as obvious, right now you are causing something to happen that will affect every actual occasion in your future. When we expand this causal network to encompass all actualities, we realize that the whole universe causes us in each moment and we in turn affect the entire future of the universe. To be actual is to be in time and space, to be communal, and to be in process.

The Process of Actualization

The above discussion of the relationship between what is possible and what is actual is important for a clear understanding of our own experience and how it relates to reality. It is crucial for science if it is ever to understand the nature of consciousness and how it relates to the physical world.

We will now look more deeply at the process through which the potential is actualized. Specifically, how does it happen that you and I become actual beings from moment to moment? And, more generally, *how do all entities become actual at every moment of their existence?*

In some significant way, this entire metaphysics may be viewed as an exploration of that question—an analysis of the process of becoming actual. Understanding this will go a long way toward opening up a new perspective for understanding what a personality is, how it persists from moment to moment, and how it may actually survive the death of its physical body.

We experience the past as it actually was. Actuality always begins in the universe and as an experience of that universe. In other words, the process of actualization is a "conformal experience" that involves the entire past history of the universe, streaming into every new moment. We always begin a new moment by experiencing the past as it actually was.

Modern thought is confused about how we experience the past or objective events. Science says we experience the outer world through our senses, and this seems indisputable. The light from the window strikes my desk. The atoms of my desk are excited by the impact and, in turn, they emit light that hits the cells at the back of my retina. Those cells respond to the light by generating nervous impulses that travel though my nervous system, coordinate with other nervous impulses from my eyes and other senses, and eventually form a representation of the world. So far, so good. This entire process is *causal*, so that the sun, the desk, and the whole world are, in some way, involved in the production of the representation. This is important: my perception of the desk is *causally* related to the desk itself, and this guarantees that my representation is relevant to the actual world outside my body. The desk (along with the rest of the world) *causes* my perception, and so my perception is really a perception of the desk.

Mind is intrinsic to matter. But modern thought loses this direct causal connection by denying that the process through which the representation of the world is formed in the nervous system involves any sort of experience. According to science, the sun, the desk, and the nerves are just physical things that do not involve any awareness or any experience. So the scientific explanation is left with a big puzzle: How is it that the pattern of exclusively physical activities in the nervous system that forms the representation becomes, for me, a conscious experience? What bridges the gap between a non-experiencing world and an experiencing subject?

We return to the hard problem. The events through which the sun and my desk are represented in my nervous system form a causal process, and this takes place in the one coherent, outer world. But if we were to accept the standard scientific story, the consciousness that actually experiences the representation is somehow outside that world, and there is no intrinsic connection between the representation and the *experience* of that representation. This explanation leaves us stuck in a kind of private theater where we are confronted with representations, but we never get access to the real things that, so we imagine, are represented.

In contrast, the process metaphysics I am developing here eliminates the hard problem by putting experience back into the world. I am working on the premise that to be *causally affected* is to *feel*. So the sun feels energetic and transmits that to the desk, which feels energized. The desk transmits its energetic feeling to the cells in the retina, which feel the light from the desk. Each entity in the perceptual process is, in itself, an experience. "I" am a key event in the perceptual process, and I feel the experiences of all of my coordinated cells. In this way, the entire perceptual process is a transmission of experience through the creative advance. There is no hard problem at all. My representation of the world *is* an experience of *and from* the world, as that experience is transmitted through the occasions of my body.[10] True, I interpret the world. My experience is an abstraction from actuality, and that abstraction is conditioned by my motives and interests. It is both less and more than

---

[10] As we will see later, the higher-grade occasions of the body can communicate with the higher-grade occasions in the rest of the universe directly, without that communication being mediated by the lower-grade occasions in which those higher-grade occasions are embodied.

the actual past. But it *is* causally connected to that past, so that my consciousness is really a part of the world, and the actual world as it is (and was) constitutes the raw material of my experience.

Causality is transmission of experience. Indeed, this way of speaking is much more natural than the strange circumlocutions forced on us by materialistic reductionism. When we are not doing science, we have no choice but to assume that we are involved in reciprocal causal interactions with the actual world we perceive. Perceptual physiology makes this obvious. It is only the strange idea that the transmission of energy is something other than a transmission of experience that forces us to think of ourselves and our consciousness as somehow outside the process.

Creativity is built into the fabric of existence. Even though the past is fixed and determines every current actuality, that is far from the whole story. At every moment, the actual world comes into being with a host of unrealized possibilities. Every present actuality is both determined by its past and has a set of open possibilities that orient it toward the future. In every moment of actuality, there are always possibilities we can realize. This is fundamental to the metaphysical nature of every actual entity. In common language: there is always something new to do.

Between the past and the future comes a conscious decision. The key to every actual process is a decision. Without beings who are capable of making choices, nothing would ever happen. We, and all other actual occasions, make decisions. The world presents itself to us as actual and simultaneously discloses a halo of possibilities. We create a new actuality as we decide among those possibilities.

Take a moment to think about this. We behold reality and we experience definite, actual things. But if we shift attention just a little and look at things differently, we can see that every actuality also presents us with a variety of options. Every actual situation is both fixed by its past and rich with the flexibility of unrealized potentials, some of which will become actual by virtue of our decisions. Every actual occasion comes into being with a range of unrealized potentials. Options are always available, the future remains open, and so there is always something new to do.

Again, take my cup as an example. I can drink from it, I can drop it, I can describe it to you, I can throw it through the window; my actual cup is surrounded by a halo of possibilities. What is true of my cup is true for every object—including human beings.

The creative advance is guided by purpose. It is also important to note that, by its very nature, no decision is ever random. The selection of a new possibility is always the operation of choice. And choice is different from randomness. Choice, because it is free, is undetermined and unpredictable. To an outside observer, a random event and an act of choice might both appear random. The crucial difference is that choice involves the presence of consciousness and purpose or "aim." Aristotle called this purpose the "final cause." I consider the elimination of purpose or final cause from the universe to be one of the greatest metaphysical blunders of reductionistic materialism. The model I am proposing restores purpose to the very nature of reality itself.

Purpose is always an aim at value. When I make a choice, I do so in order to reach a goal, to fulfill some purpose, to realize some value. I value some outcomes more than others, and I choose and act accordingly.

My choice might be right or wrong, but unless I am influenced by the desire to achieve value I have no criterion by which to evaluate the various options or possibilities that are present to me in any moment. Without value to guide my choice, my actions would, indeed, be random. And what is true for me as an actual entity is true for all actual entities. The universe unfolds through creative advance ultimately because of the presence of beings who experience value and aim, and who make choices. *There is no actuality without an aim at value and an experience of value.*

Contrary to the metaphysical mythology of reductionistic science, which tells us that ultimate actuality is devoid of value, I am suggesting that *every actuality has value for itself,* because it emerges out of a decision made in the presence of an aim or a final cause.

A Radical Revision of Science

We can now generalize what we know about actual occasions. In every moment of actualization (every actual occasion), there is the apprehension of the actualities of the past and of the field of possibility implied by the specific configurations of those actualities, and then there is a conscious, value-informed decision among those possibilities that makes one of them definite and actual. The process of actuality involves experiencing the world, discerning possibilities and deciding among them. That is what it means to be actual. Nothing is actual that does not go through that process. This is not just a philosophical statement. It is exactly what quantum mechanics tells us, too.

It is important to note that this does *not* mean—as the New Age cliché goes—that we can "create our own reality." Yes, there are always unrealized possibilities among which we will choose, but everything that happens has to be logically consistent with what has already happened in the past. Also many possibilities are mutually incompatible, and cannot be jointly actualized. For example, the reality that gives rise to me lets me speak a large number of words and lets me move in different directions, but I cannot speak two different words at the same time, and I can move in only one direction at any given moment. The possibility of going left at the crossroads, and the possibility of going right at the same crossroads at the same time cannot be jointly actualized.

What am I saying here? Well, I want to be clear that I am proposing a radical metaphysical revision of science. You could say that I am trying to correct the scientism that sometimes passes for real science. In fact, I am showing the way to replace the faulty metaphysical assumptions of reductionistic, materialist science with a new set of metaphysical premises that will give science a solid and expansive foundation and allow it to explore the full spectrum of the universe as it is revealed in our actual experience.

I am taking as my starting point the difference between possibility and actuality, and reversing the topsy-turvy assumptions that underlie the way reductionistic materialism views them. Remember, the essence of modern scientific reductionism—or *scientism*—is the assertion that reality, what is *actual,* is composed of objective, purposeless dead stuff, those infinitesimal BB atoms (updated as quarks or quanta) hurrying meaninglessly through time and space. I am saying that such a view is entirely inadequate to account for the facts of our experience.

On the contrary, actuality is not dead—automatic abstractions are. And since possibilities are abstract, non-temporal, and non-spatial, if anything qualifies as dead, purposeless, and automatic it is *possibility.*

By contrast, finite *actuality* is conscious, causal, communal, inextricably involved in time and space, purposeful, and valuable. As

I sit here at my desk contemplating metaphysics, exploring a universe of possibilities in thought, I am vitally aware of the difference between what is merely abstract possibility and what is actual, alive with consciousness, purpose, value, and a capacity to choose. *This* is actual. When I say "this" I am indicating myself, and my experiences of the world around me.

By "actual" I mean you and me and everything we experience. Every object, every atom making up our world is essentially just like you and me; it possesses a capacity to make decisions guided by its own appropriate aims and values. Strange as it may sound to ears and minds schooled in scientific materialism, every *actual* atom and molecule (not the mathematical abstractions we read about in textbooks) emerges into actuality, moment to moment, as an activity of choice, motivated by its own inherent value. Every actuality, from quarks to human beings, has value in and for itself, and it interacts with its world directed by those values.

The whole universe is permeated by purpose and choice. Consciousness is active everywhere, all the time. I am fully aware how radical this statement is compared to the "givens" of modern reductionistic materialism. But I am equally aware that this approach is not inconsistent with genuine science, at all. In fact, it can be helpful in interpreting quantum mechanics, as physicists who read Whitehead are discovering.[11]

Is Reality Atomic?

I'll conclude this chapter by looking at one more important question about the nature of actuality. Whenever we analyze something, we usually view it in terms of fundamental units. My question is, can we analyze and understand reality in terms of ultimate constituents? And, if so, *what are the fundamental ontological units?*

I've already pointed out why the mathematical abstractions that physicists call "atoms" cannot yield the world we actually experience. Nevertheless, the idea of atoms or quanta—some discrete constituent of reality—seems unavoidable.

Whitehead tended to think there are ultimate units. In his later

---

[11] See Stapp, *Mindful Universe*; and Epperson, *Quantum Mechanics*.

philosophy, he concluded that "actuality is incurably atomic."[12] And in a certain sense that is true, though not in the reductionistic sense assumed in materialistic science. Once again, we start with our own experience as a paradigm example of actuality. If we pay attention, we recognize that each moment comes as a drop of experience; we take in the world, we interpret it, we make decisions, and in doing so we become actual at that moment. The next moment we start all over again. Each moment is actualized by a new and unique decision—never to be repeated. *Each moment happens only once.* This is what Whitehead had in mind when he said that "actuality is incurably atomic."

Actuality is composed of momentary "atoms" of experience, where each moment is distinctive, discrete, and unique because of the creative acts of decision that select possibilities and make them actual. Whitehead, as we have seen, referred to these atoms or units of reality as actual occasions. That is, they are fully realized moments or occasions when *something happens.* Actuality, then, is composed of *events* when viewed from the outside, and drops of experience when viewed from inside the occasion.

I want to repeat that this understanding of atomicity is not reductionistic. Clearly, we do not experience ourselves as choppy, discrete atoms of awareness. Rather, we experience ourselves as continuous from moment to moment. While it is true that each moment gets its atomic character due to each unique act of decision, it is also true that each completed moment *causally influences* or informs the next moment, and partially *constitutes* it. The flow of causality from past to present accounts for our experience of continuity. As we will see later on, this process is a key to understanding the nature of personality and how it can survive the death of the physical body.

The bottom line, then, is that reality consists of both atomicity and continuity. They are complementary—each is needed to make sense of and allow for the other.

Continuity and Personality

In the coming chapters, I will be describing continuity in Whiteheadian terms as "personal order." For Whitehead, a society with personal order

---

[12] Whitehead, *Process and Reality* p. 61.

is a sequence of actual occasions in which there is one in each moment, like beads on a string: me, and then me, and then me, and then me. That is my personal order—my *personality*. I can now generalize and say that *societies in personal order are personalities.*

Here's how it works: I come into existence in this moment, and again in this next moment, and then again in this new moment, and so on. It's a continuous sequence. And in each one of those moments the whole universe participates in my coming to be. If the universe changes too much, I cannot have personal order, and I would cease to be. For example, if some calamity destroys my body between two successive moments of my experience, then my personality would either cease to exist, or else it would experience a radical discontinuity that changes it from a physically embodied to a physically disembodied state. And this continuity, as we will see, also depends on a continuity of conditions in the transphysical worlds. There has to be something that holds the universe sufficiently the same from moment to moment in order for me to emerge sufficiently the same from moment to moment. In other words, my continuity as a personality is intimately tied in with the continuity, consistency, and *coherence* of the universe as a whole.

Clearly, for anything to endure, whether it's a pellet, a pebble, or my personality, the universe must maintain some minimal degree of continuity and coherence. To achieve this, the universe (the totality of all that is) must itself be some kind of self-organizing system—a self-organizing system of actual occasions that maintain some degree of continuity from moment to moment. The universe is a self-organizing society of actual occasions, and so are our daily selves.

In transphysical process metaphysics, whenever there is a self-organizing system of actual occasions (whether it is the universe as a whole, a human being, a single cell, or a hydrogen atom) the system has its own consciousness, with its own aims, values, and choices. If we take the presiding occasion of a human individual in waking life as an example, we can see that personality only emerges out of a complex relationship between individuality and continuity: the texture of decisions inherent in personality breaks it up into individual events, and yet those events are part of an ongoing continuity. Also, the ongoing self-organizing system of the cells depends on the personality, and the continuity of the personality depends on the ongoing self-organization of the universe as a whole.

Now we can see that these three terms—self-organization, atomicity, and continuity—are all complexly interrelated and interdependent. We cannot have any one without all three. This is a new idea that helps resolve the issue of personal identity. (I will elaborate on this in a later chapter.)

Summary

We've seen that the overall metaphysical situation, according to science, is that reality is composed of dead matter controlled by mathematical laws and chance. I'm suggesting this is not the way things are. On the contrary, every process of concrescence that leads to the actualization of an event involves a field of structured possibilities which, through a process of conscious decision within that concrescence excludes incompatible possibilities and includes a mutually compatible set of possibilities, thus giving itself a definite character and thereby making what was merely abstract and potential into actuality. Reality, then, intrinsically and naturally involves some factor that continually renders it actual by deciding which possibilities to actualize. And that factor, I will argue, is consciousness. Consciousness is an agent of actualization.

Every instant of actualization is illuminated by consciousness and embodies a quantum of freedom. It emerges from, and then creates, a field of possibilities for the future. It enjoys the value of the past, and enjoys its own value, while anticipating value in the future. Once we adopt this perspective, it becomes clear that *every* actuality, including the actualities making up human personalities, exercise causal agency. Thus we have established a basis for the first of my five fundamental propositions: that the personality has causal agency.

In the coming chapters we will see how it is now possible to construct a comprehensive cosmology that includes the possibility of parapsychological effects, reincarnation, and life after death. The cosmology will thus provide a basis for the other four propositions, namely that: II) there are transphysical worlds; III) the personality can function independently of its body, even during the life of the body; IV) the personality survives the death of its physical body and has an ongoing existence in transphysical worlds; and V) reincarnation is part of the human life cycle.

Chapter 5: Rethinking Causality

One of the major novelties—indeed, *the trademark*—of the modern scientific perspective was its radical re-visioning of Aristotle's understanding of causality, which had dominated the philosophy and science of the Middle Ages. In modern times, science has operated on the assumption that all the important characteristics of nature are measurable, that all qualities can be reduced to quantities, and that causation unfolds with the inexorable inevitability of a mathematical calculation. This is particularly true of the hard sciences. That assumption, which opened up the possibility of modern technology, has conferred a terrible power on those who hold it, with the disastrous environmental and social consequences we now see unfolding in the world around us.

We digested this modern view of actuality throughout our education, and it can be difficult for us even to imagine that other valid modes of understanding actuality could exist. I want to discuss, then, the historical evolution of the modern position. If we can appreciate that there was an intelligible, interesting, and even valid way of understanding causality before the scientific era, we might also appreciate that a new intelligible, interesting, and *useful* understanding of causality might be arising now.

Aristotle proposed four different types of causes that account for the existence of any finite natural being. I will begin my discussion with Aristotle's four-fold division and show how our understanding of each of these four causes changed during the transition to modernity, and is, again, transforming today.

Aristotle's four causes are material, efficient, formal, and final. It is remarkable that this formulation still holds such relevance after twenty-five hundred years. A succinct example illustrating the four causes is that of a house: the wood, bricks, or other stuff out of which it is built is the material cause, the construction worker is the efficient cause, the architect's blueprint is the formal cause, and the desire to live in it is the final cause. This example is overly simple, but it helps me, at least, to keep the four causes ordered in my mind.

What we think of today as "cause" is the second of Aristotle's four causes: efficient cause. But when Aristotle uses the word "cause," he has in mind a richer and more concrete understanding of the notion. For Aristotle, a cause is a necessary factor for the appearance of any natural being (*ousia*) in the actual world. The natural being (what we would, in our rather abstract fashion, call a "thing") must be made out of something, and this something is the material cause. It must be impelled into being, and this is the efficient cause. No natural being can arise without a form, shape, and definite family of characteristics. This is the formal cause. And finally, nothing happens without a reason, and the reason why is the final cause.

Table 1 summarizes the evolution of our ideas about causation. Take a moment to review the table before we proceed.

Aristotle's Understanding of the Four Causes

Aristotle's mode of understanding these categories is different from the modern view. He proposed that the material cause of a natural being is "substance"—but by substance he did not mean, as Descartes did, something already formed that needs nothing other than itself (and God) to exist. Aristotle imagined substance as having no form of its own. Rather he thought of it as a formless something that is a passive receptacle; it receives forms into itself and holds them together as natural objects. The active factor in the natural world, according to Aristotle, is form itself, the idea. Forms are like possibilities that innately seek to actualize. This dynamic potential within the forms themselves is what makes actuality happen. While artificial things require an efficient cause, a formal cause, and a final cause (all external to themselves), in natural beings the idea or form is all three; it's the motive power (efficient

cause), the form toward which the entity becomes (formal cause), and
the reason why the entity becomes what it does (final cause).

	ARISTOTLE	CLASSICAL PHYSICS	PROCESS PHILOSOPHY
MATERIAL	Substance (a.k.a. "hylé"): Passive and formless	Atoms and matter: Passive, always already formed	Creativity: Active, chooses forms according to its aims
EFFICIENT	Agent: The specific agency that determines the various forms of substance	Transmission of energy and the power of the past: For example, the gravitational (later electromagnetic) character of past atoms	The power of the past as experience of past experience: Propositions have causal power
FORMAL	Form: The active template, or idea, that imposes its shape on matter	Natural law	The range of possibilities open to the occasion in concrescence, weighted in relation to the aim of the occasion
FINAL	Purpose: That for the sake of which the entity exists	None	The maximization of value for itself and its relevant future, with further specification determining grade and style; the power to impose aims on certain other occasions

Table 1: The Four Causes in Three Metaphysical Contexts

Because Aristotle tended to see each entity as coming into being through the operation of its own set of individual causes (and not through the operation of other natural beings), he thought of relations among natural beings as secondary to their substantial existence. In other words, natural beings first exist and then, secondarily, they have causal relations among themselves. As a result, Aristotle's logic—while very good at analyzing the categories to which a natural being belongs and what that implies—is incapable of analyzing even simple relationships such as "greater than" or "less than." Furthermore, number plays a secondary role in Aristotle's metaphysics, and he had no particular interest in measuring things. As a result, Aristotelian metaphysics tended to minimize the importance of mathematics in the understanding of the actual world.

The Modern Understanding of the Four Causes

The modern understanding, as discussed earlier, came out of an enduring Platonic and Pythagorean strain of thought that saw mathematics as the fundamental language of nature. The work of Kepler, Copernicus, and Galileo found hitherto unprecedented ways of illuminating nature through mathematical forms and so gave great impetus to the emerging modern consciousness. But once the power of number in illuminating the actual world became evident, an important question emerged: what does it say about the world if, indeed, mathematical forms are the only forms that determine the unfolding characteristics of actualities over time? Newton not only outdid his predecessors in expanding the explanatory power of the new mode of understanding, he articulated a clear vision of what this new, mathematically characterized world must be like.

The outlines of his understanding—framed in terms of three-dimensional space, one-dimensional time, and atoms—is sufficiently familiar that we need not review it here, but this new worldview required an entirely new understanding of causality.

For Newton, atoms in space and time became the material cause. While Aristotle's material cause was formless, and his idea of process was the coming to be and the ongoing functioning of definite actualities through the agency of form, Newton's atoms are always and already formed, and in his idea, process becomes nothing but the rearrangement of the atoms. For Newton, an important part of the formal cause—the form of the individual atoms—is taken for granted as an element of the material cause. Every metaphysical system assumes some factors of existence and derives everything else from those factors. Aristotle tried to account for the existence of finite entities in terms of formless substance and active forms. Newton tried to account for the characteristics of macroscopic entities through the ongoing rearrangements of entities that are microscopic, self-existing, and already formed.

The efficient cause, for Newton, was actually the will of God. This position, embarrassing to the scientific sensibility that developed after Newton's time, was a necessary consequence to the thoroughly passive nature of the atoms as Newton imagined them. Newton maintained that space and time were the "sensorium of God," and that all movements of atoms were divinely ordained in accordance with the law of gravitation. The fact that Newton and his contemporaries took this seriously explains in part the awe in which Newton was held—he had, or so it was believed, actually read God's thoughts as God manages His universe. Very quickly after Newton, scientists dropped this deistic conception and began to assign gravitational fields to the atoms themselves. From that point forward, the efficient cause for any particular atomic movement was imagined as the gravitational gradient that resulted from the positions of the other atoms in the immediately preceding instant.[1]

Although scientists after Newton ceased to discuss formal causes, formal cause reappeared in scientific thought under the guise of "natural

---

[1] It is interesting to note that when scientists began to assume that each atom is the center of a gravitational field, they destroyed the entire philosophical basis of mechanism. Mechanism was founded on the idea that there is no action at a distance, but gravitational fields were treated as the action at a distance of atoms. Relativity theory and quantum theory can be seen, at least in part, as logical consequences of the assumption of action at a distance.

law." Natural law, as understood in science, is a mathematical description of the shape of possibility. Given these particular circumstances, those particular movements are the only ones that are possible. Whereas for Aristotle, the formal cause was an active shaping factor in each individual existing thing, in the Newtonian view, natural law is an immutable factor that governs the relations among already formed actualities (atoms), the spatial displacements of which constitute the process of existence.

Like Aristotle, Newton also accepted a doctrine of final causes. For Newton, the final causes of the events in nature were the aims that God had in mind for His creation. When Newton's followers, however, rejected deism they rejected final causes altogether. *It is this rejection of final causes that renders the universe nothing but a meaningless hurrying about of atoms in empty space through uniformly flowing time.*

The process through which the Aristotelian worldview evolved into the Newtonian understanding was gradual, and can be traced over thousands of years. Ivor Leclerc has traced this movement in his remarkable work *The Nature of Physical Existence.* The important point here is that the scientific view is not an ultimate truth, but is, rather, a stage in the unfolding of human attempts to understand the world in which we live. It has advantages, but it also has significant disadvantages, which we have explored in depth in preceding chapters.

Causes in Transphysical Process Metaphysics

Transphysical process metaphysics presents a new understanding of causality that preserves the advantages of the Newtonian worldview while simultaneously allowing us to think clearly about the full range of causes that are apparent in waking life. It also gives us an understanding of causality capable of supporting the five basic propositions we have been discussing.

Material Cause

For process metaphysics, the material cause of actuality is not substance; it is process itself. In Whitehead's version of process metaphysics, this ultimate material cause is termed "creativity." Creativity is the ongoing process that generates actual occasions of experience by unifying the actualities of the past into a novel experience that, in turn, becomes a past actuality to be unified by subsequent experiences. It is this recursive function[2] of actualizing that becomes the material cause, rather than the material cause being either a passive formless substance (as it was for Aristotle) or a collection of permanently formed, substantial atomic things (as it was for Newton). Notice that in this process analysis of material cause, the material cause has become the ultimate source of activity. Whereas for Aristotle, the forms themselves were the sources of action, in process metaphysics, it is the material function that is the source of activity while the forms have become relatively passive. It is the actualizing process itself that chooses (within certain constraints) the form that will characterize it. This makes process metaphysics more adequate to the experience of personal freedom that we so highly prize in our historical epoch.

Efficient Cause

The efficient cause in process metaphysics is the shaping power of the past. The power of the past is, however, richer in process metaphysics than it is in the metaphysics of Newton. For Newton, the power of the past can be fully expressed as a gravitational gradient. Of course, later classical science added an electromagnetic gradient and, in certain cases, a strong and a weak nuclear gradient. But in all classical science (indeed, in quantum theory as well, though here probabilities are involved), the power of the past can be adequately expressed entirely in mathematical form. This is not the case in process metaphysics. Here, the actualities of the past are expired actual occasions of experience, and, as such, they are characterized not only by mathematical forms, but also by subjective forms such as consciousness, appreciation, disgust, and so forth—none of which are measurable in the modern scientific sense of that term, but all of which profoundly shape the way in which the creative advance unfolds.

A new occasion must, from its own perspective, experience the experiences that preceded it in the creative advance of nature. In other words, as we have previously discussed, in process metaphysics the causal power of the past is the power of memory: the shaping power

---

[2] A recursive function is one that takes its own output for input in its next iteration. This is elaborated at the beginning of Chapter 6.

of our experience of past experiences in all their sensory, emotive, and cognitive significance.

Propositions in the functioning of efficient causation.

Occasions of experience, in the process of their formation (concrescence), produce propositions. A proposition is simply a way of binding entities together. For example, in the process of my own concrescence, I may form a proposition that could be verbally expressed as "that flower is yellow." In this case, I am binding together an actuality (the flower) with an idea, or form (yellow).

In the process of concrescence, I sometimes bind together a potential *future* actuality with a particular form. For example, I might form a proposition that could be verbally translated as, "I will now raise my arm." If I hold this proposition with the correct attitude (the correct subjective form) then, indeed, my arm begins to rise. Somehow, the proposition I form in the course of my concrescence has a distinct, efficiently causal effect on other occasions in the next moment. In process metaphysics, the propositions that a current occasion of experience forms concerning possible future occasions of experience are an important factor in the constitution of those future actualities. Propositions are efficient causes. This shift in the understanding of efficient causation allows us to understand in more detail the causal power of personality. We will explore this issue in greater detail in the next chapter.

Formal Cause

The understanding of formal causation also undergoes a characteristic transformation in the context of process metaphysics. The material cause—creativity—is now the primary actor in the process of actualization, and it expresses itself through actual occasions that choose the forms that will characterize them for all future occasions. But each actual occasion is presented with only a limited set of forms, or eternal objects, among which it can choose. In process metaphysics, this array of choices is held to be the formal cause of an occasion. These choices are weighted in various quantitative and qualitative ways. In quantum mechanics, which studies the concrescence of very low-grade actual occasions, each emerging occasion is confronted with a "probability matrix" that specifies which characteristics it may come to have, and assigns to each one a probability. Something similar happens in the case of higher-grade occasions such as the moments in our personalities.

In each moment, we emerge out of a settled past consisting of a multiplicity of past occasions of experience. It is not the case that "anything is possible" in any given moment. In fact, only those possibilities that are logically consistent with the past are actually possible. For example, before I wrote these words I entered my office and sat down. There are many possibilities open to me now: I might keep typing, or I might get up and open the window—but all the possibilities open to me now must be logically consistent with the fact that I have already put myself in this chair. I cannot now make a decision that would have required me to have left the house instead of walking into my office.

Furthermore, the possibilities that are open to me now are weighted. I cannot assign a numerical probability to the various possibilities open to me because the higher the grade of an occasion, the more complex and potentially divided are its aims, and the more difficult it gets to predict how various possibilities will be weighted, and which one of them will be chosen. Only when very specific and narrowly defined situations are considered, and then only when large numbers of actors are considered as well, can even statistical probabilities for diverse choices be generated for high-grade personalities. Nonetheless, it is obvious that the choices open are not all equally likely. I could, for example, get up from my chair and begin attempting to stand on my head. This is possible, but it is rather less likely than my continuing to write, or my getting up to open the window. In summary, the formal cause of an actual occasion is the array of choices open to it in its concrescence, as those possibilities are variously weighted in relation to the occasion's aim.

Note that in process metaphysics, each occasion has its own unique formal cause. In modern science, however, we have become accustomed to the idea that the formal cause under which nature operates is the one system of natural law, which is the same everywhere and for all time. This system of natural law that is posited by modern science can be abstracted from the notion of formal cause that is posited in process metaphysics if we restrict our attention to systems of actual occasions that are of sufficiently low grade. Occasions of low grade confront a small number of probabilities among which they must choose. Quantum mechanics allows us to predict which choices will be available to a new quantum event, and the probabilities that govern their actualization. In an environment where the probabilities of significant choices approach unity (as they do in macroscopic systems), natural laws of the classical type can be approximated. When a set of occasions is chosen, such that the array of choices in terms of which they all operate is sufficiently simple and uniform, we can then imagine that they are all governed by a single set of natural laws, as is customary in modern science. The idea that each occasion of experience has a unique formal cause is not incompatible with the results of scientific experiments.

Formal causes also have a role in determining how fully a given occasion affects the occasions in its future. Remember that in transphysical process metaphysics, we say a past occasion "objectifies" in a current occasion and that it does so under abstraction. In other words, when I experience an occasion belonging to my past, I never feel it as fully as it felt itself. Also, by definition, the less fully I feel it, the less causal impact it has on me.

The fullness with which one occasion can objectify in another occasion is governed by many factors. The most obvious factor is distance in time and space. In general, the further away from a past occasion that I am in some given framework of spatio-temporal relations, the less fully that past occasion will objectify in me. The attenuation of causal factors over distance is of great interest to modern scientists. For example, the discovery that gravitational attraction falls off with the square of the distance between the attractive bodies was one of Newton's greatest discoveries. But distance is not the only factor governing the fullness of causal objectification among occasions.

Another important factor governing the fullness of causal objectification is that of "formal resonance." Formal resonance is an intensification of the objectification of one occasion in another occasion by virtue of their similarity of form. At the beginning of a new actual occasion, its formal cause consists of all of those possibilities that are actually relevant to it, given its past and its subjective aim. At the end of the life of an actual occasion, it has chosen for itself a specific set of forms that will characterize it for all subsequent occasions. The final form achieved by one occasion will "resonate" more or less fully with the formal causes of new occasions that are starting their concrescences. The stronger this resonance, the fuller will be the causal objectification binding the two occasions.

The most obvious application of this principle to our work in this book concerns the function of memory. As we know, memories are most often triggered by associations—which is to say that it is some formal property (e.g., "being in a museum," or "eating with a friend") of the current situation that enables a past occasion on which we experienced a similar formal property in the past ("The last time I was in a museum …") to objectify more fully in our current awareness. Because in transphysical process metaphysics efficient cause and memory are the same thing, we can easily see how these formal resonances affect the operation of efficient causation.

I do not think that this notion of "formal resonance" exhausts the influence of formal causes in the creative advance. It should be possible to articulate and develop some notion of "archetypal resonance" that would further enrich transphysical process metaphysics. This task awaits doing.

Final Cause

Final cause, as we have seen, is thoroughly rehabilitated in process metaphysics. Nothing happens without a "reason why." Every concrescence begins with a settled past *and* with an aim at value. In transphysical process metaphysics, the importance of final causes is greater than it is in Whiteheadian process metaphysics. In transphysical process metaphysics, the aim of one occasion is understood as having a direct influence on the aims of certain other occasions that take place in spatial and temporal contiguity to it.[3]

This understanding of final causes has significant ramifications. If we understand final cause in this way, it allows us to account for the fact—attested to over and over again in daily life and well established in parapsychological experiments[4]—that our aim, our purpose, or our will has noticeable effects in the world around us.

Centuries of scientific materialism have accustomed us to the idea that all interactions among entities are external, like a kinetic interaction between billiard balls. Transphysical process metaphysics, while it acknowledges the existence of efficient causes, revisions them as internal relations, as a complex transmission of experience through the creative advance. But transphysical process metaphysics also allows the purpose, or aim, of a given occasion to have an effect on other occasions under certain circumstances. This is a kind of transmission of final causes.

Recall that every new actual occasion must begin with an aim. An actual occasion does not choose its own aim because its concrescence does not begin until that aim is present. We will discuss the ultimate origin of this aim in the next chapter. What is important in this context is that the aim of an occasion can be influenced in decisive ways by the aims of higher-grade occasions in its neighborhood.[5] We can get a sense of this by noting how it is that the aims of our society, the aims of the planet as a whole (Gaia), and the evolutionary aim of the universe itself are all implicitly operative in our valuations and decisions. Of course, we make our own free decisions, but many of the aims that

---

[3] In Whiteheadian process metaphysics, this relationship operates between an occasion and its prehensions, which are imagined to happen in a way that is somewhat private to the concrescence involved. In transphysical process metaphysics, the relationship between a concrescence and its prehensions is a relationship between full, actual occasions.

[4] See Chapter 1.

[5] Technically, transpersonal process metaphysics holds that the higher the grade of an occasion, the longer its duration. The final satisfaction of an occasion cannot be reached until all its component prehensions have reached final satisfaction. The higher the grade of an occasion, the longer this will take. Strictly, a higher-grade occasion modifies the aims of those occasions that take place within its span of existence. The implications of this for the structure of time are spelled out in Weiss's *Embodiment: A Frame for the Exploration of Reincarnation and Personality Survival*, particularly in Appendix 1.

condition our decisions are inherited from the past. We find ourselves emerging into actuality moment to moment as an expression of aims that enter us through the larger systems of which we are, in some sense, an expression.

By the same token, we can create a way to think intelligibly about the effects that *we* have on the occasions of our bodies. It is not just that we form propositions and ask our bodies to perform specific actions. We can form propositions asking rocks to levitate all day, but successful levitation is rare indeed! Why? Because the occasions of our bodies have already formed under the influence of our aims, so they are predisposed to accept our suggestions whenever possible, whereas occasions that form outside the influence of our aims are much less liable to be responsive to our propositions.

The fact that our aims can influence the aims of other beings also helps account for at least one subset of synchronistic events. For example, Jung's famous example of "synchronicity"—in which he was discussing with a client a dream about a scarab beetle and, at that precise moment, a scarab beetle began tapping at his window—could be explained in this way. The therapeutic aims of Jung and his client could, in this way of thinking, have influenced the aim of the beetle in such a way that it found value in approaching Jung's office. This could also account for the frequent cases of psychic contact between people who are emotionally close. People who are very close can be imagined as influencing not only each other's behaviors but each other's aims as well. In this way, people who are emotionally close would be somewhat like cells in the same body and thus open to propositions formed by the other participant in the bond.

In a later chapter, we will see how this final causation is relevant to the explanation of micro- and macro-psychokinesis.

As we will see in the following chapters, the power of one occasion to decisively influence the aims of other occasions allows us to explain the process through which a high-grade personality such as ourselves can be embodied in systems of lower-grade occasions such as our bodies. On the basis of this understanding, we will be able to account for the difference between a live body and a dead one, and also for how it is that personalities can continue to function after the death of their bodies.

We will also be able to outline a tentative way of accounting for micro- and macro-psychokinesis.

Finally, subjective aims are an important factor in governing the fullness of causal objectification among occasions. In general, the more the aim of a new occasion "resonates" with the aim of an already expired occasion, the more fully the expired occasion will objectify in the new occasion. We will explore this relationship more fully in the next chapter.

From the point of view of materialistic science, such speculation seems useless. Reductionistic scientists are reluctant even to acknowledge the existence of final causes, let alone their power beyond the individual in which they occur. Nonetheless, this way of understanding does make intelligible some of the anomalous data with which we are working. It may be that science needs to acknowledge this new form of causal interaction, and to begin working out ways of exploring it more deeply.

In the next chapter, we will look in detail at how these various types of cause play out in the creative advance.

Chapter 6: The Creative Advance and Paranormal Phenomena

The "creative advance" is Whitehead's phrase for the ongoing process of actualization that constitutes the actual world. In this chapter, we will do two tasks. First we will explore in greater detail how the four causes outlined in the previous chapter play out in the creative advance of actual occasions. Second, as ideas develop that permit an approach to the explanation of various parapsychological phenomena, we will pause to explore the possibilities that are opened up.

With a deeper understanding of the causal interactions that bind the universe into a coherent whole, we will be better positioned to understand the transphysical worlds, their role in everyday life, and their role in life after death. We will also see how understanding the creative advance illuminates the five fundamental propositions I outlined at the beginning of this book.

First, let's look at one of the most important key terms that defines the very possibility of the creative advance—*Creativity.*

Creativity

In transphysical process metaphysics (following Whitehead), we call the ultimate source of all actuality "Creativity." Because this is a technical use of "creativity," I will capitalize it whenever I use the word in this sense. Creativity, here, serves the function that earlier philosophies ascribe to substance. It is the material cause, the ultimate ingredient of all actual entities. However, unlike classical philosophies in which the material cause, substance, is thing-like, in process philosophy we think of the material cause as a recursive function, an activity that feeds back into and builds on itself. We can make this clear by thinking of Creativity as a set of instructions, something like a computer program.

- Our initial assumption is that the creative advance is beginning-less and endless. Note that this does not deny the possibility of a Big Bang; it merely makes the Big Bang a particular incident in an ongoing process of actualization.
- Given this assumption, we can then assume that Creativity always has a past to work with. At the inception of each new instance of Creativity, the past shows up as a universe of completed actual occasions. We can symbolize actual occasions with the letter a, and then we can write the formula:

$$Past = (a_1, a_2, a_3 \ldots a_\infty)$$

which indicates that the past consists of an infinite number of already settled actualities.

- Creativity, then, operates on the past to produce a new actual occasion that we will designate as a_{new}. Note that each operation of Creativity embodies a quantum of freedom in the interpretation of the past and in the choices that are made among the mutually incompatible possibilities for the future. Note also that every occasion, arising as it does out of a unique and never-to-be-repeated past and involving free decisions, is a novel and unique actuality. We can then can write:

$$\text{Creativity(Past)} = a_{new}$$

- Finally, this new actual occasion becomes part of the past for a new instance of Creativity. We symbolize this by:

$$\text{Past} = \text{Past} + a_{new}$$

- Now we can put this together into a simple, informal program:

$$\text{Past} = (a_1, a_2, a_3 \ldots a_\infty)$$
REPEAT THE FOLLOWING STEPS:
$$\text{Creativity(Past)} = a_{new}$$
$$\text{Past} = \text{Past} + a_{new}$$
FOREVER.

This formula is oversimplified, given that many instances of Creativity are taking place simultaneously, but it gives us a sense of Creativity as a recursive function. It also illuminates some of the difficulties inherent in describing this process, since we must know what actual occasions are like before we can describe the process of their formation.

Concrescence and Prehension

Concrescence is the process by which an actual occasion attains actuality. If we analyze a single instance of concrescence, we find it is composed of other concrescences of the same or of lower grade than itself.[1] In other words, an actual occasion is a "drop of experience" and if we attend to a single drop of experience, we can always decompose it into smaller

---

[1] Whitehead generally holds that actuality consists of God, actual occasions, and prehensions. Prehensions, which belong exclusively to one actual occasion, are themselves like actual occasions, except that they get their aim from the occasion to which they belong. In transphysical process metaphysics, I regard prehensions as actual occasions in their own right. For a more extended discussion of this difference between Whitehead's process philosophy and transphysical process metaphysics, see the appendix in Weiss, *Embodiment*.

and simpler drops of experience. At this time, we can leave open the question of whether there is a definite bottom or a definite top to this hierarchy of actual occasions. Each actual occasion, while engaged in maximizing its enjoyment of value for itself, also thus plays two other roles in the creative advance:

- First, an actual occasion may order the experience of many other occasions (of a grade similar to or below that of its own) into the unity of a new drop of experience. An example of this would be the way in which the experiences of the actual occasions that are the cells and organs of my body all form part of one drop of experience that is me at the current moment (me/now). When I analyze my experience (or the experience of some other actual occasion) in this way, I will say that the drops of experience that are making up the drop of experience that is me/now are functioning as "prehensions" in my concrescence.
- Second, any actual occasion may serve as a prehension for one or more actual occasions of a grade similar to or higher than its own.

Thus the terms "concrescence" and "prehension" are relative. Every prehension is a concrescence in its own right, and every concrescence may serve as a prehension in one or more other occasions. As we will see later, this doctrine is helpful in explaining how it is that we are a personality embodied in a physical body.

When an occasion is functioning as a prehension in the concrescence of another occasion of the same or higher grade, the prehending occasion in the relationship experiences just so much of the prehended occasion as is relevant to its own aim and its own position in the creative advance. For example, the concrescences forming the retinas of my eyes are contemporary with some member of my personality and are strongly influenced by my subjective aim and so I prehend them more vividly than I do, for example, the occasions in my fingernails. Each of those actual occasions prehends the entirety of its world and makes its own choices as it comes into being. However, my influence on the occasions of my retina disposes them to pay particular attention to color and form as they construct their appearance of the world. I then prehend those cells, under the abstraction appropriate to my aim, as visual elements in my experience. I abstract from the full experience of the cells in my retina only those elements that are relevant to the formation of my own "appearance" of my own world.[2]

One occasion can function as a prehension in the concrescence of another in a variety of ways. Let's look at some of these now.

Causal Prehensions

Occasions completed at the time a new concrescence begins serve as "causal prehensions" for the new occasion.[3] The way in which the new occasion abstracts from the experiences of its own causal prehensions is strongly conditioned by several factors.

The first of these factors is *the relative positions of the two occasions in time and space*. Each new occasion has a position in the creative advance—it is somewhere in time and space—and so it has a perspective on its own past. In general, the greater the temporal and spatial distance between the new occasion and the already completed occasion, the more abstract is the experience of the old occasion by the new one. In other words, the further away something is from us, either in space or in time, the fewer details about it are relevant and perceptible to us. Furthermore, certain features of the old occasion may be hidden. For example, in the normal course of events I cannot directly prehend the back of your head while I am looking directly at your face. Distance

---

[2] I will sometimes refer to prehensions as objects in the world of the occasion in which they function; at other times, I refer to them as elements of subjective experience. This ambiguity is important: each prehension is an actual occasion, a drop of experience on the inside (for itself), and a causally effective event on the outside (for others). For a concrescence in which an occasion is serving as a prehension, it can be considered both as an object *of* experience and as an element *in* experience. Because occasions (and prehensions) can be described in these two complementary ways, we can use phenomenological methods to identify them as elements in experience, and simultaneously we can consider them as objects involved in networks of causation.

[3] Whitehead refers to these occasions as "physical prehensions." This terminology, however, makes the mistake of confusing the actual with the physical—a mistake I aim to avoid in this work. Since the completed actualities that enter into the initial phase of concrescence can be of various grades, not just the lowest, or "physical" grade, I refer to them as "causal prehensions."

in time and space strongly condition the fullness with which a causal prehension is experienced.

The second factor we will call "resonance."[4] Resonance, like time and space, is a factor that governs the fullness of objectification among occasions but operates in a very different way. The space-time relationship, in general, establishes that the greater the space-time distance between a past occasion and a currently concrescing occasion, the more abstractly the past occasion will objectify in the current one. But the greater the resonance between a past occasion and a current one, the more full the objectification will be—*independent* from the space-time distance between the occasions. For example, it may be the case that all high-grade actual occasions contemplating the Great Pyramid may enjoy, in that moment of contemplation, a special resonant connection with all other high-grade occasions that have contemplated that same form at any point in its history. Or it may be that there is an ongoing resonance between all the members of a single political movement.

The term "resonance" is used here with no appeal other than to intuition. This term is in need of philosophical analysis. It should be pointed out, at least, that resonance is not the same as similarity. For example, two forms might resonate by virtue of their vivid contrast or by virtue of their complementarity.

In transphysical process metaphysics, we recognize two forms of causal resonance: formal resonance and resonance of aim.

Formal Resonance among Causal Prehensions

Each actual occasion has a form. We can speak of that form in two ways. At the concrescence of an actual occasion, there is its formal cause, or the full spectrum of possibilities that are available to it given the past out of which it is arising. Then, at the end of its concrescence, its final satisfaction is a complex proposition, the form of which is the character that the occasion will present to its future. To the extent that the final form of a past occasion "resonates" with the formal cause of a

---

[4] My use of the term "resonance" is inspired by Rupert Sheldrake and his notion of "morphic resonance." However, I am defining the term in my own way, and I have not worked out in any detail the similarities and dissimilarities between my use of the word and his.

new occasion, that past occasion will objectify in the new occasion with greater fullness and intensity.

Formal resonance is an important factor in memory—i.e., our memories tend to be triggered by experiences in the present that are resonant with the relevant past. Since memory, in process metaphysics, is efficient cause, here we see the direct causal relevance of formal resonance.

Should the causal efficacy of ritual and sympathetic magic be sufficiently established, formal resonance would give us a way of beginning a conceptual analysis of that power.

Finally, it seems possible that the simple idea of formal resonance being presented here might be elaborated into a fuller doctrine of "archetypal resonance" that would significantly enrich transphysical process metaphysics.

Resonance of Aim among Causal Prehensions

The second form of resonance among occasions is the resonance among their aims.

Every actual occasion aims at a maximization of value. This includes the value it experiences in its own moment of existence and the value that may be realized by virtue of its current existence in the various futures relevant to it. More specifically, each occasion has its own particular way of valuing its world. The subjective aim is a tapestry of values. All of us work toward the realization of values such as truth, beauty, justice, power, convenience, wealth, and so forth. And each of us weighs differently the various values we hold. Each of us, then, is characterized by our own individual way of aiming at value.

Transphysical process metaphysics holds that the aims of actual occasions are more or less resonant with one another and that *the greater the resonance between the aim of a new occasion and the aim of an expired occasion, the more fully the expired occasion objectifies in the new one.* This explains, for example, why the occasions of our own personal past, which are extremely resonant to us in aim, objectify so fully in our present moment. This principle will also be important when we come to discuss reincarnation in Chapter 11.

The Binding Problem, and How a Living Body Differs from a Dead One

The idea that the aim of one occasion can be an important factor in setting the aim of another occasion of lower grade offers a novel solution to what is called the "binding problem." This is the problem of how a collection of entities can come together into a new and higher whole (e.g., how the multiple "little" consciousnesses of my cells bind into the single unit consciousness that I experience as "me"). Whitehead, in his process metaphysics, uses this idea to explain the wholeness and unity of actual occasions. He says that all of the prehensions within an actual occasion are just like full actual occasions except that they share an aim in common with the concrescence to which they belong.[5] Thus the unity of an occasion consists in its unity of aim. The unity is not an expression of the physical pole—it is not the result of some arrangement of efficient causes. Rather the unity is an expression of the mental or conscious pole, and it consists in a unity of aim. Transphysical process metaphysics generalizes this idea by maintaining the relativity of concrescence and prehension. In this way, we can explain the wholeness of macrocosmic entities, such as living bodies, in the same way that Whitehead explains the wholeness of individual occasions. All of the occasions making up a human body are functioning as prehensions for the inhabiting personality of that body, and it is in this unity of aim, or final cause, that the body finds its unity. It is precisely this unity of aim that is lost at death, causing the individual occasions of the body to lose their unity, and initiating the process of decay.[6] This understanding of the unity of the body solves the conceptual problem of explaining what occurs at the death of a living body. If the body's unity over time consists in the presence of a higher-grade personality that makes all of the occasions in the body into its prehensions by means of influencing

---

[5] Whitehead, *Process and Reality*, p. 19.
[6] This understanding of the unity of the body permits an interesting speculation about cancer. It is said that, in cancer, individual cells of the body cease to respect their place in the unity of the body and begin to function more like parasites. This suggests that cancer does not result from an interaction of efficient causes but rather from a breakdown in the sharing of final causes among the occasions involved. This could explain the "miraculous" cures sometimes reported in cases of cancer and could validate the effectiveness of psychoneuroimmunology, possibly opening new avenues of research.

their subjective aims, then the liberation of this higher-grade occasion from the body would free the occasions of the body to pursue their own individual aims, and so the body would begin to disintegrate.

Causal Prehension as Simple Feeling, Empathy, and Telepathy

The subjective forms of actual occasions of different grades differ along an important qualitative dimension. The subjective form of a low-grade occasion tends to be one of simple, taken-for-granted certainty. Thus, a low-grade occasion, such as an atom, objectifies itself as having a certain gravitational and electromagnetic field, and a certain vector in time and space, and it entertains no doubts or questions about these characteristics. We register our causal prehensions of low-grade occasions as simple feelings, or (in the context of an appropriate theory) facts. Science, which tends to concentrate on low-grade occasions and on the sensations that give us access to them, borrows its certainty about the validity of experiments, in part from the subjective forms of the occasions it studies.

By comparison, medium-grade occasions mix and augment simple causal prehensions with considerations of possibilities (by means of propositional prehensions that I will discuss shortly) and evaluate those possibilities with various shades of appreciation, disgust, hope, and fear. These more complex subjective forms are possible because medium-grade occasions consider the relationship between the actual and the possible. This way of understanding highlights a crucial difference between sensation and emotion: emotions always involve some form of comparison between the actual and the possible. To say that I am disgusted by some particular experience, for example, implies that I evaluate this experience by contrasting it to what it might have been. The subjective forms of medium-grade occasions are *emotional*. This accounts for the feeling that accompanies the prehension of life. Not only do we experience sensations that inform us of the presence of living beings, we feel life vividly and emotionally because that is how living occasions experience their world, and our experience of those occasions is necessarily an experience of them just as they were. The causal prehension of one medium-grade occasion by another medium- or high-grade occasion has the quality of *empathy*.

High-grade occasions go a step further. Not only do they consider (or prehend) the immediate possibilities of the current situation, they also consider possibilities in the abstract. As a result, high-grade occasions have subjective forms characterized by meaning. The subjective form of "meaningfulness" arises when the mere contrast between the actual and the possible (characteristic of emotions) is supplemented by a consideration of the relationship between a particular experience and the whole of all experiences, and also a consideration of the relationship between a particular experience and the larger context of aims in which it is being evaluated. We could say that the causal prehension of a high-grade actuality by another high-grade actuality is telepathy, where telepathy is defined as "the prehension of a proposition with a feeling of meaning."

In short, I am suggesting that the subjective forms of actual occasions, while they are each distinct, share certain forms that are appropriate to their grades. Low-grade occasions have a "sense certainty," medium-grade occasions have an emotional vividness, and high-grade occasions have a feeling of meaningfulness.

Such an understanding of subjective form opens the way for a metaphysics that includes *simple feeling*,[7] *empathy*, and *telepathy* as modes of causal transmission in the creative advance. This is a major epistemological step forward beyond the limits of the metaphysics of materialism and sensory empiricism that dominates modern science. It allows us to account for a wider range of phenomena and research data.

The reality of empathy and telepathy is well established both by anecdotal and laboratory data, yet modern science is unable to explain such phenomena. They simply do not fit into the materialist paradigm. Transphysical process metaphysics covers a broader range of experiences and data. While fully accounting for the behaviors of low-grade occasions observed by physicists, the new metaphysics makes it clear that each occasion—every actual event—is capable of empathic and telepathic interactions. Given the new metaphysics, we no longer have

---

[7] Note that a "simple feeling" is not the same thing as a "sensation." A simple feeling is a direct causal prehension on the part of any occasion. A sensation is a complex presentation of some aspect of the world elaborated by the various intelligences of an animal body and presented to the presiding personality of that body as a representation.

to attempt the impossible task of explaining empathy and telepathy as the outcome of merely physical forces. Indeed, we now have to explain why empathic and telepathic interactions are so minimal among the merely inorganic occasions studied by physicists. This is easily done, as we have just seen, by a consideration of the properties that differentiate the three grades of occasions from each other.

We will now consider two other ways in which occasions can function as prehensions—*conceptual* prehensions and *propositional* prehensions. Both differ from the causal prehensions of a given occasion in that they must be in "unison of becoming" with the concrescing occasion for which they are prehensions. The phrase "unison of becoming" requires clarification.

The concrescence of an actual occasion is restricted to a finite quantum of time. Only an abstraction has existence at an instant. All actualities are finite in both time and space. While process metaphysics recognizes no abstract, absolute time in which actualities transpire, different durations can be defined by comparisons among occasions. Whitehead suggests that the duration of a human-grade event is something like one-eighth of a second (as measured by oscillations of inorganic occasions in some form of clock). We know that many cellular events go into the making of one human moment, and that millions of atomic events go into the making of one cellular moment. All the events that transpire during a concrescence of one occasion are said to be in "unison of becoming" with that occasion.

The subjective aims of occasions that serve as causal prehensions for a new concrescence are not influenced by the aims of the new occasion. This is because the causal prehensions were already fully actual before the prehending occasion began its actualization. But *all occasions that are in unison of becoming with a given concrescence are influenced by its aims.* This influence is a matter of degree, so that those occasions that are more proximate in spatial terms are more powerfully influenced than those that are further away; those occasions that are more formally resonant are more powerfully influenced; and those occasions whose aims are more resonant with that of the new occasion are also more powerfully influenced.

The important point here is that each concrescence has a potent influence on the aims of some set of occasions that are in unison with it and are resonant with it in the process of becoming. These are, in particular, the occasions Whitehead has in mind when he discusses the prehensions that make up the later phases of an occasion of experience.

Confirmation and Novelty in Causal Prehension

No matter how fully an expired occasion may be objectified in a new occasion, the new occasion further abstracts from the old occasion only that which is relevant to its current aims. Note, however, that even though there is the imposition of abstraction on the objectification of the old occasions in the new occasion, all causal prehensions are "conformal." That is to say each new occasion, even though it experiences only some portion of the experience of the old occasion, experiences those portions it has selected *exactly* as they were. Since each of the old occasions had a subjective form—its own mood of certainty or of questioning, its own emotions of attraction or aversion, its own degree of meaningfulness, and so on—the new occasion prehends the subjective form along with the objective data. In addition, and crucially, *the new occasion generates its own subjective form*, its own individual reaction, to the objective data and the (now-expired) subjective form it receives from the old occasion. The subjective form of the new concrescence influences how this particular prehension will figure in the further reaches of the creative advance.

Review

In this chapter, we have been exploring the creative advance of actual occasions that make up the cosmogenesis in which we are participating. In this section, we have discussed causal prehensions, which are the relationships that a nascent occasion forms with those occasions that were fully realized in its settled past. We have seen that the fullness with which a past occasion objectifies in a new occasion is affected by space-time distance, by formal resonance, and by resonance of aim. Also, we have seen that low-grade occasions objectify elemental eternal objects with the subjective form of simple feeling, that medium-grade occasions objectify complex comparative forms with subjective forms that are emotional, and that high-grade occasions objectify complex forms with subjective forms of meaningfulness. Causal prehensions in transphysical process metaphysics are, depending on the grade of the occasions involved, either sensation-like, empathic, or telepathic.

Conceptual Prehensions

For each causal prehension, an occasion must have a conceptual prehension that abstracts from the causal prehension some subset of those eternal objects that are ingredient in it. For example, let us return to the example of the retina of my eyes. Let us say that a particular cell in my eyes is prehended by me as a patch of color. My further concrescence then demands another prehension of the eternal object characterizing that particular color. Thus, under the influence of my currently concrescing occasion, another occasion (of lower grade) will take place in unison of becoming with it, and that occasion will be missioned, by me, to pay particular attention to some of the eternal objects instantiated or ingredient in its environment. This new occasion will serve as the needed conceptual prehension in the new concrescence. Whitehead, in his formulation of process metaphysics, suggests that the conceptual prehension is a very simple matter. For example, if the relevant causal prehension were of a concrescence that had an experience of redness, then the eternal object abstracted from it would be "red." But Whitehead then needs another mechanism (he calls it "conceptual reversion") to permit the concrescing occasion to experience the character of its prehension in ways other than as red.

In order to simplify Whitehead's scheme, and to bring transphysical process metaphysics more in line with quantum physics, I suggest that a conceptual prehension objectifies itself as something like a probability matrix. We know from physiological studies that the way in which that particular color will ultimately be perceived by an occasion in my personality is heavily dependent on context. Therefore, the initial conceptual prehension of that occasion in my retina will be a prehension of the various colors that might, ultimately, come to characterize that occasion for me. Only as my concrescence proceeds, and as various causal and conceptual prehensions are formed and compared will the final decision be made as to which of the possible colors will characterize that past entity in my formed perception.

The importance of conceptual prehensions cannot be overstated. It is by virtue of conceptual prehensions that freedom enters into the creative advance. By eliciting into relevance the gap between what was and what might be for a new occasion, a conceptual prehension creates an opening for free interpretation, and permits the contemplation of new possibilities for actualization.

Propositional Prehensions

Once an occasion has assembled its causal prehensions and its conceptual prehensions, it begins the work of unifying these prehensions into a single experience of the past and a set of intentions regarding the future. Unification is done by means of propositional prehensions, but before we can understand what these are, we must first examine how propositions function in process metaphysics.

Whitehead introduces the word "contrast" as a useful technical term. A contrast is a togetherness of two entities in which the individuality of each is preserved. Thus we could put two peanuts together and say we have a contrast of peanuts. We could also put those two peanuts together with an almond, and call it a contrast of nuts.

A proposition is a specific type of contrast in which at least one of the terms is an eternal object (an idea, a possibility, or a form). Some propositions (for example, 1 + 1 = 2) consist of contrasts between eternal objects alone. Other propositions, such as "the machine is green," hold together an actuality (the machine) and an eternal object (green). Note that the propositions I am using here as examples can be verbally expressed. Most propositions, however, operate below the threshold of fully lucid consciousness and thus are never verbally expressed. For example, we can deduce from the behavior of a bacterium that it interprets its environment in terms of a chemical gradient that points toward food and away from toxins. If the bacterium could speak, it might form the verbal proposition "there is food in that direction." But of course it can't speak. Indeed, it doesn't have to speak in order to entertain a proposition in this sense.

All propositions belong to actual occasions. In other words, the elements in an actual proposition are held together in the conscious experience (the mental pole) of the actual occasion that entertains the propositions. Propositions play a number of very important roles in the process of concrescence.

- First, the unifying activity of concrescence is accomplished by means of propositions. This happens in at least three ways:

  o An actual occasion takes one or more actualities of its past and holds them in contrast with some eternal object that belongs to all of them. It then forms a proposition, judging the actualities to be a single entity. Whitehead calls this particular act of unification "transmutation." For example, say some collection of actualities in the past of an actual occasion share the characteristics grey, cold, and hard. Then these may be judged to be "a rock." What is particularly important here is that this rocklike collection of actual occasions will be prehended by future concrescences—through the transmuting occasion—as a single entity. This is important in perception where, for example, some concrescence involved in the perceptual process carried on by my body has performed just this transmutation, and so I, the high-level personality inhabiting the body, see that collection of gray, cold, hard occasions as a single entity—a rock. Because of this operation, we can apprehend our world—a vast multiplicity of occasions—as a collection of discrete entities.

  o An actual occasion may hold several entities together as a recognizable group. It then forms a proposition linking those entities together under a single category. This differs from transmutation in that the individual members of the group still stand out within the group as individuals. Nonetheless, it is an important unifying move in that future concrescences can then form propositions concerning the group as a whole, abstracting from the individual members. For example, it might hold a group of people as "my family" or as "citizens of the United States."

   o   Ultimately, in the final satisfaction of the occasion, all of the entities prehended by the concrescence are held together as "elements of this experience."
- An actual occasion can form propositions that function as questions—which, in effect, a concrescence asks of itself. For example, as we saw before, a concrescence might hold "machine" and "green" together in a proposition with the subjective form of certainty, in which case the proposition would translate as "that machine is green"; but it might hold that proposition with the subjective form of a question, so that the proposition would translate as, "Is that machine green?" When a proposition is held by one occasion in the interrogative mode, it may inspire a subsequent occasion to re-examine the original causal prehensions that had been transmuted into "a machine." Thus it forms an interrogative contrast between "the green machine" and the original concrescences involved. This interrogative contrast may then be resolved into an affirmative or negative judgment: is the machine really green or not? In other words, propositions enable concrescences to form hypotheses and to test them.
- Propositions are the means by which novelty is introduced into the creative advance. An easily understood example of this is a situation where I mistake a stick for a snake. In the train of concrescences that constitute the body's perception of its world, some particular concrescence prehends the actual occasions making up the stick and forms the affirmative proposition, "That is a snake." As far as I am concerned there is a snake in the path in front of me, and I experience all the reactions that are usually attendant on that discovery. In this case, I might subsequently form the interrogative proposition, "Is that really a snake?" and then by means of another proposition test it against the original prehensions. But in other cases, the novelty introduced in this way remains effective in the creative advance. For example, some water-breathing ancestors of ours formed a proposition expressing a pleasurable evaluation of sunlight

and dry air, ultimately leading to the emergence of life from the oceans.

- Actual occasions form propositions that function as lures for feeling. A concrescence in a plant might hold a proposition such as "there is more light over there," leading to a new direction of growth. Or a concrescence in the life of a human personality might hold the proposition "this society could be more just," and that proposition might come to dominate much of its behavior.

- Actual occasions form propositions that function as efficient causes for particular occasions that might happen in the future. In transphysical process metaphysics, this is an especially important function of propositions that has not, to my knowledge, been explored in the literature on Whiteheadian process metaphysics.

Let us consider then our own personalities as sequences of actual occasions. An actual occasion feels its world (as causal prehensions), interprets its world (by means of propositional prehensions), and makes whatever decisions among possibilities that it must in order to become actual. Then it expires into "objective immortality," which is to say that henceforth it is available as a causal prehension for any subsequent occasion. That's all it does. It has no hands, no voice, no feet. So how does it have causal effect in the actual world? Quite simply: it does so by means of propositional prehensions.

For example, let's say I want to raise my right arm over my head. I form a proposition predicating that movement of the actual occasions making up my arm. That's all *I* do, and then my arm moves. In terms of transphysical process metaphysics, here's what happens: because the occasions in my arm are under the influence of my subjective aim, they are tuned into the propositions that I form. They then prehend those propositions, and, most of the time, they make the relevant decisions necessary to effect the action I am contemplating. Admittedly, important details need to be further explicated, but the point here is that actual occasions make a bid to influence the future by means of the propositions they form concerning it. All actual occasions, like the occasions of experience making up our own personalities, influence the world only by means of propositions they form. Understanding this helps explain the widely reported phenomenon of psychokinesis, discussed in Chapter 7.

The very last stage of the concrescence of an actual occasion is a special propositional prehension called the "final satisfaction." The final satisfaction of an occasion enjoys a causal prehension of all of the previous occasions that contributed to its formation. It resolves any last decisions among possibilities that may be left at that point, and it contributes to this synthesis its own subjective form—its own freely generated aesthetic response to the process that led to its coming into being. This subjective form may include emotional tones such as anger or boredom, any mode of aesthetic appreciation or even aesthetic disgust, attitudes such as certainty or questioning, and some degree of awareness. This could be anything from the extremely dim and simple awareness of a subatomic occasion to complex mental self-consciousness.

Finally, propositions are an essential element in the formation of personalities. This point requires explication.

Remember that we have defined personalities as societies of actual occasions so arranged that they have one and only one member in each of a string of successive moments. We have seen that atoms can be considered personalities in this sense, as can the society of high-grade occasions presiding over a human body. If we examine more closely the formation of societies, we will see that they are, in effect, bound together by a skein of propositions.

We imagine quantum events as constituting one vast society, but we do not imagine quantum events as personally ordered. In other words, quantum events do not have a personal past or a personal future. For them, the past is a simple fact, and the future is a matrix of probabilities. They do not recognize any particular event in their causal past as having been "mine," nor do they anticipate some future event which might claim them as "mine" in an analogous sense.

In order for an occasion to participate in a personally ordered society, it must be of sufficiently high grade so that it can claim some occasions in its past as belonging to the same society as it does. This is clear in the case of human experience, where out of all of the experiences flooding in on me in each moment, I clearly identify those that were me in recent moments, and some significant subset of those that were me in earlier times, and identify them as having been "me." But it must, in some sense, also be true for any personally ordered society, even one composed entirely of inorganic occasions. In order for an occasion to be able to identify, or indicate, certain occasions of the past, it must form a proposition concerning the systematic space-time relations obtaining among the occasions of its past. In Chapter 9, I will call this a prehension of the "time-space relation" in the context of which an occasion is concrescing. It then must form a proposition which makes use of the time-space relation to indicate certain specific past occasions, and predicates of them membership in "my" personality.

When an actual occasion makes its decisions about how to be actual, it does so with the aim of maximizing value in its own moment of functioning as well as in what is, to it, the relevant future. The anticipation of future satisfaction is a significant component of present satisfaction. For an occasion that is a member of a personally ordered society, the relevant future is often dominated by the future that will be experienced by subsequent members of the same society. In other words, when I am making decisions, they frequently concern the satisfaction that will be experienced by future occasions of my personality, often by those occasions that will, I hope, take place in the immediate future.

For example, I may choose to walk now so that some future occasion of my personality will reach the destination I have in mind. What is true for high-grade personalities must, by the Hermetic Principle, be true for lower-grade personalities as well. Each member of a personally ordered society must form a "continuity proposition" anticipating a future concrescence at a position defined in terms of the relevant time-space relation (and having an appropriate grade) so that it can function as the next member of the personality.

One of the tragic features of the creative advance is that the continuity propositions formed by members of personalities are sometimes disappointed. For example, I might be walking on the street and anticipating the enjoyment of the next moment of my waking life when I am hit by a bus, and that expectation is disappointed. Clearly the continuity proposition is limited in its causal efficacy. It remains, however, an important factor in the creative advance.

If the continuity proposition can be disappointed, then there must be factors other than the personality itself dictating its next position. In a general way, we have identified God, or what I am calling the "ultimate ordering factor," as having the responsibility for final decisions regarding the position of a new occasion. When one occasion expires, a new actual world emerges on which Creativity will operate to produce a new occasion. God's aim is the intensification of value in the creative advance. Thus God will choose to provide the new occasion with the perspective that can create the most value out of this actual world. If the occasion that has just expired is a member of a personally ordered society, then it will most often be the case that maximum value can be achieved by maintaining the continuity of the personality. Thus God is likely to consult the continuity proposition, and to ratify it unless some other, overriding value intrudes. This argument is of a type not usually offered in modern thought. It is an argument couched in terms of final causes. As we have seen, process metaphysics takes final causes very seriously.

Without a proposition such as this, it would be impossible to construct a "process mechanics." Consider a situation in which two atoms are about to collide. Each of them must prehend the other, and form a proposition concerning the probable location of the next member of the series of occasions that makes it up. Then, it forms a proposition concerning its own next instantiation. If that instantiation would put it in the same position as the other atom involved, it must form a new proposition suggesting a new trajectory for itself. Extending this explanation to larger systems of occasions will enable us to form a process metaphysical understanding of the interactions among billiard balls and other macrocosmic entities.

Societies of Actual Occasions

I have already spoken of "societies of actual occasions" and have informally defined them as self-organizing systems of actual occasions. Now we are in a position to give a more precise and interesting definition of societies of actual occasions.

Four Types of Systems

Systems theorists have identified various types of systems that emerge in the interaction of actual entities. For our purposes, it will be sufficient to identify four types:

- *Crowd*—a group of actualities that can be identified merely in terms of their proximity and, usually, in regard to some character they share. For instance, we might speak of a crowd of gas molecules in a box, or a crowd of people on a street.[8]
- *Assembly*—a group of occasions that remain together as an identifiable unit by virtue of some pattern of efficient causes. For example, a rock is an assembly of actualities. The electromagnetic interactions[9] among the various molecules making up the rock are so arranged that the path of least resistance for those molecules involves their staying in close association. All types of machinery, including computers, are assemblies in this sense.
- *Dissipative System*—a system that is similar to an assembly defined by the efficient causes operating among its constituent entities. But it is unlike an assembly in that it takes place only in the context of entropy flows.[10] Dissipative systems are interesting to scientists because they draw their own boundaries in space, exhibit some adaptive behavior, and undergo occasional re-organizations. Thus, they mimic certain properties of life.
- *Autopoietic System*—a self-organizing system. Maturana and Varela[11] introduced the concept of autopoietic systems in the 1970s in an attempt to specify the nature of living systems.

---

[8] Whitehead refers to crowds as "nexus."

[9] The task of fully describing these efficient causal interactions in terms of actual occasions and propositions is fairly straightforward in principle. The electromagnetic field of an event, for example, can be described as a proposition formed by that event concerning the motions of all future events. A detailed working out of a process-oriented physics is an important and urgent task.

[10] Entropy awaits coherent and adequate interpretation in terms of process metaphysics.

[11] Maturana and Varela, *Autopoiesis and Cognition: The Realization of the Living.*

Such a system is held to be organizationally closed and recursive. That is, it produces the products and processes needed to allow it to keep producing those products and processes. With this idea, Maturana and Varela attempted to reduce life to systems of efficient causes. They seemed to have come close to capturing the essence of life, but they failed in several important respects. In the next section, we will consider the difficulties inherent in their idea, and propose a new definition of self-organization and life.

Embodiment

The problem with the idea that life consists of self-organizing systems of entities interacting entirely through efficient causes is threefold:

- *Coordination of spontaneities.* First, scientists have no idea how it is possible for self-organizing systems to come into being. To be sure, some have a good understanding of how dissipative structures emerge, and it is generally assumed, in a vague sort of way, that self-organizing systems are a further complexification of dissipative systems. But exactly how a dissipative structure can actually become fully self-organizing is not understood. When we take into account the insights of quantum mechanics, particularly the intrinsic spontaneity of each component in a self-organizing system, it quickly becomes apparent that full self-organization requires *a coordination of spontaneities.* This is clear when we consider living systems of great complexity, such as human bodies. If we try to stop ourselves from blinking, the fact that our organs retain some degree of their own independent will becomes clear very quickly. We can tell our eye to stay open, but without some extraordinary effort on our part, it will close when it wants to. And yet, by and large, our eyes are willing to let us tell them when to open, when to close, and where to look. In general, at a deeper level, all of the uncounted cells in our bodies make free decisions in a way that works to our overall benefit. How can there be a coordination of spontaneities in a complex system if the system is held together only by networks of efficient causes?

- *Discerning possibilities.* Secondly, living systems, as a whole, are able to discern possibilities in their worlds that none of their components could access. Back to the example of a cell: It is clear that no macromolecule (macromolecules are probably assemblies) could possibly identify or follow a chemical gradient. How can any mere assembly of entities discern possibilities that none of their individual members can discern?

- *Unified consciousness.* Third, and most telling, the theory of self-organization by means of efficient causes entirely fails to account for the unified central consciousness that belongs to every living being. To make this clear, let us consider human beings. Humans are certainly living beings, and we know that each of us has a central consciousness—a central personality—around which we are organized. Clearly this is so for other animals as well. In the case of plants, we might imagine, as Whitehead suggests, that they are more loosely organized and are something of a democracy. They may fall in some intermediate ground between assemblies of living beings and integrated living beings, such as animals, which possess (in addition to the myriad "little" consciousnesses of the individual beings that constitute them) a central unified, presiding consciousness. But even individual living cells act as if they are operated by a central personality. Confronted with a chemical gradient, for example, they will decide, as an individual being, which way to go. I have heard scientists who work with cells under microscopes say that if they were large enough, they would make good pets.

Transphysical process metaphysics enables us to redefine living systems in a way that overcomes the difficulties with the idea of self-organization or autopoiesis. Rather than considering the essential property of living systems to be organizational closure, I propose that living systems are the *embodiment* of actual occasions of higher grade. In other words, a living system behaves as it does because the aims of each of its components have been conditioned by the aim of some higher-grade occasion. Indeed, each of these lower-grade occasions is functioning as a prehension for the higher-grade occasion to which they belong. Organizational closure is possible because the subjective aims imposed on the lower-grade occasions of the system makes them into prehensions for the higher-grade occasion involved. Organization closure is the unity of an actual occasion writ large.

From this point forward, I will no longer speak of living systems as self-organized and will refer to them as *embodied* systems. As we will see in subsequent chapters, this understanding of life will allow us to comprehend the life of the personality after the death of its physical body.

The Process of Concrescence

With all of these definitions in place, we can now review the entire process of concrescence. While I have previously discussed this issue in terms of three broad stages of feeling, interpretation, and decision/ enjoyment, here I will discuss concrescence in terms of prehensions, thus laying a firm ground for our discussion of transphysical worlds and their involvement in our waking and postmortem lives.

The Inception of a New Actual Occasion

A concrescence begins from a universe of settled actualities. Somewhere, a concrescence has completed and has added to the totality, and now a new instance of Creativity is about to begin.

Several determinations must be made as the concrescence begins. First, the new concrescence must have an aim. Part of this aim is inherent in Creativity itself—that is, the new concrescence must have an aim at integrating the universe in which it finds itself into a novel experience that maximizes value for itself and for its relevant future. The new concrescence must also have a position within its universe that will establish its perspective on that universe, and will thus determine the societies to which the new concrescence belongs. For example, an atomic concrescence with an appropriate aim, taking place in sufficient proximity to the other molecules of a particular cell belongs to (or is a prehension for) the society of that cell, and also, indirectly, belongs to all of the societies to which that cell belongs (or for which it functions as a prehension).

The position and the aim jointly determine the grade of the new occasion. A high-grade occasion can emerge only if the actual world out of which it grows is sufficiently interesting to support the construction of an elaborate appearance. A sufficiently interesting actual world is a necessary condition for a higher-grade occasion, but it is not a sufficient condition. An occasion with a deficient aim might arise in a very interesting environment and yet ignore most of its richness. Thus both an interesting world and an appropriate subjective aim are needed as conditions for the formation of high-grade actualities.

Finally, the aim of the new occasion is partially determined by the aims of the societies to which it belongs.

Note that all of these determinations must be made *before* concrescence begins. Who or what makes these determinations? To answer this question, Whitehead calls upon a factor in actuality that he calls God. If the aims of actual occasions were somehow spontaneously chosen by the occasions themselves, or if they were random, then the spontaneities of the various occasions would be in no way coordinated, and so there could be no evolving order in the universe. Every occasion would just go its own way, and no stable patterns could form.[12] There must be in the actual world some agency that coordinates the aims of occasions in such a way that they tend, generally, toward order. In Whitehead's system, this function is played by God.

For the purposes of Part One of this book, I will accept Whitehead's explanation.[13] In short, I will assign the function of providing an aim and a position for a new concrescence to God. Note that God, by hypothesis, is also aiming at maximum value. "God" in this Whiteheadian sense is purged of mythic significance Whitehead's God is not the God of any particular religion. It is only a factor in actuality that persuades occasions to participate more or less cooperatively in the creative

---

[12] It might be suggested that some kind of statistical ordering of spontaneities could emerge out of "natural selection." But what is natural selection? It must be, at minimum, a tendency in the environment to encourage certain sorts of behavior over others—and where does that tendency come from? In terms of transphysical process metaphysics, this tendency itself must be a function of the aims of God and of other relevant occasions.

[13] In Part Two I will outline an expansion of transphysical process metaphysics that brings its theology more in line with Sri Aurobindo's as articulated in *The Life Divine*.

advance by providing them with appropriate aims. Thus God places the concrescence where it is most likely to achieve maximum value, and it coordinates the aims of the new occasion to the aims of the societies to which it will belong.

How Concrescence Unfolds

As soon as the aim and position are established, the already-settled occasions of the world out of which the new occasion is arising become, for it, causal prehensions. Several limitations on this process must be noted:

- *Abstractions from the past.* First, as discussed earlier, causal prehensions experience the experiences of the past under abstraction. While everything that an occasion experiences of its past conforms to the actuality of the past, it does not experience the past in its entirety. Rather it abstracts from the past those features that are relevant to its own aims. Because of distance in space and time, or because of a lack of a significant resonance among aims, some occasions of the past may be largely irrelevant to a current concrescence. It that case, they would tend to fade into the background of experience.

- *Downward causation.* Occasions of higher grade than a new concrescence may have an effect, as previously discussed, on the aim or purpose of the new occasion. If the higher-grade occasions are prehended—if they function as an efficient cause in the new concrescence—they will do so under a high degree of abstraction. For example, a rock in my garden may prehend me as a factor in the overall gravitational gradient, but it will not, and cannot, prehend me as an element in an operating, high-grade personality. However, a lower-grade concrescence may prehend, and be affected by, propositions formed by higher-grade occasions, especially if those propositions have specific relevance to it. The casual effectiveness of these propositions explains, in the context of transphysical process metaphysics, our partial control of our own bodies, as well as the phenomenon of

144

psychokinesis, as we will discuss in Chapter 7. If a new concrescence is partially shaped by the aim of a higher-grade occasion, it will be especially attentive to propositions formed by that higher-grade occasion. In this way, transphysical process metaphysics accounts for the particularly intimate relationship between a personality and its physical body.

Disembodied Actual Occasions

A new occasion, even if it is of a very high grade, need not prehend any lower-grade occasions at all. This doctrine is crucial to transphysical process metaphysics, and I want to pause to elaborate on this idea.

In the modern world, we have lived with the notion that the actual world *is* the physical world, and nothing but the physical world. In transphysical process metaphysics, we define the physical world as a system of low-grade, inorganic occasions. Physics is the study of these low-grade occasions by the higher-grade occasions making up human personalities. Standard modern science is grounded in the assumption that these low-grade inorganic occasions are the fundamental actual entities. However, transphysical process metaphysics recognizes that the high-grade occasions making up human personalities, and indeed, the high-grade occasions embodied in living beings in the physical world are also actual—and constitute a different form of (nonphysical) matter and embodiment. In the next two chapters, we will consider these "higher types of matter" in some detail.

In the waking world, that is, the world that has evolved out of physical processes over many billions of years, all higher-grade occasions are closely associated with systems of low-grade, inorganic occasions. This has led to the notion that living and thinking beings are nothing but arrangements of low-grade, physical entities. In contrast, I am granting these higher-grade occasions full actuality. For example, I understand a living cell to be a system of macromolecules organized by a higher-grade personality that has its own existence, independent of the existence of the macromolecules.

The living personality organizing a cell is intimately associated with its system of macromolecules. Indeed, it could not function *in the world of our waking experience* without using those macromolecules as its prehensions in the physical world. But the personality of a cell does not prehend only its macromolecules, it also prehends other occasions of its own grade. This allows us, for example, to account for the way all of the cells in our bodies directly feel each other in a kind of empathic web. It also leads us to expect direct communication between the cells of our own bodies and the cells of the bodies of others, and also with disembodied intelligences that are of its own grade.

The point to notice is that the personality of a cell is not *dependent* on the macromolecules though which it expresses itself in the world of evolution. It could come into being, and stay in being, merely on the strength of its interactions with other occasions at is own grade. I will return to this point when I discuss the transphysical worlds in more detail in subsequent chapters.

Following its initial causal prehensions, the currently concrescing occasion is partially involved in the concrescence of other, lower-grade occasions that will serve as its conceptual prehensions. This gives it creative access to the forms, or eternal objects, that were ingredient in the past, and also to other eternal objects in terms of which that past may be experienced and the future may be imagined.

With this grasp of its actual world, the concrescence begins to construct its coherent appearance of that world by means of layers of occasions of successively higher grade that function as its propositional prehensions. Thus we can imagine actual occasions as hierarchies of subsidiary actual occasions.

This hierarchy culminates in the final satisfaction, which is the last concrescence in the process, and is the concrescence of highest grade. In the process of this concrescence, the past is experienced coherently, propositions concerning possible futures are formed (the "probability matrix"), and decisions among those possibilities are made. The completed occasion is enjoyed with a specific subjective form.

This new occasion, and all of the concrescences that were involved in it, is now added to the universe, and a new iteration of Creativity is initiated.

Understanding the creative advance, as presented in this chapter, we are now in a position to discuss my second proposition: *the actual universe in which we live includes transphysical worlds.*

Chapter 7: The Waking World

This chapter serves two functions. First, it explores the way in which the transphysical worlds[1] already pervade our waking lives. I call this the "transphysical dimension of the waking world." Second, I review and expand on many of the metaphysical ideas we have considered in previous chapters.

Let's begin by clarifying what I mean by "the waking world." It is the world as we experience it when we are awake, in our "normal" state of consciousness, the state of consciousness most highly privileged in modern science.

In general, we tend to confuse the *waking* world with the *physical* world. They are not at all the same thing. During the day, and under normal circumstances, we live in the waking world and can experience the richness, complexity, and subtlety it offers. We perceive things with our senses, feel our emotions, and interact with other people and animals and the world around us. We engage in a variety of personal and social relationships and spend at least as much time dealing with other living beings as we do with the inorganic portions of the physical environment that surrounds us.

The physical world per se is nowhere near as rich as the waking world. It consists only of low-grade occasions interacting in metrical time and metrical space. If we try to imagine how the world appears to, let us say, an atom, it probably appears as nothing but a gravitational and

---

[1] "Transphysical" refers to worlds of high-grade occasions existing on their own, with no dependence on the low-grade occasions studied by physics.

electromagnetic gradient. It's not complex compared to our richer and more nuanced experience. An inorganic actuality can know nothing of chairs and cups, even when it is part of one, and it can never know a living being in the way that one living being can know another.

Our waking experience is richer than that of an inorganic occasion. Not only can we know about systems of atoms, but we also know and engage with living and thinking beings that are embedded in systems of inorganic occasions (physical bodies). Higher-grade occasions can know about their lower-grade constituents in ways simply not available to the low-grade occasions themselves. In short, the living beings in the waking world construct a more luxuriant appearance of the world than do the inorganic entities constituting the physical world.

In this chapter I will distinguish between the physical world and the waking world, and I will discuss properties of the waking world that are richer and more complex than the properties of the physical world itself.

A Metaphysical Review

In order for us to account more fully for the difference between the waking world and the physical world, we have to work with the idea of "grades" of actual occasions. Before we get to that, let's review key aspects of this new metaphysics.

In the last few chapters, I have been speaking about "actual occasions." This is Whitehead's technical term for the ultimate entities making up the actual world. An actual occasion is simply a moment, or occasion, when something actually happens. Actual occasions are "events." Instead of being composed of things or ideas, the world is composed of events. Human beings are fine examples. As I write these words, my personality is a sequence of events, and my body is a more complex society of events. Together, these events compose all of who I am (e.g., beating heart, pumping blood, metabolism of energy, activated nerves and muscles, as well as thoughts, feelings, emotions, and other physical and mental activities). And you, as you read these words, are likewise a sequence of actual occasions. Actual things are happening, and that's what makes a world—any world—actual.

When we re-conceptualize the world in terms of actual occasions, instead of merely physical atoms, the appearance of the world we construct is transformed. We no longer get caught in the problematic oppositional dualisms of Western philosophy—particularly, the split between matter and mind. Instead, we realize that everything consists of *actual occasions that are both material and mental.* Remember in Chapter 2 we saw that every moment can be viewed as a "drop of experience" (mind) on the inside, and as a causally effective event (quanta of energy) on the outside? The causal transmission of experiences from past to present is the transmission of energy; it is the physical, or material, pole of an occasion. A *re-experience* of past experiences occurs in the new mental pole, felt in the new consciousness of each new actual occasion. In other words, we use the word "energy" to mean the experiences of the past made present. Energy and experience, then, are always bundled together in every moment, composing every actual occasion.

The technical term for this feeling of causes streaming in from the physical pole is, as noted in Chapter 6, *"causal prehension."* A causal prehension is the *re-experience of an experience* that was already complete when the current experience began to concresce. Notice the symmetry: every *cause* (a past drop of experience that has become actual) is later a *prehension* (a mental accounting of the cause in a new present). Matter and mind always go together. Their difference is essentially a question of perspective.

The material and the experiential cannot be separated. They always occur together in everything actual. This means, in case you hadn't already noticed, that some degree or *capacity for experience* is present *at every level* in the actual world—whether electrons or elephants, atoms or apes, molecules or mice. All actualities have the same essential psychophysical nature, and they differ only in the richness and complexity of their structures and processes.

Every actual occasion is an experiential process. There is no such thing as a vacuous actuality that can exist or persist from moment to moment, devoid of self-experience and self-enjoyment of value. Nothing actual exists independently of time, like the hypothetical insentient atomistic BBs of Newtonian physics and materialist metaphysics. To repeat: everything actual is an experiential *process.*

Although everything actual is a process, there is more to reality than just actuality. To help you grasp what I mean, I should point out that I am making a distinction between what is "real" and what is "actual."

Possibilities and actualities both exist; they are *real.* We can and do entertain real possibilities, and by choosing them we make them actual. But only what has been actualized *actually* exists. Every occasion, as it comes into being (or concresces) must possess the *capacity to experience* past causes, the capacity to organize them into an appearance, and the *ability to choose* among the possibilities *presented* to it. Once its decisions are made and it has become actual, the occasion then exercises *causal efficacy—the ability to participate as a causal prehension in future occasions.*

Every process enacts these four phases: experience, interpretation, choice, and causal efficacy. That is how something new emerges in every moment; it is what Whitehead calls "creative advance."

Unlike actualities, possibilities (or abstractions) do not exist *in* time or space—rather, they exist *with* all time and *with* all space.[2] The particular pattern of possibilities surrounding an emerging actual occasion is unique, and so is the pattern it ultimately chooses to actualize. Neither pattern will ever be repeated. But each of the individual possibilities making up these patterns—both simple possibilities such as colors and sounds, and more complex possibilities through which simple possibilities are related—do not change; they are "eternal objects," like Plato's forms or ideas. They are identical with themselves wherever and whenever they are experienced. Yet these forms or possibilities do contribute to change in the actual world when they are incorporated into an actual event as one of its defining characteristics. Everything actual comes into being in a process that involves feeling or prehending its past (causal efficacy), feeling the halo of possibilities surrounding the emerging moment (conceptual prehension), forming an interpretive cascade of propositions (propositional prehensions) and deciding whatever needs to be decided along the way. This process is guided by an aim at the maximization of value.

Every process is both material (causal) and mental (experiencing and choice-making). All of this happens, for every actual occasion (from proton to primate), within the context of the entire history of all past events. In other words, every actual occasion emerges out of an *already*

---

[2] For a more detailed consideration of this issue, see my 2009 article, "A Commentary on Chapter 10 of *Science and the Modern World* by Alfred North Whitehead," in *Process Studied,* Supplement I(14). http://www.ctr4process.org/publications/ProcessStudies/PSS/

existing actual world. It always begins its coming-into-being at a specific moment in the creative advance, following a particular actual universe alive with the immortal experiences of the past. Thus, it occurs at a specific moment in time.

In addition, every actual occasion also has a position in space. For example, not only do I exist right now, at *this moment,* I am also somewhere in the world, in this position, at this *place.* I am right *here* in relation to everything else. This place determines my perspective on every other place.

To be actual, then, means to exist some*where* in space and some *when* in time. That is to say, every actual occasion exists at a *position in the creative advance of actuality.*

But that is not all. Every actual occasion is an *experiential* process. It feels, or is aware, that it is located and in process. A spark of consciousness is always present. Every actual occasion is aware of the world, in some way, however abstract. Along with consciousness, each actual occasion always possesses a quantum of free will.

Furthermore, every actuality is guided by an aim; it is going somewhere. At every moment we make choices (sometimes conscious and explicit, sometimes unconscious and implicit). Our choices always have some motive behind them. We act for a reason. We may not be able to articulate that reason fully, but we sense it.

This leads to a bold and stark conclusion: *if there wasn't a reason to exist, existence wouldn't happen.*

In dramatic contrast to the doctrine of materialism, which denies any purpose at work in the universe, transphysical process metaphysics holds that purpose or aim (final cause) is intrinsic to the actual universe.

Following Whitehead, I start with the assumption that each of us is a perfectly valid example of what it means to *be.* I then acknowledge the obvious fact that we experience ourselves as having goals and aims, and that we choose and act with purpose (despite the materialist worldview that tries to tell us this isn't possible). What is true in our own case must also be true of every other actual occasion because they are all *experiential processes,* just as we are. There is no *essential* ontological difference between actual occasions. Therefore, since *we* have a motive or a reason directing our existence, it follows that *everything* has an aim or motive for existing.

That's the starting point of Whiteheadian process metaphysics: every actual occasion begins as a moment in an actual world, located at a position in space, possessing a spark of consciousness motivated by an aim, and equipped with the capacity to interpret its past and to choose freely among the possibilities implied by that past, and even among novel possibilities never before actualized.

The world is made of actual occasions—but they are not all alike. Every actual occasion is unique. We can, however, usefully group actual occasions by their grade. The simplest, lowest-grade actual occasions discussed by science are quantum events, the tiniest processes identified by postmodern science. Quantum events are so unimaginably rapid that from our perspective they are hardly distinguishable from instantaneous blips. To a quantum, the speed at which we change and grow would probably be as undetectable and as uninteresting as it would be to us to observe the changes taking place in a rock in the course of an afternoon. In fact, the duration of actual occasions is one of the characteristics that distinguish the different grades—higher-grade actual occasions take longer to happen than lower-grade occasions.[3]

In the theory I am suggesting here, an atom (a system of subatomic blips) is itself a higher grade of actual occasion that organizes a series of lower-grade, subatomic occasions. On a higher level, a cell is an actual occasion that organizes macromolecules, and so forth. Like nested Russian dolls, the waking world is composed of actual occasions all the way up and all the way down. Technically, waking reality is dynamically structured in layered networks of actual occasions within actual occasions within actual occasions. The higher we go in this hierarchy, the higher the grade of the occasions involved.

---

[3] This does not imply some objective temporal framework by which duration can be measured. It simply means that during the concrescence of a high-grade occasion, it can prehend the concrescences of many lower-grade occasions. For example, my decision to turn left or right at an intersection spans many nerve impulses, each of which spans many subatomic events. I believe this idea differs from the ideas that Whitehead was working with in *Process and Reality*, where he sees each concrescence as beginning with a particular four-dimensional slab of nature, and remaining entirely closed and private during its concrescence. Occasions in transpersonal process metaphysics are radically open, and continue to receive information from the world as they concresce. This is a part of what distinguishes transphysical process philosophy from the Whitehead version. I have discussed this issue in Weiss, *Embodiment*.

Two Worlds: Waking and Physical

We are now in a position to make a more precise distinction between the waking world and the physical world. The world that we see when we are awake, the world perceived through our physiological sensory apparatus, is the physical world—as apprehended by higher-grade actual occasions. For example, when we see a cell in a microscope, we see inorganic macromolecules organized into a glorious dance by the presence of a higher-grade occasion—a transphysical occasion—that is using those macromolecules as its prehensions in the physical world. And when we gaze into the eyes of other animals, we see thinking beings gazing back at us, animated not only by medium-grade occasions like cells but by high-grade mental occasions that *think* about the world around them, giving it *meaning*.

The waking world is profoundly shaped by higher-grade occasions that exist beyond the reach of physics. They are transphysical in the sense that they are less predictable in their actions than physical occasions, and although they produce causal effects in the waking world, they do not exist in the same time and space as the actual entities studied by physics. I will return to this issue in greater detail in chapters 8 and 9.

This notion of "grades" is so important, let's pause to look more closely at the anatomy of an actual occasion and see how process metaphysics accounts for different grades that make up the multilayered complexity of our actual world.

A Three-Phase Anatomy of Process

Once an actual occasion comes into existence and begins to function, we can further analyze its process into three distinct stages:

1. We Feel What Causes Us. First, moment-by-moment, every one of us is emerging into actuality—right here, right now. You opened your eyes this morning and there you were, existing again. And, thankfully, it's still happening. Well, how *does* that happen? Where do we come from? How do we exist? That's what we're going to look at.

The beginning of each actual occasion is profoundly mysterious. Whitehead attributes this beginning to the ongoing activity of what he calls Creativity, as discussed earlier, the ultimate principle by virtue of which "the many become one and are increased by one"—which is to say that the many actualities of the past are unified into a single experience by a new actual occasion in the present, and this adds one more occasion for all subsequent concrescences to unify in their experience. The actual world is evolving and constantly growing.

As we continually emerge into our world, the first thing we do is to take it in—we behold it. The universe flows into us, and, for our part, we experience the world. As Whitehead said, we experience the world "conformally." In other words, we experience the world *as it was.* The world I emerge from is there for me to behold, and I have to behold it just as it was, otherwise there could be no continuity in the universe at all. As noted earlier, I am *caused* by the world, and as the world causes me, I *feel* it.

I want to emphasize this point—and it's one of the deepest shifts in perspective that comes with the new paradigm I am describing here: the distinction between causality and feeling is transformed into a difference of perspective.

To be caused by something is to feel it. To feel something is to be caused by it.

The efficient causes from the world rush in on us and we feel the effects—every occasion does.

2. We Interpret the World. Next, as we emerge into actuality, we interpret the world. Notice that you are exactly at the center of your own universe (just as every other actual occasion is at the center of *its* world). While you may not be in the center of the room where you are right now, or at the center of your town or city, state, or country, you are in the center of your *experienced* world. If you move across the room, city, or country, you will still be in the center of your world.

You are always precisely right at the center of your universe.

When you look out and behold the world, your experience always has the structure of a mandala—which is a complexly structured, more or less symmetrical image. Mandalas are always circular and always have a center and a fringe. They are a central motif in Eastern religious art. They also play a large part in Jungian psychological symbolism, where they are interpreted as representations of psychic wholeness.[4]

---

[4] For example, note that two-dimensional mandalas in Tibetan paintings are mere abstractions. The mandalas they represent can be three-dimensional or can even take place in non-metrical spaces such as those I will discuss in Chapter 9.

In Chapter 9, we will see that actual time-space, as we experience it, is always mandala-like. We begin each new moment with a diversity of objects spread around us and ordered by the relevant time-space relation, and, as we take them in, we interpret them into the aesthetic unity of one moment of actual experience.

First reality, then interpretation, and every interpretation shapes how reality appears to us. For every actual occasion, the world has a certain appearance. That appearance is always inevitably mandala-like, with us at the center. What appears can be rich and detailed or can be poor and abstract. Nevertheless, every actual occasion constructs an appearance of the world for itself.

Imagine the experience of a hydrogen atom in practically empty interstellar space; its experience is poor. The appearance of the world it constructs is abstract. It probably experiences the entire universe as a fairly flat gravitational gradient and nothing else. By contrast, we have a more elaborate experience, involving a multitude of objects, forms, and forces that share our immediate and distant environment in a massively rich and meaningful way.

The point to realize here is that the appearance constructed by each actual occasion is causally connected to the reality out of which it emerges. The world impinges on me, or as Whitehead would say, "I prehend the world;" it comes into me. Then I begin to pay attention to certain things and ignore other things. Patterns emerge from my experience of the world—my mandala. By selective emphasis and abstraction, I begin to construct my appearance of the world, but what I pull from the world is always causally connected to the world from which it comes.

I am now addressing one of the longest-standing problems and debates in philosophical thought: the relationship between appearance and reality (it goes all the way back to Plato and his allegory of the cave). Typically, we think appearance is something that shows up "inside," while reality is "outside." Modern thought assumes there is no intrinsic connection between what shows up "inside," in our experience, and what is really "out there." All we know are the appearances in our minds, and because we cannot step outside our minds to know what lies beyond them, it is assumed that we can never know reality *as it is in itself.*

German philosopher Immanuel Kant described this split between appearance and reality in great detail in his influential book *Critique of Pure Reason*. He distinguished between the "phenomenon" (what shows up in our minds) and the "noumenon" (the unknowable reality as it really exists in itself).

But now we can see this split does not really describe our own experience. We *can* know reality as it is in itself because the world impinges on us at every moment and we feel it.[5] We then abstract those features that are interesting to us (relevant to our aims), and that is how we construct our appearance of the world. True, we don't do justice to all the details of the entire world in our experience at every moment— that would be unimaginably overwhelming. But what we do select is, nevertheless, actual. It is not "just" an appearance; it is a real part of the real world as it was just a moment ago. And, once again, *what is true for us is also true for every actual occasion.* Countless times in every second, every entity in the world is constructing an interpretation of the world (the world's "appearance") for itself.

This has some profound and practical implications: the way we interpret the world conditions what we experience as possible. For example, when I apprehend my cup, I see that I can pick it up and that I can drink from it. A particular set of possibilities was actualized by the actual occasions making up the cup, and I experience them conformally, as they were. I select among the possibilities and even arrange them in novel ways as I construct my appearance of the world. But if my cat saw the cup, a different set of possibilities would be selected, or prehended— the world would show up differently for her. My cat might, for example, conceptualize drinking from the cup but would never conceptualize the possibility of picking up the cup; she would pull out a different set of possibilities relevant to her history and aims.

The first phase of actualization, then, is to feel the world *conformally* (exactly as it was), and the second phase is the formation of an interpretation of the world relevant to our aims. And this leads us to the third stage.

3. We make decisions aimed at enjoyment. I pull the world in, and I construct an experience of it. That experience comes with a halo of

[5] See de Quincey's "Reality Bubbles: Can We Know Anything about the Physical World?," *Journal of Consciousness Studies,* Vol. 15(8), August, 2008.

possibilities radiating out in all directions. As I become actual in this moment, I choose which possibilities I am going to actualize, and I enjoy the value that comes from that decision.

A Deeper Look at Grades of Actual Occasions

I have said that all actual occasions are identical in that they undergo the same essential process of actualization: feeling the world conformally, interpreting the world, and deciding about and enjoying the world. However, these elements of the process are experienced differently depending on the complexity, or grade, of the actual occasion in question—whether a low-grade *physical* occasion, a medium-grade *living* occasion, or a high-grade *mental* occasion. An atom does not experience the world the way an ape does. As we move along the evolutionary continuum, different grades of actual occasions experience the world with different emphasis (see figure 1).

	Feeling	Interpretation	Decision/ Enjoyment
Low	X	x	x
Medium	X	X	x
High	X	X	X

Figure 1: Grades of Actual Occasions

Note that even though every actual occasion goes through the three stages of feeling, interpreting, and deciding, each differs in the emphasis given to the three phases depending on the complexity of its grade.

Although I have divided actual occasions into three grades, I want to be clear that these grades are not entirely distinct. In fact, there is a continuous variation in grade, from the lowest to the highest. The threefold distinction I am using is similar to our convention of dividing the color spectrum (which is continuous) into seven distinct colors. The threefold distinction is convenient because it corresponds to our usual differentiation between inorganic, organic, and thinking beings. Yet, as we know, even that distinction represents a continuum. The fuzziness of the distinction between inorganic and organic, for example, is often remarked upon.

Low-Grade

Low-grade occasions emphasize *feeling*, the first of the three stages in concrescence, or the process of actualization.

A low-grade actual occasion, such as a hydrogen atom, mostly just feels the world and interprets it in an abstract way. The interpretation is entirely lacking in nuance and does not disclose the vast richness of concrete actuality. Also, there is a bare minimum of exploration of the possibilities that are revealed. The atom, most of the time, just repeats what it did a moment ago.[6] It does not exercise elaborate decision making. As an actual occasion, it is comparatively simple.

Medium-Grade

Medium-grade occasions emphasize the first and second stages of concrescence—*feeling* and *interpretation*.

A medium-grade actual occasion—for instance, the personality of a cell or an organ or an animal—feels the world but interprets it in a more elaborate way. We can easily observe that this is the case. A bacterium can identify a chemical gradient and follow it to food. However, these medium-grade, living occasions do not seem to spend much energy in deciding what to do. Plants, for example, experience a limited range of possibility for novelty; they follow the sun and grow this way or that. They just do it with minimal choice. Similarly, simpler animals (i.e., those without the complexity associated with a frontal cortex) simply follow their impulses or instincts.

Just to be clear: this is not intended as a biological treatise, so I am not concerned about consigning any particular species or phylum to a specific grade. Those kinds of details need to be worked out later by a science informed by this alternative metaphysics. I am simply noting that actual occasions do occur in different grades, and I'm indicating the kinds of entities and organisms that, in general, can be assigned to each grade. The important point is that understanding the differences

---

[6] Of course sometimes it does do something different—as when, for example, it gets together with oxygen to become water. But it does this under external pressure, and in any case its behavioral repertoire is comparatively small.

between grades will help us later when we come to discuss what kind of entity the human personality must be in order to survive the death of the body.

Keep in mind (as mentioned earlier and will be important later) that medium-grade occasions always prehend other medium-grade occasions, and may or may not (depending on their own aims) prehend low-grade, inorganic occasions. In other words, medium-grade occasions can form a world of their own, not dependent on the physical world in any way.

High-Grade

High-grade occasions emphasize all three stages in the process of concrescence—*feeling, interpreting,* and *deciding.*

High-grade occasions, like ourselves, feel the world and interpret it in an elaborate way. In addition, we actually *think* about what we are going to do next. At many moments, we consciously evaluate possibilities and choose those that best suit our aims. We have an elaborate decision making process; we go for the possibility that will yield the maximum value over sometimes considerable ranges of time and with many intervening steps. For example, we may decide to go to school and then realize we need to work to make the money for tuition, and then we prepare ourselves for a job that will accomplish this.

Again, high-grade occasions always prehend other high-grade occasions, but they need not (depending on their own aims) prehend occasions of medium or low grade.

The process of actualization or concrescence always involves these three stages, but the emphasis placed on each stage, along with its richness and depth, varies for different grades of occasions.

Here in our everyday lives we are in the waking world, where inorganic or low-grade occasions play a significant role; they make up the physical bodies of the objects that surround us: walls, roofs, furniture, tools, toys, and so forth. As societies of high- and medium-grade occasions, we are actualizing from moment to moment, in a rich way. Meanwhile, the atoms and molecules around and inside our bodies are low-grade occasions actualizing in their own, comparatively poorer way. When we study them, we are doing physics—which is the study of low-grade occasions by high-grade occasions.

Until the advent of quantum mechanics, physics didn't have any place for high-grade occasions; they were irrelevant to the professional concerns of physicists. Consequently, because physicists concentrated on studying low-grade atoms and molecules, that's all they observed. And then, mistakenly, they many made a leap and declared, "That's all there is." Reality, they claimed, consists exclusively of low-grade inorganic occasions, and anything else is either a configuration of those inorganic occasions, an epiphenomenon, or an illusion. Hence the awkward metaphysical tangle we know today as "physicalism," which is the assumption that only what is physical (low-grade) is ultimately real.

Clearly, this is not satisfying philosophical reasoning. Good philosophy does not require us to explain away our own existence. The whole purpose of philosophy is to allow us to explain our own existence to ourselves.

Then came quantum theory, and physicists began to realize that, in fact, reality must include something other than the low-grade inorganic entities they study. Famously, they have had to deal with the metaphysically shocking discovery that *somehow* their little inorganic blips, now limited in time as well as in space, can come into actual existence only when *observed*. The shock was probably intensified because they assumed that the observer had to be a *human* observer. That assumption leads to the absurdity that the whole evolutionary past didn't exist until human beings evolved to notice it.

I agree with the quantum physicists who believe it always takes a conscious decision to make anything actual. This is the truly radical and paradigm-shattering discovery of quantum physics that should send every serious physicist, scientist, and philosopher scrambling for a textbook on metaphysics. *How could such a thing be possible? How or why is it necessary for consciousness to be present for the actual physical world to come into being?* Answering that question will open the way for understanding that we live in a vastly more complex and interesting world than science previously suspected, though spiritual traditions have known this for millennia.

What I will suggest, following Whitehead—and which many quantum theorists are beginning to think too—is that *each occasion has the consciousness needed to make itself actual.* Each actual occasion makes the decisions by virtue of which it becomes actual. This realization now forms the basis for a number of interpretations of quantum theory.[7]

Understanding Measurement

In this chapter, let's remind ourselves that we are working to understand the waking world by focusing on the various grades of actual occasions. In doing so, we have highlighted the distinction between what we normally call "matter" (actual occasions of a low grade) and "life" (actual occasions of a higher grade), which organizes matter into the interesting and beautiful forms we observe in the waking world. However, in order to refine our understanding of the difference between the waking world and the physical world, we also have to examine the question of measurement.

In this discussion, when I use the word "measurement" I am indicating what it means in classical science (which I will elucidate below). In quantum mechanics, by contrast, the word tends to connote "detecting," where what is detected can be any quality whatsoever.

Physicists understand inorganic occasions in the language of mathematics. Since the late 1600s, it has been assumed that numbers are the language of nature. To "get nature's number," or to understand nature mathematically, we have to *measure* it. Only through measurement can we transform our experience of the world into numbers we can manipulate mathematically.

But what is measurement? Well, in essence, it is an operation that reliably produces a number in relation to some observation. This much is taken for granted. But then we can ask: How is measurement possible? This is a deeper question.

We need to understand what measurement is if we are to understand what science can effectively tell us about the actual world.

Measurement is central to almost every scientific procedure, yet few people have paid sufficient attention to this deceptively simple process. One of the great merits of Whitehead is that he devoted an enormous amount of attention to unearthing and explicating the conditions under which measurement is possible.

To make this really simple: all measurement involves either a ruler

---

[7] See, for example, Epperson's *Quantum Mechanics*.

(which physicists rather suggestively call a "rigid rod") or a clock (which physicists call a "periodic oscillator"). Measurement requires a fixed standard for comparison, and standards are either spatial or temporal.

If I want to measure something in time, I compare its duration to the ticks of a clock. If I want to measure something in space, I take a ruler and count[8] how many units designated on that ruler it takes to equal the extent of the object I am measuring. It is very plain. Whenever you measure something—whether reading a dial, a digital readout, or anything else—it all comes down to comparisons between what we are measuring on one hand, and rulers and clocks on the other.

But why are rulers and clocks good for measurement? What gives them this ability? If you think about it you will realize that the reason rulers and clocks work is because compared to the characteristics we care about, they are invariant. Periodic oscillators continue to oscillate regularly even when they are moved, and rulers hold the same length over time and across space. For very good reasons, we don't use the songs of birds as periodic oscillators, or snakes and rubber bands for rulers.

So far so good. It all seems so effortless and obvious. But then we ask, what are the conditions under which things can either oscillate periodically or hold a rigid length? Now the answer is no longer as obvious. However, given what we already know about actual occasions, we can see that rulers and clocks work because they are made up of low-grade occasions that tend to persist in their habits unless disturbed. You could not make a ruler out of living tissue, which is always adapting to its environment and won't hold still to function as a standard. Measurement works only with rulers and clocks that are composed of inorganic entities. Basically, it involves comparing inorganic entities to inorganic entities (including the inorganic features of living things, such as size or velocity).

Measurement is possible only in the inorganic world.[9]

---

[8] Note that measurement presupposes counting. We must *count* the number of units that correspond to the extent we are measuring. Counting is a complex activity that many of our ancestors (whose whole-number system consisted of "one," "two," and "many") did not possess. See Ernst Cassirer's *The Philosophy of Symbolic Forms*, pp. 226–48.

[9] Psychologists will sometimes claim to "measure" experiences like "anxiety." What they are doing, however, is either measuring something else (such as electrical resistance in the skin), or asking people to assign a number to their experience

The stubbornness of inorganic occasions is not the only factor necessary for measurement to be possible. Space must also be structured in a certain way. If I measure my chair to see whether it will fit through the front door, I have to assume that one-and-a-half feet here is the *same* one-and-a-half feet over at the door. As I move in space, the definition of distance does not change. If it did, measurement would be useless. By contrast, think of what happens in dreams, where distance does change. In a dream, I could measure my chair over here and think that it would fit, but when I go over to the front door, it might not fit at all. Unlike in the waking world, dream space is fluid.

In Whitehead's terms, the only way measurement can work is in a space pervaded by (imaginary) parallel lines. For example, in our physical space, a set of parallel lines connects the width of my chair to the width of the door. Being parallel, the distance between the lines is constant, and so the ruler remains the same here and over there. That's what makes measurement possible. In other words, measurement is possible only where actual occasions are interacting in a stable, grid-like, metrical space-time. (I will discuss the structure of time and space more deeply in Chapter 9.) Bottom line: measurement is possible only in a space-time that permits Cartesian grids with parallel lines.

The inorganic world, studied by physics, is populated by low-grade inorganic occasions operating in a time and a space in which, for all practical purposes, parallel lines never meet. As we will see in Chapter 9, measurement is possible only when the time-space relation is defined by a metrical geometry.[10]

Inorganic entities form the inorganic physical world, and when we are awake we are very much involved in the physical world—but we are not inorganic. We are actual occasions of a higher grade. In other words, the "matter" that constitutes us *is not physical.* Yes we are

---

("how anxious are you on a scale of one to five?"). In the former case, what is being measured is something physical (electrical resistance), and the connection between that and what is supposedly being measured (anxiety) is purely speculative. In the latter case, there is no way to replicate the measurement and so it is hardly scientific. These methods may or may not be useful in some contexts, but they can be called "measurements" only by analogy.

[10] The metrical geometries are those in which parallel lines are defined. These are Euclidean, elliptical, and hyperbolic geometry. (In order to be metrical, a time-space must also have a constant curvature.)

material beings, but we are not physical beings. This is an important distinction to grasp. It is central to the model I am proposing here. We could regard different grades of actual occasions as, in effect, different types of matter. For example, I am an actual material being—as actual as any atom anywhere in the universe. But I am nowhere in the physical world. I inhabit the living, or vital, world—what we will call the mental world. While it is possible to locate and measure the physical atoms that compose my physical body, *I* cannot be located or measured—because I am of a higher grade than my physical atoms and molecules.

One of the challenging and controversial consequences that follows from this radical worldview is the realization that no scientist has ever detected a living being per se. All they have detected are complex systems of inorganic beings. The qualities that inform the lives of living beings cannot be quantified, and the relationships between them cannot be reduced to relationships among numbers. The causal relations among living beings are richer and more complex than any equation that can describe numerical relations. Your personality and mine are actual entities, sequences of actual occasions that are as actual as anything else in the universe. We are, in that sense, material beings that are not physical beings. *We exist in a different world*—beyond the domain studied by science. We are high-grade actual occasions—*we are transphysical.*

This gets a little tricky because one of the fundamental tenets of the modern world is the equation "physical = actual." It goes with the assumption that everything actual can be measured by a physicist. In fact, in our culture, if you want to know if something is real, you go to a physicist (or an engineer) and ask for it to be measured. This belief runs so deep it is even a major factor in our legal system where forensic science is called on to provide "physical proof" of what is real, of what actually happened.

But you simply cannot prove the existence of a human being in that way. Our personalities do not exist in such a world—a world of low-grade physical occasions operating within a metrical space-time relation. Once we realize this, we can see that what I am calling the waking world is not at all the same as the physical world. *Physical does not equal actual.* The actual world is *more than* physical—in fact, the actual world is *both* physical and *transphysical.* The waking world is profoundly shaped and formed by these higher-grade occasions—and these form a very different kind of material than that studied by physics and the other sciences. We could call it "transphysical matter" or "subtle matter."

This is not a new idea. It has been around for a long time, showing up in the cosmologies of all pre-modern peoples, and more recently, in the writings of Theosophists and spiritualist-oriented scientists during the 1890s and early 20th century. But to my knowledge, no one has yet come up with a definition of transphysical matter that makes sense in relation to scientific ideas. I aim to rectify that in this work by offering a robust and coherent set of metaphysical ideas that not only makes sense of the discoveries of modern science but also extends to what are sometimes referred to as esoteric disciplines.

The Theosophists and others tried to explain subtle matter in terms of density, saying that solid matter is dense, liquid matter is less dense, gas even less so … moving along a continuum of density until eventually reaching transphysical matter. But that approach doesn't work; no matter how rarefied and tenuous low-grade matter becomes, it is still low-grade matter—still subject to mathematical laws. Explanations in terms of density don't correspond to the experiences we have of transphysical worlds in dreams, and waking dreams, lucid dreams and out-of-body experiences.

Nor does it work when people talk about "higher dimensions" (as the Theosophists do) because as long as these are, in principle, measurable, they are merely complications of the familiar *physical* world.[11]

I am suggesting something very different. The key factor that differentiates transphysical matter from physical matter is the proportion of *mental* activity involved. Entities higher on the gradient of actual occasions are capable of more elaborate interpretation and decision-making. The crucial difference between grades of actuality is not an issue

---

[11] The Theosophists were fascinated by the "fourth dimension" because it gave them a way to answer the question, "Where are the transphysical worlds?" I propose replacing this idea of "higher dimensions" with the idea of transphysical worlds that are configured in terms of less restrictive time-space relations (see Chapter 9). I cannot say with any authority what string theorists are getting at, but in any case, their eleven dimensions are all orthogonal to one another and are complications of an essentially Newtonian time-space relation. Such "higher dimensions" are not, as far as I can tell, relevant to transphysical worlds.

of energetic vibrations, material density, or physical complexity—the difference is the comparative *richness and complexity of consciousness.*

Once we acknowledge that every actuality involves consciousness and matter—that every actual occasion is a drop of experience on the inside and an event on the outside—then we can see how the respective proportions, or dominance, of materiality and consciousness can change from physical to transphysical. In higher-grade occasions, the process by which they become actual involves more elaborate mental activity like interpretation and decision making. Actualities that involve more mind are *qualitatively* different (not just a difference in quantities such as vibrational frequencies or material density). Higher-grade, transphysical entities are still material; they are still fully actual like physical atoms are but are actual in a more robust and mentally elaborate way.

Given this, we now realize that matter itself comes in grades along a continuum from low-grade physical matter to higher-grade transphysical matter. Physical and transphysical are equally actual. It follows then that we cannot explain everything on the basis of the properties of physical matter alone. Higher-grade actualities (such as human beings) literally consist of a *different kind of material* than matter formed of low-grade atoms and molecules. Atomic material is physical; human material is *transphysical.* We are "transphysical" beings because we have more elaborate capacities for interpreting what shows up in experience and for choosing among the range of possibilities that present themselves than do the inorganic occasions of the physical world.

If we accept this analysis, we may then ask: how do transphysical entities interact with physical entities? How can entities from one kind of world cause anything to happen in a different kind of world? How are high-grade and low-grade occasions related? These are legitimate and metaphysically important questions. In fact, they lie at the heart of the modern scientific and philosophical conundrum known as the hard problem. Answering these questions will put us right on track to understanding the relationship between human personalities and survival in a postmortem realm.

Scientists have been trying to understand reality by restricting analysis to causal interactions among low-grade occasions. But if we accept the idea that there are various grades of matter, then we also have to look at the causal interactions among high-grade actualities themselves (intragrade), as well as the causal interactions between high-grade occasions and lower-grade occasions (intergrade). Understanding the difference between intragrade and intergrade interactions will go a long way toward elucidating the nature of transphysical worlds.

When we take on this task, we are faced with a network of causes far more elaborate than those recognized by modern science. In fact, this investigation demands that we radically expand our conceptual toolkit to embrace a richer and more complex reality than hitherto accepted by our culture—a reality that includes the possibility of consciousness surviving the death of the physical body.

In the next section, we will move one step closer to understanding this by examining the causal interactions among different grades of actual occasions—how different worlds form and interact.

Embodiment in Different Kinds of Matter

We are now ready to talk about how causal interactions take place among occasions of different grade. Specifically, we will explore how high-grade occasions, like ourselves, interact with lower-grade occasions like those that make up our bodies. The mystery we are about to unravel is: How do we inhabit a body?

Many scientists tell us that we *are* our physical bodies—nothing more. They say, for example, that to be conscious is just to be a complex pattern of electrical activity in the brain. They are trying to tell us, in other words, that all actuality—including our own consciousness—can be reduced to causal interactions among low-grade occasions.

I reject such extreme reductionism on intellectual and emotional grounds. Intellectually, the notion of minds emerging from purely physical brains is incoherent—no one can even *begin* to explain how such a "miracle" could happen. This mind-body problem has befuddled modern science and philosophy for centuries.[12] Emotionally (aesthetically and morally), I refuse to be objectified as merely a collection of physical atoms. As an actual occasion of higher grade, I am not only physical matter. Because of my proportion of consciousness, I am a *different kind* of matter. I do not inhabit the physical world, as atoms and molecules do.

---

[12] See de Quincey's *Radical Nature* for a detailed philosophical analysis of the mind-body problem.

How then do I (a mental-grade personality) control or coordinate the activities of my body (which consists of medium-grade organic occasions and low-grade physical ones)?

To understand this, we have to remember that we come into being out of an existing world that presents us not only with pre-existing actualities but with a field of structured possibilities. We are determined by the past, yes; but the future is always open because every actuality exists in the present surrounded by a halo of possibilities. Given these possibilities, we can *choose* our future. However, our choices are not entirely open and free. There are things we can and cannot do. Also, some options are more probable than others.

The choices we make are always in reference to our aim or purpose at that moment. Aim, (remember Aristotle's final cause), is intrinsic to actuality—every actual occasion is imbued with purpose. But just what is this purpose? What is the general aim of all actuality?

We have already seen that aim is intimately related to *value*. Whitehead says that the general aim of actuality is the maximization of value in the present and in the relevant future. And so now we go a little deeper and ask, "What is value?" In simple terms, value is the richness of experience—the essential capacity for enjoyment or bliss. That's what we aim for. That's what motivates every actual occasion from low-grade atoms to high-grade human beings. We all live for value in that sense. We want to maximize value. And that's what guides our decisions.

Metaphysically, this general aim is built into the very fabric of reality itself. In addition, each of us has our own specific aims directed at a certain type of value. For example, each of us has a personality, developing over many years, that expresses itself (at least in part) as preferences for certain kinds of value. And what makes life interesting is that we all have different tastes and, thankfully, we share many preferences too. In my own case, as a philosopher, I happen to greatly value intellectual understanding, and in my day-to-day decisions I sacrifice other values in order to achieve this one. Other people place greater value on artistic, ethical, or pragmatic issues and sacrifice other values to achieve those. We each have our own individual aims that we develop over time.

We also have social aims. Our values are in part conditioned by our environment, for example, by our families, friends, community, or nation. We have a certain set of values that come to us from the larger social environment in which we exist and out of which we emerge.

Beyond individual and social aims, and also influencing them, are more broadly encompassing cosmic aims. Take evolution, for example: Why does it happen? Why is there, as Teilhard de Chardin would say, a "privileged axis of evolution," or a consistent aim at "complexity and conscious interiority"? Somehow, it seems, the universe itself has an aim, and this aim conditions all of the occasions that participate in it.

The aims that influence our existence, therefore, are multilayered—coming to us from our personal past, from society, and from the cosmos. The particular aims that coalesce in us as individuals determine how we evaluate the possibilities available to us at any moment.

With this in mind, the issue at hand gets really interesting. In general, how do high-grade occasions interact with low-grade occasions? And specifically, *how do I cause my body to act?* I am suggesting that at every moment *we influence the aims of the actual occasions that make up our bodies.* I'm saying that we actually shift the taste for value of our organ systems, so that, for example, when I form a proposition concerning the moving of my arm, my muscle cells are predisposed to act out that decision because the very aim under which they have come into existence is influenced by my aim. In short, I persuade my cells to accept my suggestions; I influence their aim.

In a similar way, occasions larger than I am—those that organize human society, Gaia, or the universe as a whole—affect the aim or motive guiding the choices I make. I, in turn, affect the choices of my cells by influencing their aims.

We can now view the whole waking world as a cascading hierarchy of actual occasions, where the larger, higher grades persuade the activities of the smaller, lower grades, which then begin to organize in new ways.

Let's now focus on this process in terms of a single cell. We know from science that cells are vast collections of complex molecules, called macromolecules, such as proteins and DNA. Scientists have boldly tried to recreate simple living systems in the laboratory—and have actually made some significant progress. For example, they have succeeded in stimulating groups of macromolecules to perform as dissipative systems that actually form their own boundaries or membranes, creating little sacs around themselves. But that is not life.

Living systems are more than the organization of macromolecules. Three additional factors are needed for life beyond what can emerge simply as the result of dissipative structures of macromolecules.

1. A living cell is a center of consciousness. Every living cell has its own unified, central consciousness—it's not just a sac of chemicals. We can make this assertion with confidence based on our rehabilitation of the Hermetic Principle. We know that we are a center of consciousness that directs our own bodies. In general, our bodies enact our purposes. It is clear that the bodies of higher animals also respond to the will of a central consciousness in a similar way. We should be able to make this analogy all the way down. We may doubt that this is the case in slime molds or plants, for example, which seem to be, as Whitehead suggests, more of a democracy. This is analogous to the difference between rocks and cells. Rocks seem to be associations of molecules merely held together by networks of efficient causes. There is no reason to think the various molecules in the rock share a common purpose. But cells, autopoietic structures, do seem to have a unified interiority over and above that of their constituent molecules. Slime molds and plants, analogously, may be more like "living rocks," or associations of cells in which no higher-grade occasions have been embodied.[13] Multicellular organisms, however (beings such as snails and mammals), are presided over by actual occasions of higher grade.

2. Living systems actualize a greater range of possibilities. Every actuality—from atom to molecule to cell to human—as part of its coming-to-be (its concrescence) surveys a range of possibilities and decides among them. The higher the grade of the actuality, the larger the field of possibilities open to it, the more options it surveys, and the larger its behavioral repertoire will be. Because of its greater complexity of matter and consciousness, a cell pursues possibilities that would not make any sense to macromolecules. Living cells respond, in recognizable ways, to gradients of value or satisfaction. Put a cell in a petri dish with

---

[13] We might speculate that the occasions of a rock, because they share many formal properties, may objectify more fully in each other than they would if they were not forming a rock, and so may exist at a somewhat higher grade than they would if they were not aggregated with similar occasions.

some food such as sugar, and it will spontaneously move toward the food source (or away from some toxin). Macromolecules don't do that. In other words, the cell can penetrate deeper into the halo of possibilities that always surrounds every actual occasion.

3. *The organization of life requires a coordination of spontaneities.* Not only does a cell decide among the possibilities open to it at the cellular level, it employs its consciousness to influence the aims and direct the organization of its own constituents at the molecular level.

A living cell manifests qualities that a macromolecule cannot because the cell coordinates the spontaneities of its constituent macromolecules.[14] I am convinced that if we examine the behavior of molecules within a living cell we will find that they move in different ways than they do outside the cells. *Molecules in a living cell behave differently.* The behavior of macromolecules is not totally determined. We know this from quantum theory; there is always some indetermination in every moment of actuality. The momentum and position of a macromolecule are not fully determined by its past. It has a degree of freedom.

I am proposing that the consciousness of the higher-grade occasion embodied in a cell influences the aims of its macromolecules so that they begin to behave differently than they would if left to themselves. Macromolecules within a cell behave as what appear to be self-organizing systems under the influence of the higher-grade occasion embodied in the cell. The phenomenon of self-organization, so prized by biologists as an explanation for life, can itself be understood only as a result of the intervention of actual occasions of higher grade.

We are not stuck with the properties of the atoms or molecules, and we don't have to derive everything from them. Every actuality surveys a range of possibilities and decides among them. And because higher-grade actualities have a larger field of possibilities, they can manifest

---

[14] I am assuming that a macromolecule is not an embodied system. It is, rather, an association of atoms in which each atom, pursuing its own individual purpose, finds it natural to associate itself with other atoms. I make this assumption because the behaviors of molecules can be fairly well understood by the methods of classical physics, while those same methods cannot be used fruitfully to predict the behaviors of cells. I am assuming, that is, that a macromolecule is more like a rock or a crystal than a cell. It is probable that the most complex macromolecules, such as DNA or viruses, occupy a position intermediate between rocks and cells in this regard.

a larger repertoire of behaviors, allowing for entirely new behaviors to emerge.

I call this a theory of embodiment.[15] Personally ordered societies of higher-grade occasions become embodied in self-organizing systems of lower-grade occasions. These higher-grade embodied occasions influence the purposes of the lower-grade occasions in which they are embodied, through a kind of final causation. Because the purpose, the subjective aim of these occasions is modified, the possibilities they notice are different, and thus they can behave in ways that would otherwise be impossible for them. The presence of apparently self-organizing societies in the waking world is always a sign of the presence of the unifying will of a higher-grade, personally ordered society.

The Waking World Revisited

At this point we come full circle to the waking world. As we know from physics, the real world beneath our feet—the world we actually experience—does, in fact, consist of physical inorganic atoms and molecules. They are really there, fully actual. But that's not all. The waking world we experience also consists of equally actual higher-grade actualities, transphysical material—but this aspect of the world is beyond the reach of our bodily senses and, therefore, of our current physics.

We know from common everyday experience that higher-grade beings such as humans are constantly manipulating and changing the appearance and the actuality of the physical world around us. Living systems reorganize the elements of the physical world. For example, we turn physical matter into objects of art, into houses and cathedrals, into cities and civilizations. Higher-grade human occasions have produced technologies that enable us to radically transform our waking world. *Human transformations of the physical world cannot be explained merely in terms of the principles of physics.* Clearly, other factors come into play— such as our goals and desires, our aims and values, our consciousness, and our choices.

And this same principle extends to all life. All living beings achieve

---

[15] I have further elaborated the doctrine of embodiment in an unpublished paper: "Embodiment: An Explanatory Framework for the Exploration of Reincarnation and Personality Survival," 2004.

complex organizations and pursue novel and interesting possibilities through the influence of higher-grade occasions, and these higher-grade occasions are not part of the physical world.

Thus, we see that the transphysical worlds thoroughly pervade the waking world, and this is what I call the "transphysical dimension of the waking world."

We can now explore a remarkable implication of this transphysical dimension.

Recall, in Chapter 6, I discussed the subjective forms of actual occasions of different grades. I noted that actual occasions of a low grade achieve final satisfaction with the subjective form of simple certainty. Prehensions that are characterized by this subjective form play a crucial role in the constitution of the scientific "facts" that are central to scientific work.

Actual occasions of a medium grade achieve final satisfaction that may fail to realize simple certainty, but does acquire a vividness and complexity of appreciation that I am calling "emotional." Actual occasions of medium grade necessarily objectify other actual occasions of medium grade, and they objectify those other occasions in a way that is conformal to their emotional experience. Thus the waking world, to the extent that it is embodied by actual occasions of medium grade—and is, therefore, alive—is pervaded by a network of empathic connections.

We are aware of the network of empathic connections that pervades our bodies. If even a few cells in our little toe are in pain, our entire body feels the discomfort. In Chapter 1, I pointed to cases where people can make geometrical blisters, or even writing, appear on their skin merely by willing or imagining it. It has been shown that the patterns that appear on the skin do not correspond to patterns of nervous tissue in the skin and so cannot be accounted for by reference to the nervous system.[16] However, when we understand the body to be pervaded by a network of mutual feeling, these skin patterns begin to seem more intelligible.

Our metaphysical position, moreover, leads to us believe that these empathic networks are not confined to the interiors of bodies. Rather, we can justifiably assume that the living occasions in our bodies also

---

[16] Kelly and Kelly, *Irreducible Mind.*

prehend living occasions in other bodies. Certainly, when someone near us is angry or desires us in some way, we can *feel* it. The living occasions in our bodies are directly prehending the living occasions in the bodies of others.

Furthermore, because the living occasions of our bodies are not part of the physical world, the causal prehensions among them are not restricted by distance in the same way that the causal prehensions of inorganic occasions are. For example, someone I care for deeply is *empathically* closer to me, even if physically distant, than someone I don't care for who may be physically close. In an important sense, this network of empathic connections is worldwide, spanning the web of living systems.

Finally, high-grade occasions—possessing subjective forms involving some shade of "meaning"—also causally prehend each other, and do so in a world-spanning way. This web of telepathic connection can help us find a metaphysical basis for terms such as "zeitgeist," and for phenomena such as simultaneous discoveries, in which two people, entirely unaware of each other, simultaneously arrive at the same discovery. One famous example of this is the simultaneous development of the calculus by Newton and Leibniz.

When we recognize that the waking world is not just the physical world but is also constituted by the pervasive texture of medium- and high-grade occasions that give it so much of its characteristic form, then we realize that the entire waking world is pervaded by empathic and telepathic networks.

At the very least, this metaphysical model allows us to intelligibly account for all the data of parapsychology confirming empathy and telepathy. In addition, it is also fully consistent with what we already know about the universe through modern and postmodern science.

It has other implications, as well. If our intuitive sense of feeling the emotions of others and of telepathically knowing what they mean is valid; and if these empathic and telepathic connections are elaborately interconnected in complex ways that transcend mere physical proximity, then it means we are awash in an ocean of feelings and thoughts that we usually fail to notice, in the way a fish fails to notice water.

We might think that our thoughts and feelings are safely sealed up in the private domains of our own individual minds or personalities;

however, according to this new model, we are always participating in complex networks of feeling and thinking involving beings all over the planet—indeed, throughout the universe (and even from transphysical worlds). The Internet is just a pale shadow, an infinitesimal abstraction from the flows of sensation, feeling, and thinking that bind the planet into a living and thinking community of sentience.

Any attempt to account for the unfolding of history that does not take into account the unifying influence of transphysical communications (effectively binding us into a single community of sentience) is necessarily incomplete. History is not just a series of external physical events influenced by the internal force of great personalities; it is, rather, powerfully influenced by participation in the shared network of emphatic and telepathic influences operating through the transphysical worlds. The waking world, then, is understood as an ongoing interaction among physical and transphysical domains of being.

Psychokinesis (PK) and Embodiment

The first of the five propositions around which this book is built— that the personality exercises causal influence in its world—is most dramatically revealed in cases of psychokinesis (PK). As we come to the end of this chapter, we have now developed the intellectual tools that will enable us to say something interesting about that phenomenon.

PK is usually understood to be an interaction between a personality and some society of low-grade, inorganic occasions. It is then roughly divided into "micro-PK" and "macro-PK." Micro-PK involves a situation in which an embodied personality can, through the power of its intention, bring about very subtle changes in the inorganic world. For example, a great deal of micro-PK research has been done with random number generators and has worked to establish that personalities can, by the force of intention, affect these random number generators in such a way as to make them produce results that deviate from statistical expectations. Macro-PK, by contrast, involves situations in which a personality, by the force of its intention, brings about displacements in position of macroscopic entities, such as human bodies, books, spoons, or pianos.

As we will see in what follows, in the context of transphysical process metaphysics, micro-PK and macro-PK are explained in the same way, and this explanation is a straightforward extension of the process that we have been calling "embodiment."

Why Is PK So Hard to Explain?

In the context of the classical notions of science that so strongly condition modern common sense, macro-PK seems particularly difficult to account for. Let us examine the assumptions that make it seem so odd.

- Modern scientifically informed common sense insists, as we have seen, on the vacuous nature of physical matter. In spite of the fact that many quantum physicists no longer think of matter in this way, we still tend to assume that inorganic matter is dead, insentient, purely automatic, and devoid of value. In other words, we tend to think of physical matter as purely objective and "substantial" in the Cartesian sense.

- If bits of matter are vacuous, and, therefore, passive, they must be moved by external forces and laws. Thus, we are encouraged to imagine that the physical world is operating under the control of immutable natural laws. In process metaphysics, we must assume the existence of God, or the ultimate ordering factor, to account for the provision of aims and positions for new occasions. Some, or indeed many, scientists might have difficulty with this hypothesis. And yet the scientific account of reality is utterly dependent on it own ultimate ordering factor that somehow applies the natural laws and calculates trajectories for all of the particles that it hypothesizes. If scientists would ever ask themselves who or what does the calculating that directs particles on their trajectories, they would realize this.

- We are asked to imagine that the physical world is causally closed, so that it is necessarily indifferent to any "subjective" or "transphysical" influences.

- Finally, we are supposed to think of macroscopic entities as enduring through time and as possessing intrinsic inertia.[17]

---

[17] Post-Newtonian materialism harbors a paradox: while unquestioningly accepting

Given these assumptions, any attempt to explain PK is a non-starter. By definition, there is simply no way an epiphenomenal consciousness could have any impact on dead, inert, automatic objects that are entirely controlled by immutable laws external to themselves and that respond only mechanically to physical contact with other objects. If we accept the reality of PK phenomena (or even try to explain the data), we must reject this classical way of looking at the universe.

A New Approach to the Problem

In the context of transphysical process metaphysics, the problem of PK is entirely transformed, because process metaphysics

- Insists on the full actuality of each event making up the universe. In other words, it recognizes each event as aware, communal, purposeful, sensitive, valuing, and decisive.
- Reduces the number of functions assigned to God, or the ultimate ordering factor. In process metaphysics, as we will see, enduring entities actually play a role in calculating their own trajectories.
- Complexifies the notion of causality (Chapter 5) so that it includes both a principle of *formal* resonance and a principle of *final* resonance.
- Completely revolutionizes the problem of movement. Recall that actual occasions, the basic building blocks of process metaphysics, do not move at all. Each one is uniquely situated in time and space. Movement, then, is not the inertial displacement of a self-existing substance but is, rather, a property of personally ordered societies of actual occasions. Movement is the ability of such a society to arrange the universe so that another appropriately positioned member of the series will appear in each successive moment at a particular point in space-time. This ability to influence the position of subsequent occasions is accomplished by means of the continuity proposition referred to in Chapter 6. Each member of a personally ordered society must anticipate

---

the doctrines of mechanism, it blithely ignores those doctrines when it treats atoms as "possessing" a gravitational field and inertia.

the position of its next member, and the ultimate ordering factor must take this continuity proposition into account as it decides on the position and grade of the occasion that will concresce the actual world left behind by as the current occasion expires.

Within the framework of these ideas we were able to articulate a doctrine of embodiment. Now, in the context of PK, I want to look more deeply into the issue of embodiment.

In order for a high-grade personality to become embodied in a society of low-grade occasions, it must enter into an intimate relationship with those low-grade occasions such that they come to function as its prehensions.

In order for such a high-grade personality to enter into intimate relations with some specific society of lower-grade occasions, it must "pay attention" to those lower-grade occasions in some special way. This notion of paying attention needs to be clarified.

Each actual occasion forms it own appearance of the world out of which it arises, and in forming that appearance it elevates certain elements into prominence and relegates others to obscurity. It is clearly possible for an actual occasion to pay selective attention to some society of actual occasions in its world.

We now make the following assumption: the more closely a current actual occasion (a) attends to some occasion in its world (b), the more fully (a) objectifies (b) in its experience. When a past society is weakly objectified we can treat it as a mere abstraction, as we often do with the inorganic things in our worlds. But as we objectify (or prehend) another personality more fully, we come to feel greater concern for and participation in its being. This is clearly true in waking life, where the more attention we pay to another human or animal personality, the more deeply we come to participate in its existence. That participation can deepen into something that resembles an actual identity between the two personalities involved. We can observe this in the way that our personalities come to identify so closely with our waking bodies that we imagine ourselves to depend on them for our very existence (psychologically, a similar phenomenon of "identification" can occur in relationships between lovers or close family members, and even with a community, tribe, or nation).

In general, it seems that personalities most easily form deep relationships with other personalities that are functioning at their own grade or just a little lower. In this way, we have deep relationship with the personalities presiding over our various sensory organs, with higher mammals, and the other people in our world, but less intimacy with, for example, the occasions in our fingernails or hair or in the inorganic world around us.

Because actual occasions tend to relate most intimately with occasions of their own grade or a little lower, our bodies are structured as an elaborate hierarchy of personalities of various grades, each organizing personalities at a somewhat lower level—all the way down to the cellular personalities embodied in societies of macromolecules.

From this point of view, we can imagine medium-grade personalities in the vital world selectively attending to a dissipative society of macromolecules, bringing them together under the guidance of its aims and propositions, and inducing the macromolecules to move in what looks from outside like a self-organizing system. In this theory of embodiment, some element of PK is involved even in the formation of a cell.[18]

In waking life, however, high-grade personalities such as ourselves usually find it very difficult to selectively attend to low-grade, inorganic societies in such a way that we can influence their aims and, thus, significantly affect their behavior. Difficult—but not impossible.

While we habitually operate in the waking world through the hierarchically ordered occasions of our waking bodies, a high-grade concrescence has the ability to selectively attend to any society of occasions in its world—even to societies of low-grade occasions —and to embody itself in that society in such a way as to make that society amenable to accepting value shifts and propositions that induce it to calculate the continuity proposition in a way that it wouldn't ordinarily do. (In short, through focused attention or intention, a high-grade occasion can choose to selectively embody itself in inorganic matter—such as spoons, tables, chairs, or pianos—and, by sharing aims and

---

[18] It is possible that transphysical occasions might be the bearers of what Rupert Sheldrake has dubbed "morphic fields."

values not usually held by those inorganic entities, induce them to move. Colloquially, we call this "mind over matter" or "mind moving matter," in other words, psychokinesis, PK.)

Note that lower-grade occasions "cycle" more rapidly than higher-grade occasions do. Thus, once a high-grade personality tunes in to an ongoing lower-grade society, the occasions of that society start concrescing in simultaneity with that high-grade occasion, meaning that their aims are strongly influenced by the aims of the higher-grade society in the interaction. Thus, for example, a human personality can actually embody itself in societies that are external to its body. In this way, transphysical process metaphysics can explain PK.

However, this explanation leaves an important issue unresolved. If it is possible for a human society to embody itself in a society of lower-grade occasions external to its body, thus producing psychokinetic effects, where does the energy come from to cause motion?

A full answer to that question requires working out a detailed "process thermodynamics." Current ideas about thermodynamics seem to be rooted in Newtonian substance physics, which has long been superseded. What is needed is a rethinking of thermodynamics in the context of process metaphysics—a project I hope to undertake in the near future. However, two preliminary considerations of that larger work will be helpful here. First, Creativity (Whitehead's "principle of the ultimate") is not subject to entropy. It simply renders the many one and inexhaustibly increases the many by one. There is no way for Creativity to "run down." The problem in process metaphysics is to account for the notion of entropy at all. It may turn out that entropy is merely an abstraction that applies to a system under consideration only insofar as it can be, for some purposes, regarded as closed.

Second, although we may, for some purposes, regard some systems as closed, in process metaphysics no such closure can be complete. Process metaphysics leaves the entire universe, and every situation in it, open to energetic interactions with still larger systems. In particular, every situation in waking life is open to energetic interactions with transphysical worlds. So, in general, the activities of a high-grade occasion that is embodied in a low-grade system bring into that system the potential to move in ways that would be impossible were it not for that high-grade influence. In less technical terms, we could say that the low-grade system gets "energy" from the high-grade occasions that are embodied in it. So it should be possible to work out a theory of PK in which the energy needed to move macroscopic entities against gravity can come from the higher-grade occasions involved in the PK event. These ideas need to be worked out in more detail.

The Value of This Explanation

First, this explanation of PK in terms of process metaphysics gives us a way of plausibly accounting, at least in principle, for the apparent contravention of natural laws. Additionally, it provides some suggestions for how PK might be approached experimentally.

From this perspective, the ability of a high-grade personality to influence the macroscopic behaviors of a low-grade personality is a function of the level of "rapport" between them. Further, this rapport is a function of the intensity and concentrated focus that the high-grade personality can bring to bear on the lower one. Thus, we could hypothesize that the ability to concentrate effectively is a determining factor in PK success.

Also, this theory would lead us to suspect that it should be easier to influence the behaviors of medium-grade occasions more easily than the behaviors of inorganic systems. Experiments might be designed to test this. However, the higher the grade of the occasion being influenced, the more freedom it has to interpret the influences that are impinging on it, and this might complicate experimental efforts in this direction.

This last section has established that the problem of PK, while entirely intractable under the terms of modern scientific materialism, is entirely workable within the framework of transphysical process metaphysics.

In the next chapter, I will discuss the ways in which the transphysical world actually transcends the physical and waking worlds.

Chapter 8: The Transphysical Worlds

Up to this point I have outlined a new metaphysical model for the physical world and its relationship to what I call "the waking world." While I aimed to provide a rigorously logical alternative to the standard scientific-materialist view of reality (and I feel reasonably confident I have done just that), in some ways the first seven chapters are a prelude—laying the foundation for what is probably the most radical departure in this new metaphysics.

Beyond the physical world, beyond even the waking world, we need to expand our understanding of how the cosmos is structured and how it operates to include a transphysical dimension—a transphysical world. Only then can we hope to have a comprehensive metaphysical cosmology that can account not only for the data of modern science and our own waking, daily, lived experience but for the truly remarkable and anomalous data from parapsychological research—especially the ostensible phenomena of survival of consciousness or personality after the death of the biological body.

As before, my approach is inspired and informed by process philosophy—in particular, the work of Alfred North Whitehead. However, in this chapter, I will take process metaphysics beyond where Whitehead explicitly took his philosophy while always staying true to his profound metaphysical vision. Here I will extend what we might call "conventional process metaphysics" to a broader or deeper transphysical process metaphysics, largely inspired by the work of the great Indian philosopher and sage Sri Aurobindo.[1] I believe this is a necessary move if we are to achieve our objective of developing a cosmology that can account for survival of personality after death.

In short, the transphysical process metaphysics I am proposing here is solidly grounded in Whitehead's process philosophy expanded and augmented by the multileveled ontology of Sri Aurobindo.

Transphysical process metaphysics, like Whiteheadian metaphysics in general, describes all worlds as composed of causally interacting drops of experience. It reveals the physical world as a society of low-grade actual occasions operating in a metrical time and a metrical space. It also reveals the waking world as the physical world pervaded by actual occasions of higher grade. These higher-grade actualities organize the world into the exquisitely beautiful and endlessly fascinating patterns of order that give it its grandeur. They bind the whole planet into webs of empathic and telepathic interactions that suggest whole new ways of imagining the evolutionary process.

This is in stark contrast to the modern scientific worldview, which insists that the ultimate constituents of actual things are nothing but vacuous physical matter. Many of us were raised to think that everything, including ourselves, is made of intrinsically dead or insentient atoms or insentient brute energy. Everything that exists, and all their properties, we were told, could ultimately be reduced to interactions among atoms or energies. This reductionist project achieved a great deal of success when dealing exclusively with the physical world, but encountered serious difficulties when applied to an understanding of life. It is extremely hard to see how life, as we feel it in ourselves and in each other, could ever be accounted for in terms of mere movements among insentient things, little atomic billiard balls, or mathematically directed flows of insentient energy.

Of course science has undergone a major revolution since then with the advent of quantum physics. The old mechanistic view of reality inherited from Newton and his successors has given way to a very different understanding of the nature of reality. Today, those quaint atoms and insentient energies have dissolved into patterns of events, and

---

[1] Transpersonal process metaphysics is also very much influenced by the ideas of Teilhard de Chardin, Jean Gebser, Ernst Cassirer, Sri Aurobindo, and others.

process metaphysics has resolved these events into conscious, purposeful actual occasions. With this move, the relationship between matter, life, and sentience can be approached in an entirely new light. No longer are we faced with the insoluble problem of how life and sentience could emerge from dead matter or energy. Instead, we now approach the issue in terms of the relationship between inorganic low-grade occasions (the physical components of a body) and the higher-grade living occasions that are embodied in and through them.

Transphysical process metaphysics resolves this question by its doctrine of embodiment, which I have already discussed. But there is a further critical issue of whether or not all complex entities must always rest on a foundation of low-grade physical actualities. Even if we accept the idea that life is the embodiment of higher-grade occasions in systems of lower-grade occasions, is it necessarily the case that the higher-grade living occasions depend for their very existence on the lower-grade occasions in which they are embodied? This is a crucial question—because the answer we give will determine whether or not we can account for the phenomenon of personality survival beyond the death of the body and resolve the question at the heart of this book.

Unlike in scientific materialism, process metaphysics doesn't start out with an assumption that, ultimately, all that exists is insentient matter. Rather, our starting assumptions are these: first, that actuality ultimately exists as the consequence of an ongoing intrinsically experiential Creativity (the fact that many become one in a drop of experience, and that this drop of experience becomes one of the many for all subsequent drops), and; second, an ordering factor (which Whitehead called "God") that keeps a universe of free occasions from dissolving into mere chaos by the provision of coordinated aims for all new occasions. Given this metaphysical background, the occurrence of an actual occasion of some particular grade depends on just two factors: first, an aim toward a sufficient depth of value; and second, a sufficiently interesting actual world to allow the fulfillment of that aim.

The question of whether life and intelligence depend on physical matter for their existence now takes on an entirely new complexion. Clearly low-grade actual occasions can no more supply the aim for a higher-grade actual occasion than they can supply their own aim. Yet, the presence of an aim is a precondition for concrescence. But is a higher-grade occasion dependent on the presence of low-grade occasions to give it the kind of environment that it needs? As we will see in detail in this chapter, from the perspective of transphysical process metaphysics, the answer is no. The final satisfaction of a living occasion is incomparably richer than the final satisfaction of an inorganic occasion. One living occasion, even at the level of a single cell, has an experience capable of unifying the prehensions from millions of molecules. Certainly such occasions, interacting with each other, could produce a much more complex and interesting environment than anything constructed by the simple, habitual inertia of the low-grade occasions that constitute the physical world.

By contrast, a system of actual occasions of higher grade, receiving their aims from the primordial ordering factor,[2] and providing for each other a rich and interesting environment *is* the "transphysical world." Transphysical worlds are not dependent on the physical world in any way but exist in their own right as fully actual environments capable of supporting the adventure of personality. And it is this transphysical autonomy that makes possible the survival of personality after biological death.

In the next section, I will use transphysical process metaphysics to help us figure out what transphysical worlds are like.

The Nature of the Transphysical Worlds

As noted, grades of actual occasions vary on a continuum from low to high. The division into low-grade, medium-grade, and high-grade occasions is somewhat arbitrary. Nevertheless, we have good empirical grounds for assuming that the universe of human experience consists of three relatively distinct domains: the physical world, the vital world, and the mental world. Indeed, our usual divisions of evolutionary process support this idea of a tripartite metaphysical system. After all, standard evolutionary theory has little difficulty describing evolution in terms of three great stages: matter, life, and mind. [3] Also, as we will see in the

---

[2] This and the "ultimate ordering factor" are terms I like to use to describe what Whitehead calls "the primordial nature of God."

[3] This idea of a threefold division of worlds is also found in the *Upanishads* and is picked up by the theosophists. Both Michael Murphy and I independently noticed the fit of this threefold division to our usual scientific way of describing the major

next chapter, a consideration of the various geometries that hold sway in these different worlds also suggests a clear-cut distinction among them. In this section, however, I will simply make the provisional assumption that there are three distinct worlds, with significant variations of grade within each. I have already discussed the physical world—of low-grade, inorganic actualities operating in metrical space and metrical time. Now it's time to turn to the living or vital world.

The Vital World

The vital world is the region of the transphysical world closest to the physical. We catch confused glimpses of the vital world in our dreams, and a better sense of the vital world in lucid dreams, out-of-body experiences, and near-death experiences. All of these reveal that the vital world resembles the waking world in many important respects; it contains distinct places and various independent individuals other than us who operate in accordance with their own autonomous wills. However, the vital world is different from the physical world because it lacks many of the restraints on what is possible that we encounter in our waking world. It is also more responsive to our moods and thoughts, and it differs significantly in how cause and effect relate to measurable distances.

Given the similarities and major differences between the vital, waking, and physical worlds, how can we best understand the transphysical world in terms of our metaphysical ideas?

Let's begin by considering the physical world as we have come to know it through contemporary science. Modern research and theory tell us that the macrocosmic physical world is composed of 103 different atomic elements. When we assume that all other entities in the physical world are composed of these primary elements, we learn a great deal about the physical world. Now let's see what happens if we approach the vital world by examining its basic elements.

The first thing we note is that the simplest elements of the vital world are much more complex than the physical elements. The various types of atoms—each a personally ordered society of low-grade actual occasions that endure through time and move more or less continuously[4]

stages in evolution.

[4] Quantum mechanics leads us to expect some quantum discontinuities even in the

through space—form the lower border of the macrocosmic physical world. The upper boundary of the macrocosmic physical world consists of ultra-complex molecules, such as DNA, proteins, and viruses. If we assume a continuous variation in grades beyond the physical, then the lowest entities of the vital world have just that degree of complexity and intelligence that is reflected in simple biological cells. Several consequences follow from this:

- Because cells are so much more complex than atoms, they can be structured internally in many more ways, so we can assume there is a vastly greater variety of simple vital elements than there are simple physical elements.

- Because the simplest elements of the vital world are so much more complex (the final satisfaction of those simple entities entertains a much richer eternal object through which it represents its past and strives to influence its future), the varieties of behavior vital elements are capable of is much greater than those possible for elements of the physical world.

- The greater complexity of elements in the vital world is, in part, a function of the deeper aim at value intrinsic to those occasions when they begin their concrescences. This deeper aim is focused not only on the preservation of value (which is the aim characterizing the low-grade occasions studied by physics) but also on the active pursuit of satisfaction and the enjoyment of novelty. Thus, the occasions of the vital world are more actively and imaginatively responsive than the occasions of the physical world.

- As discussed earlier, the final satisfaction of higher-grade occasions have a subjective form that is emotional rather than merely sensory. Thus, as the higher-grade occasions of the vital world prehend each other, they are involved in empathic interactions. In a sense, the transphysical "inside" of our bodies is a kind of island of the vital world surrounded by an ocean of low-grade, physical actualities. The way in which the various cellular and organic occasions in our

---

movements of atoms.

188

bodies feel each other is very like the way all entities in the vital world feel each other.

- Causal interactions among actual occasions in the vital world are more complex than in the physical world. While the final satisfactions of low-grade occasions are characterized by simple eternal objects, held with a subjective form of unquestioned certainty, the final satisfactions of medium-grade occasions are complex eternal objects animated by a play of emotional intensities. In the waking world, our bodies are more or less responsive to our feelings and thoughts, but the physical world around us is not.

In the vital world, there is no stubborn, unimaginative, and relatively unresponsive medium separating us from one another. Nonetheless, in the vital world, there is still a distinction between a personality and its body. If we consider the core of our personality to be the personally ordered society of high-grade mental occasions that I call "me," then that personality is embodied in the vital world though a vital body, and those two bodies (the mental body and the vital body) are then embodied in the physical world through a physical body.

In the vital world, the mental personality is still embodied in its vital body, but the experience of embodiment in the vital world is quite different from the experience of embodiment in the physical world.

- In the vital world, the boundaries of bodies are more fluid than the boundaries of physical bodies, and every entity around us in the vital world is strongly affected by our moods and our intentions.
- Furthermore, any body in the vital world is free from the profound inertia of physical occasions. For example, my vital body is more able to shape itself to my intentions than my physical body is.
- The rules of locomotion for vital bodies are different from the rules of locomotion for physical bodies. It seems that in the vital world, the location at which we find ourselves is largely a matter of our moods and intentions. Not only are our own bodies more or less responsive to our intentions,

so are other entities in the vital world. Levitating objects, for example, would be easier in the vital world. Thus the world around us would respond to some extent as if it were our own body, making the body boundary rather difficult to establish.

- Finally, the personality in the vital world need not be confined to one position at a time. This reflects the experience that people often report in which they are not quite sure which person they were in a dream scene, or in which there is a sense of occupying a vital body in a dream while simultaneously being a disembodied witness to that same scene. In Whitehead's attempt to derive the metrical geometry of physics from the structure of experience itself, he was forced to make the assumption that the consciousness of the observer in the scene must define an unequivocal here and now throughout the duration of a given experience. He called this "cogredience." Cogredience does not necessarily apply in transphysical worlds.[5]

If we contemplate the vital world in terms of these characteristics, we can see that it corresponds closely to the worlds described in dreams, lucid dreams, and out-of-body and near-death experiences. The vital world comprises every scene that is imaginable. In fact, Sri Aurobindo and many other Vedic and theosophical teachers locate all of the heavens and hells described by the religions in the vital domain. Pleasure, pain, good, and evil are all vividly expressed in the vital world, freed from the constraints imposed by physical bodies.

It seems logical to speculate that the physical world is a region of the vital world in which what is being lived out is a highly constrained set of behaviors. In other words, we could interpret the waking world as a very rigid dream.

We now have a way of understanding the vital aspects of waking life and the existence of the vital world itself.

---

[5] Weiss, *Doctrine*, pp. 155–58.

The Mental World

The mental world is more difficult to describe. Nevertheless, we can say something meaningful about it:

- The variety and complexity of the elemental occasions making up the mental world are even greater than those in the vital world.

- The mentality we experience in the waking world usually operates under the domination of the vital and physical entities in which it is embodied. Thus the mind usually operates in the service of habit and desire. But the aims of mental occasions are wider and deeper than those of lower-grade occasions. While low-grade occasions are dominated by the aim at preserving value, and the aims of medium-grade occasions are dominated by the desire for novelty, high-grade mental occasions are dominated by the pursuit of harmony and coherence. Both for the personalities to which they belong and for the larger world their personalities inhabit, high-grade occasions take into account as relevant to their aims, and correspondingly make decisions about, a much greater range of the future. Thus, they are able to operate in subtle harmonies far beyond those achieved in the waking world.

- While the subjective forms of physical occasions involve simple certainty, and those of vital occasions involve the full play of emotion, the subjective forms of high-grade mental occasions are concerned with something more akin to "meaning." Meaning, here, is not simple denotation or arbitrary definition; rather, it is the kind of feeling we get when contemplating deep truths. Meaning here is not something less than emotion but is, rather, emotion sublimated and glorified by a wondrous generality of outlook. In religious and psychological terms, high-grade meaning is experienced, for instance, in numinous and synchronistic events.

- In the mental world, the normal mode of causal transmission is by means of telepathy. Actual occasions of high grade directly communicate profound meaning to one another, irrespective of physical distance—a quality common to many synchronistic experiences.

Given these attributes of high-grade occasions, it is not at all surprising that visualizing forms and events in the mental world is extremely difficult. Personalities in the mental realm are in telepathic contact, and therefore spatial distances so familiar to us in the waking world, and which allow us to perceive distinct boundaries between bodies, simply do not apply in the mental world.

Another aspect of the mental world as described here—a view generally held in many esoteric traditions— is that it is entirely beyond the distinctions we call good and evil. As a result, it is sometimes described as a kind of heaven.

It is logical to imagine that

- The vital world is a limitation of the mental world, in which meaning is limited to emotion, and only possibilities expressible in terms of a spatial continuum are developed.
- The physical world is a limitation of the vital world, in which emotions are limited, sense certainty is the dominant mode of apprehension, and the spatial continuum is limited to a metrical geometry.

Summary

We have now come a long way toward establishing the validity of the five fundamental propositions outlined in the first chapter. In this book, and in this chapter in particular, I claim that the results of modern and postmodern physics can be fruitfully explained in terms of process metaphysics.[6] We now see that transphysical process metaphysics can account not only for the results of science but can make fully intelligible the existence of transphysical worlds.

In light of what we have covered in this chapter, let's now revisit the five propositions.

---

[6] A number of theorists have worked this out in great detail. See, for example, Stapp, *Mind, Matter, and Quantum Mechanics*; Stapp, *The Mindful Universe*; and Epperson, *Quantum Mechanics and the Philosophy of Alfred North Whitehead*.

Proposition I, which affirms the causal power of the personality, follows directly once we adopt the perspective of process metaphysics.

This chapter has established Proposition II, the existence of the transphysical worlds. I have shown that we can fruitfully interpret the waking world as a physical world pervaded by vital and mental personalities. In particular:

- Our physical body is the embodiment of a medium-grade vital personality, which is the embodiment of a high-grade mental personality. My personality, along with personalities in each of my organs and each of my cells, belongs to the vital and/or mental world—causally prehending physical molecules, but not itself physical.

- A whole panorama of human experiences—visions, hallucinations, dreams, out-of-body experiences, lucid dreams, and near-death experiences—are all phenomena of the transphysical worlds, and life after death is existence in the transphysical worlds freed of embodiment in the physical world.

- Experiences of the vital and mental worlds are happening all the time. But while we are awake we shift them out of conscious awareness, and allow our attention to be monopolized largely by the objectifications of our various sense consciousnesses.

Our focus of attention is variable. We might start in our normal waking state and then slip into a daydream, from which (should we fall asleep) we might drift into a dream. That dream might become lucid, and in that lucid dream we might find ourselves out of our bodies. Finally, in extreme circumstances, an out-of-body experience might transform into a near-death experience. Thus, we do experience transphysical worlds even while we are alive (Proposition III).

Finally, because we already exist in the vital world, survival of bodily death becomes immediately plausible. If we already exist as a mental personality embodied in a vital body, then if the consciousness in our cells should lose interest in the macromolecules through which it prehends the physical world, it is reasonable to expect that the mental personality embodied in a vital body would continue its adventures, only now without a physical body. The difference between a dead body and a living body is that the dead body is no longer ordered by the aims higher-grade occasions that had been embodied in it (Proposition IV).

Proposition V, regarding reincarnation, will be discussed in Chapter 11.

Next we turn our attention to the nature of time and space in the waking and transphysical worlds.

Chapter 9: Mandalas of Time-Space

When we think about actuality, most of us usually imagine space, or space-time, as a kind of vast container populated by objects such as human beings, giraffes, galaxies, and atoms. Indeed, we tend to think of space as a kind of extended, substantial nothingness. In this chapter, I will show why this old Newtonian view of space is metaphysically unproductive and why even Einstein-inspired ideas of geometrical space-time are also inadequate as long as we hold on to the notion of space and time as some kind of *extended emptiness*. In the following pages, I will make the case that we need to radically revise our ideas of space and time (or, more accurately, unified "time-space"—as I prefer to call it, for reasons I will explain shortly) as the arena in which actual events or things take place.

- First, I will demonstrate that it is intelligible and plausible to imagine that time-space is *not* neutrally "out there" (external to conscious observers) but rather that *it is a relationship among actual occasions*.
- Second, I will show why the particular geometrical time-space of physics, rather than being the environment shared by all actuality, is only a relationship among low-grade actualities. In fact, I will argue that all existence (including *human life and death)* plays out in the context of a more complex and interesting time-space structure. And, further, once we expand our metaphysics to include this elaborate understanding of different kinds of time-space, the task

of explaining survival of the personality after death and reincarnation becomes much easier.

This chapter will probably be the most challenging and arguably the most important. I intend to spell out my arguments as clearly and simply as I can. Nevertheless, because many of the core ideas proposed here will be unfamiliar to most readers, I encourage you to take sufficient time to grasp and digest them. It may well serve you to read this chapter a second time.

The ideas presented here amount to a radical reorientation of our fundamental way of understanding the world. I expect that many readers will—at least initially—find themselves caught in a recurring tension between habitual ways of thinking about space and time and the novel insights developed in this chapter. But getting out of the old mind-set is crucial for understanding the metaphysical model developed in the rest of this book.

If we are going to expand science so that it can account for phenomena such as survival and reincarnation, I believe we have no option but to revise our fundamental cosmology to include what I have been calling the "transphysical worlds." And this will require a radical revision of our understanding of time-space—beyond what we have inherited from physics and from scientifically informed common sense. Making this difficult paradigm leap, I believe, is the most important obstacle we have to overcome.

Time, Space, and Time-Space

I will begin this examination of time and space by dealing with a common misconception. Our scientific education, which is still deeply influenced by the ideas of classical physics, leads us to think of space and time as if they are somehow separate from one other. Scientifically, we have the idea that reality exists at any single instant as a spatial configuration of matter. In other words, take away or freeze time, and space with its distribution of objects would still persist. Underlying and related to this assumption, we have the philosophical idea that space is "objective" while time is "subjective."

In the twentieth century, Einstein's special theory of relativity gave us a new understanding of space and time based on the realization that, *in actuality*, there is no movement in space that is not also a movement in time. Einstein came to this conclusion through a long chain of reasoning when he attempted to explain the movements of light in a vacuum. This idea revealed the perplexing relations between time and space that famously emerge in relativity theory. Notwithstanding the profound advances in physics that resulted from Einstein's insights and equations, the mind-boggling conundrums of relativity obscured a simple fact: the interconnectedness of space and time is also deducible from common sense.

Imagine two large rocks spaced well apart on a field. I am standing at one rock, and I ask, "How far away is that other rock?" The distance between this rock and the other one determines how long it will take me to walk there. The greater the distance, the longer the walk. So there is some important relationship between movement, time, and distance. Now, suppose I could walk infinitely fast. Then it would not take *any* time for me to get from here to there. But if it doesn't take any time for me to get from here to there, that means here and there are essentially the same place, so distance between them would be meaningless. An entity that could travel infinitely fast would have no experience of distance, and, thus, no notion of extended space.

Influenced by classical physics, we tend to think of space as more fundamental than time, and, following Einstein, physicists now often reduce time to a dimension of space. But when we think more deeply about this, it becomes clear that time is more fundamental than space. We can imagine time without movement, or we could imagine time with infinitely fast movements, but we can imagine space only where velocity of movement has a finite limit (whether we imagine this as a movement of bodies or a movement of causal influences). *Only in the context of finite velocities does space exist at all.* Time, therefore, is more fundamental than space, and because of this I choose to refer to the complex of time and space as "time-space."

Time-Space: Scientific and Experiential

As we begin our investigation of time-space, the first thing I'd like you to notice is a bifurcation in our ordinary, scientifically informed, commonsense notions. On one hand we have the mathematically defined space-time of physics. We imagine this to be self-subsistent and objective in the sense that it would still be there even in the absence of any entities occupying it, and in the absence of any consciousness whatsoever. And even in a relativistic framework—where time-space is said to be conditioned in important ways by moving masses within it, and where, therefore, time-space, matter, and energy are shown to be intrinsically interrelated—there is no mention of consciousness.[1]

On the other hand, we are all familiar with the very different "inner time-space" of our actual experience. Let us examine, for example, time-space as it presents itself to our visual sense and contrast the physicists' understanding of time and space:

- Visually, time-space is bounded by an outer edge of what we can directly see. By contrast, the space of physics has no outer boundaries and is either infinite or closed (which, in this context, means that if you go far enough in any one direction you will end up coming back to where you started).

- In the time-space of perception (in all senses), we are always dead center, always at the origin of our own set of coordinates. By contrast, in the time-space of physics there is no privileged point in this same sense. The time-space of physics is "isomorphic." Every point in time-space is exactly like every other point. But the time-space of experience is "anisomorphic." In the time-space of experience the center is a privileged point, and there are qualitative differences

---

[1] In the general theory of relativity, mass conditions space by changing its curvature. The curvature of space is a difficult notion that, fortunately, we will not have to deal with in this chapter. It is sometimes thought that relativity physics implies a subject because it talks about an observer. But in relativity physics, what is relative are actually mathematically defined accelerating frames of reference. Whether or not those frames of reference are occupied by subjects is irrelevant to the theory itself.

between what is "in front," "behind," "above," "below," and "to the side."

- The time-space of experience is fragmented, or discontinuous, in the sense that the contents of our experience are not necessarily mutually interrelated in a single time-space relationship. For example, a given moment of experience may include ordinary perceptions, memories from various time-space regions of waking reality only loosely interconnected by a common feeling tone, memories of experiences that took place in dreams, and purely imaginal experiences. The relations among these different perceptual entities cannot be expressed in geometrical terms. How many miles would I have to cover to visit the magnificent castle I saw in last night's dream? By contrast, entities in a mathematical time-space are all interrelated by the simple geometrical relation of distance.

The Relationship between Scientific and Experiential Time-Space

What then is the relationship between these two time-spaces—the smooth, geometrical, infinitely extended, isomorphic time-space of physics, and the rough, bordered, anisomorphic, conceptually elusive time-space of perception?

It is usually assumed that the time-space of perception is, through some mysterious process, *generated* by causal processes in the outer time-space of physics. In other words, the time and space that I subjectively perceive are assumed to result from various complex interactions between my nervous system, my sense organs, and the rest of the objective external world. The major efforts of cognitive neuroscience are directed at producing some plausible way in which energy and matter operating in mathematical time-space can generate not only representations of themselves in perception, but also *generate consciousness itself.* The idea is that the "real thing," the ontologically privileged domain, is "outside" in mathematical time-space, whereas perception (all that exists subjectively "in here") is either epiphenomenal or derivative.

I want to suggest that this approach is decisively backward. That is, if our explanations are to be empirical, we have to ground those explanations in what we *actually experience.* And what we actually experience is the "inner" world of perception.

Current, classically oriented scientific explanation leads us to a curious impasse. It tells us that the real world exists outside experience and that it consists of atoms or energies all operating in a smooth, continuous, geometrical time-space. This is all very interesting, and it allows us to predict and control many features of the physical world. But there's a problem—indeed the now infamous hard problem: that if the real world actually is what classical science describes, there is no coherent way of accounting for the emergence of consciousness, and, thus, no way of accounting for our *experience* of the world at all. So the classic scientific story seems to undercut the very existence of conscious experience while simultaneously claiming that science is empirical and rooted in the actual, conscious experience of scientists.

Quantum mechanics has been a major player in helping us to find a way out of this classical impasse. And the core ideas of quantum physics have found a philosophical expression in the work of Whitehead.[2] He sets out to show the precise way in which fundamental scientific ideas are, in fact, developed by a process of abstraction that brings to our conscious attention certain invariant features of our direct experience. Thus the everyday objects that populate our lives and the scientific objects (such as electrons and quarks) that populate our scientific explanations can be understood as ways of recognizing and naming *permanences within experience*, rather than *hypothetical realities outside experience.*

---

[2] Whitehead articulated his philosophy science in various works, including the following three books: *An Inquiry Concerning the Principles of Natural Knowledge*; *Concept of Nature*; and *The Interpretation of Science*. See also these book chapters: A. N. Whitehead, "The Principle of Relativity with Applications to Physical Science," in *Alfred North Whitehead: An Anthology*; and A. N. Whitehead, "Time, Space, and Material: Are They, and if So in What Sense, the Ultimate Data of Science?" in *The Interpretation of Science*.

Let's return to our examination of the perceptual world. I suggest that we can understand experiential space by describing it as a mandala. As I noted above, our actual experience of time-space is always centered on a privileged point—the point defining the here and now. (Technically, because we're dealing with time-space, it's really a "point-instant," or, more accurately, a "moment-point.") The rest of the world is structured for us as a display around this point. In other words, the world shows up for us as a mandala—always intrinsically coherent, with every one of us at the center point of conscious perception.

We are each at the center of our own experienced world, from which we apprehend a variety of entities arrayed around us in a mandala-like configuration; this is the time-space of our experience.

I am proposing that this mandala-like structure of experience is the actual time-space in which the world unfolds its creative advance. In other words, perceptual space is not derived from events in outer, geometrical space. Rather, perceptual time-space is time-space itself, and geometrical space is an abstraction that allows us to describe certain invariant relations that we can recognize and name in the perceptual time-space from which it is abstracted.

Having explored this issue in a phenomenological way, let us now look at it in terms of the ontology of actual occasions being developed in this book.

The key to this exploration is the notion that each actual occasion contains, or "houses," the entirety of its past. This is a difficult notion to grasp because we are accustomed to thinking of things or substances or events as being contained, or housed, in time-space, and I am suggesting that we reverse the figure/ground relationship.

We know that we each have our own experience of the world.

• From the purely subjective point of view, I can say that my world exists *in* my experience. The world that I see, for example, disappears when I close my eyes.

- Most of us, at some time, have played with the idea of solipsism, the idea that the entire world is just a figment of one's imagination.

Without absolutizing either of these ideas, I want to suggest that they both point to an important aspect of truth. The world as I know it *is* contained in my experience. Even the objective world can be understood to consist of experiences that I have, and ideas that I entertain about those experiences, and is, in this sense, contained in my experience. In the modern world, and *in the context of a substance ontology*, the fact that the world is contained in my experience is easily dismissed. My experience, after all, is either epiphenomenal, or it consists of qualities characterizing the mental substance that is my mind. Remember that in a substance ontology, a substance is something that needs nothing other than itself to exist. The qualities of a substance belong to it alone. So if my varying experiences are just qualities inhering in the substance of my mind, then there is no intrinsic connection between my experiences and the qualities of other substances outside me.

We usually imagine that our brains are part of the one physical world and that the external causal processes bring about electrochemical configurations of the brain that are somehow (quite miraculously) converted into conscious experiences. But in the ontology we are developing here, we are making the assumption that there are no substances and qualities in the old sense. Rather, there are *processes of relationship*. Concrescences are the coming together of past experiences and timeless possibilities, and the character of an actual occasion consists of simple eternal objects brought together in a complex pattern. Causal transmission of energy is, according to process metaphysics, a transmission of *experience* through the creative advance.[3] That which causes me *is* that which I feel. We no longer have a situation in which efficient causality on one hand and consciousness on the other hand inhabit different ontological domains. Rather, efficient causality and feeling are inseparable from one another; they are two sides of the same

---

[3] I use "creative advance" here rather than the more familiar "time" because I am viewing time (as it is understood in the modern sense) as an abstraction from the process of creativity that issues in the ongoing actualization of occasions of experience.

coin. In this sense, causal expressions of past occasions are felt in—and only in—the experiences of occasions that follow the past occasion in the creative advance. When we imagine our experience to be a mere *representation* of the outer world, it is as if we are in a glass bubble and some outer reality is being selectively represented on the surface of that bubble. I am saying there is no bubble. *Our experience is the real thing.*

Actual occasions have their moment of subjective immediacy, and then they expire into objective immortality. Their effects are felt by subsequent occasions. Each occasion houses, or contains, the causal expressions of its past. It actualizes, and then its causal expressions are felt by actual occasions that occur in its future. Each occasion houses its past, and is, in turn, housed by future occasions.

Outside this process, as Whitehead says, "There is nothing, nothing, nothing, bare nothingness."[4]

Because each actual occasion houses its own causal past, and because actual occasions are contained only in other actual occasions, we can now say intelligibly that each actual occasion is a creative unit of time-space.[5]

---

[4] Whitehead, *Process and Reality*, p. 167.
[5] Whitehead refers to actual occasions as "atoms" of time-space. The word "atom," however, carries so much metaphysical history that it would be somewhat misleading to use it in this context.

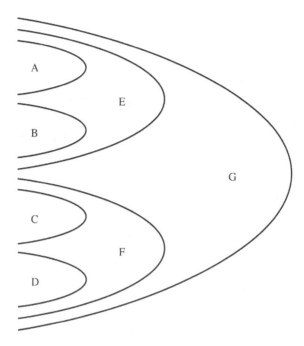

Figure 2: In this highly simplified diagram, each parabola represents an actual occasion. The past is on the left; the future is on the right.

Figure 2 (above) is an abstract picture of the creative advance. Each parabola represents one actual occasion.

- Each actual occasion in the diagram contains, or houses, the entirety of its causal past, and is, in its turn, housed by the occasions of its future.
- The space inside the parabola is mandala space. The center around which each actual occasion constructs its own mandala (the point of the parabola) is its mental pole, its own consciousness.
- What we have been thinking of as "external space," or the "substantial extended nothingness" in which things take place is no longer necessary. Actual occasions are simply contained in subsequent actual occasions.[6]

---

[6] Someone might be tempted to say, "But what about the paper on which the drawing was done? Doesn't that represent objective, outer space?" The answer to this

• The geometrical properties of time-space are still important. But rather than being properties of the "substantial extended nothingness," they are now understood as patterns of causal relations among actual occasions. We will discuss the importance of these patterns later in this chapter.

An interesting result of this analysis is that it creates an intrinsic connection between time-space and consciousness. Scientific work in the past century has demonstrated a deep connection between time-space and energy. But if time-space consists of actual occasions, and if actual occasions are structured around a mental pole—a pole of consciousness—then time-space itself cannot be separated from consciousness.

What distinguishes experience from mere existence of objects is (along with aim or purpose) the factor of existence we call consciousness. Whenever we prehend anything, we are aware of what we prehend. In a very important sense, consciousness, which pervades and contains all that we know, *is* the time-space in which experience unfolds. This brings us one step closer to a truly unified theory that shows the fundamental coherence of time-space, energy, *and* consciousness.

Because our experiences of the waking world are transmitted to us through our bodies, and because our bodies consist of occasions that *feel, interpret,* and *decide,* a considerable amount of interpretation intervenes between us and the waking world in itself. This leads us to posit two different modes of experience.

First, we experience the world in the "mode of causal efficacy," which is to say that every actual occasion in our past has some, however negligible, causal effect on the structure of our experience.

Second, we experience the world in the "mode of presentational immediacy," which is to say that as our experience of the actual world is interpreted in the process of concrescence, we form an interpretation, or an "appearance," that shows us the world in a way relevant to our own history and our own purposes. This takes place for any actual occasion

---

question is no, since any area of the paper not apparently occupied by the largest parabola is to be imagined as contained within a still larger parabola that cannot, given the nature of the medium, be represented here.

in any actual world. We objectify the waking world (which we discussed in Chapter 7) through the occasions making up our bodies. Our bodies, then, are deeply involved in structuring the way in which the waking world is immediately presented to us.

This does not change the general principle: *what is in our experience is the actual world out of which we grow.* Even the occasions of our own bodies, the objectifications that dominate our waking perception, are other occasions of experience in the actual world.

The Relational Theory of Time-Space

The metaphysics of Newtonian science posits the existence of absolute space and absolute time. It treats space and time as if they are actualities in their own right. Leibniz, on the other hand, developed a relational theory that reduces space and time to the status of relations among actualities. The idea of time-space I am developing here is like that of Leibniz (and Whitehead); it is a relational theory of time-space.

This is important. In general, science and common sense grant time-space the status of an actuality. We tend to think of space and time as empty expanses that "contain" all other entities, and, it is assumed, that impose certain geometrical forms on actualities (shapes) and other geometrical relations (distance) among those entities.

If, however, we try to imagine empty time-space as "extended," we run into some interesting difficulties. For example, we find that to make the idea of extension intelligible, we must call on some notion of plurality. A single point is not extended, so extension must involve more than one point. Or, to put it another way, we cannot call space extended unless we can imagine it as a plurality of points. But can we, in fact, imagine a collection of unextended points?

Leibniz articulated a fundamental principle of logic that he called the "principle of the identity of indiscernibles." This principle states that every individual actuality, or every individual object of attention, must be different from every other entity if it is to be recognized as such. In other words, if we say there are two entities, but there is *nothing whatsoever* that distinguishes one from another, then there are not, in fact, two entities. There is only one.

If we apply this to empty time-space, which is entirely isomorphic, and in which all points are identical, there is no way to differentiate one point from another. In this case, by the principle of the identity of indiscernibles, our collection of points collapses into a single and entirely unextended point.

The conclusion is that time-space, to be extended at all, must be a relationship among entities that are somehow discernible one from another. Whitehead and Leibniz, each in his way, offer *occasions of experience*, or "monads," as the entities that are needed. Thus, time-space is a systematic pattern of relationships among actual occasions.

A relational theory of time-space is inherent in postmodern science. In the Newtonian theory of time-space, distance is a function of position only, and position is a function of placement within absolute space and absolute time. In the special theory of relativity, there is no absolute space and time, and the distances between enduring entities are a function of their positions *and* their velocities. Thus the configuration of time-space is a function of the dynamic relations among actualities. What is invariant in the special theory of relativity is the *causal order* among occasions. That is, if A caused B, then the fact that A caused B is invariant in all frames of reference.[7]

The time-space of special relativity makes distance dependent on relative velocity, and so it is relational rather than absolute. Nevertheless, it enables us to trace the causal order among occasions and so to order the past in a particular, generally unambiguous way.

---

[7] There is considerable confusion about this particular feature of special relativity. This is due to the following situation: if two occasions, A and B, both in the past of occasion C, are too remote from each other to have causally interacted with one other, then occasion C may see either one as preceding the other depending on its own frame of reference. This does not change the fact that all causal relations that do, in fact, take place will be experienced by all future occasions as having that same causal order. The point is that special relativity, does not imply a "block universe" in which everything that ever will happen has, in some sense, already taken place. This confusion may arise from the fact that Einstein, who was a determinist, did think of the universe as a four-dimensional block. But the fact that Einstein was, on philosophical grounds, a determinist should not suggest that the theory of relativity itself implies determinism. Clearly, it does not. For an excellent discussion of this point, see Chapter 11 in Milik Capek's *The Philosophical Impact of Contemporary Physics*.

The general theory of relativity is even more relational. In this theory, gravitation is imagined as a "curvature" of time-space, and that curvature is a function of the distribution of mass/energy.

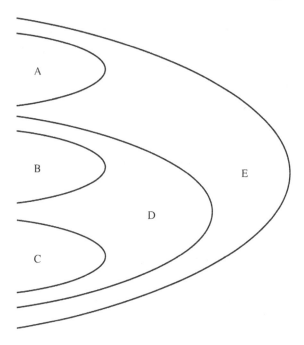

Figure 3: In this highly simplified diagram, each parabola represents an actual occasion. The past is on the left; the future is on the right. Note that A is in the immediate past of E, while B and C are in a more distant past.

Finally, in quantum mechanics, with its abrupt and statistically uncertain transitions of position, we encounter situations such as that in Figure 2, where occasions A, B, and C are contemporary, B and C (but not A) are in the immediate past of occasion D, but both A and D are in the immediate past of E. In this situation, an entity in the past (A) can objectify in the present (E) without having been objectified in any of the other occasions (such as D) intervening between A and E. The importance of this relation will emerge when we discuss memory below.

In general, for purposes of science and of common sense, we can model the positions of actual entities by points, and the distances between actual entities as lines. A set of postulates specifying relations between points and lines is a geometry. Newtonian mechanics, Einsteinian physics, and quantum mechanics each posit a somewhat different geometry of time-space.

From this discussion, we can conclude that the structure of time-space—the geometry that defines both position and distance among points—is not absolute, but is a function of relations among occasions.

Time-Space, Causality, and Memory

We will now consider the relationship between occasions from another perspective. According to process metaphysics, to be the subject of an efficient cause *is* to have an experience. What I am experiencing is the objectification—or causal expression—of the prior experiences of past actual occasions. I receive those experiences into myself, I interpret them, sometimes I modify them, and then I transmit them to future occasions. Thus, the transmission of energy is always the transmission of experience. In this sense, all objective experience is the experience of past experiences. In general, that's what *memories* are: experiences of past experiences.

Given the finite velocity at which efficiently causal transmissions propagate,[8] all my experiences of other actualities are of past experiences. Some of those experiences are of occasions I now identify as having been "me" in the past. We usually reserve the word memory for those particularly intimate experiences of our own past experiences. But in principle, experiences of my own past experiences are no different from experiences of past experiences originating from a more remote source,

---

[8] There are, of course, non-local effects as well, but non-local effects are not the same as efficient causes. Non-local effects, as I understand them, instantaneously affect probabilities of other events, but they are not prehensions of actualities.

for example, my momentary experience of a person who is sitting across from me is my experience of her past experience; my experiences of moments in my own history are simply more intimate. The point is that efficient causation and memory are, at this level, one and the same.

In previous chapters, I used the term "prehension" to refer to the basic connection between actual occasions. What emerges from this discussion is that prehension is a basic notion, from which we can abstract three crucial features of actuality.

- *Containment*: Each occasion can be said to contain, or to extend over, all of the occasions in its past, which it prehends.
- *Efficient cause*: Each occasion is, in part, the outcome of the efficient causes reaching it from the past. To prehend a past occasion is to be efficiently caused by that occasion.
- *Memory*: To be efficiently caused by a past occasion is to have *an experience of the experience* of that occasion. If we define memory as the experience of a past experience, then to prehend a past occasion is to remember it.

This way of regarding the primitive relationship among occasions has three significant advantages.

- First, it allows us to abandon any attempt to explain memory by a neural trace theory. There is no need for any physical record in the brain to explain memory. Memory is just the objectification of a past occasion in a present occasion. Because all of the past is causally effective in the present, there need be no special route of transmission to connect a memory to a present occasion.[9]

---

[9] Classical science has left us with the unfortunate habit of assuming that the only real efficient causes are those that come from the immediate past. But this notion is undermined by quantum theory, which says that all causal transmission of effects through time can be described by the Schrödinger wave function, which, because it is a linear equation, never loses any information. Thus, in quantum mechanics, an effect from the distant past may be transmitted indefinitely, entirely unchanged and not experienced by any intervening occasions through the creative advance—until the right conditions emerge under which it can be expressed.

- Second, we don't have to construct some elaborate theory to account for parapsychological phenomena in terms of physical causes. We can, rather, expand the mechanism of efficient cause in the following way. Every efficient cause is an experience of a past experience, including the feelings of "emotion" and "meaning" that characterized the occasion being prehended. A mental-grade occasion will objectify in a future mental occasion in a way that is a direct transmission of meaning—a *telepathic* interaction. A medium-grade occasion will objectify itself in a future medium-grade occasion in a direct sharing of emotion—an *empathic* interaction. Low-grade, inorganic occasions will objectify in future low-grade occasions as *physical* interactions, as simple forms or facts in the mode of sense certainty. So depending on the grade of the occasions involved, the very mechanism of efficient cause can function as a simple transmission of physical fact, as an empathic interaction, or as a telepathic interaction.

- Third, memory, we have seen, is a direct sharing of experience. Empathy and telepathy can now be understood as different modes of memory.

The Ordering Function of Time-Space

Whitehead holds that each nascent occasion feels (or, in his technical language, "positively prehends") every actual entity in its past. As this chapter develops, and we discuss what I will call "non-extensive networks," we will come to see that, in fact, an occasion need not feel *each and every* occasion of the general past, but (assuming we allow for extremely trivial experiences) it seems obvious that every occasion must feel the entirety of its *causal* past.

However, although every actuality in my casual past does have some effect on me, however minimal, the occasions of my immediate past are still distinguishable from the occasions of *their* immediate past, and so on. This because the occasions of my immediate past contain experiences of events in the more distant past, but occasions of the more distant past do not contain experiences of the immediate past. In this way, we can speak of spatiotemporal distance, and we can (as we do in relativity theory) sort the past into a meaningful, causal order.

I propose to call this causal ordering of the past the "time-space relationship"—and it plays a number of important roles in the creative advance.

- Every society or self-organizing system of actual occasions must share a common time-space relation. Since we usually assume that all of actuality operates in terms of one, and only one, time-space relation, we usually don't have to state this condition. But in transphysical process metaphysics, there may be many time-space relations functioning in parallel or intricately overlapping ways, and so it becomes necessary to point this out.

- The time-space relation characterizing the occasions in a society serves as a "scheme of indication." A scheme of indication is a set of systematic relations among actualities that allows us to use terms such as "this one," "that one," "over there," "the one I saw yesterday," and so forth. Without a scheme of indication that allows us to designate particulars for each other, we could not form propositions, such as "*that* ball is blue." Also, in the transmission of experiences through the nervous system, it is important that successive occasions can recognize inputs from various other occasions as pertaining to the same actualities outside the body. This is an aspect of the binding problem. For example, I see a bell, and I hear a bell, and both the high-grade occasion that is me and the occasions that are my eye consciousness and ear consciousness must all recognize the visual and auditory impressions as belonging together so they can be bound into a single experience of the bell. They can perform this function only if they share some systematic way of designating particulars.

- The time-space relation conditions the transmission of causal efficacy. Much of our science is concerned with the idea of the attenuation of causal efficacy as distance increases. For example, gravitational and electromagnetic influences fall off with the square of the distance. And distance is always defined (not necessarily mathematically, as we will see) by the time-space relation.

In physics, the time-space relation is what I referred to in the last section as a particular geometry. Thus, we could say that classical physics, relativity physics, and quantum physics each describes actuality in terms of a different time-space relation.

Possibility, Actuality, and the Time-Space Relationship

In Chapter 4, I discussed the relationship between possibility and actuality in terms of the relationship between forms and events (which I have also been calling eternal objects and actual occasions). We saw that each occasion becomes actual by deciding in each situation which possibilities it will choose, of all the possibilities open to it. Actualization is a process of *decision* (or "cutting off") that narrows the possibilities until only one is left.

Now let us focus on the structure of the field of possibility itself. But first: What is a "field of possibility?" The simplest way to understand this idea is to think in terms of what scientists call natural law. If we know a natural law, then given a particular set of circumstances to which the law applies, we know the range of possibilities relevant to the immediate future of that situation. Suppose I am standing on the surface of the Earth, and I am holding a rubber ball in my outstretched arm. My knowledge of the laws of gravity give me an accurate idea of where the ball will go, and of how fast it will go there, after it is released. My knowledge of natural law is useful because it lets me know the field of possibilities that extends outward from the current event that is my experience in this moment.

Any actuality is, of course, more complex than any set of mathematically expressed natural laws could ever encompass; nonetheless, it is clear that what happens in our experience is always relevant to and conditioned by what has already happened. There is a structure of possibility.

We also saw in Chapter 4 that the eternal objects (or forms of definiteness) that we prehend in the world and in our thoughts are possibilities. A specific eternal object is just the possibility that some actual occasion might possess that particular character. Thinking is the process whereby we recognize the possibilities that were actualized in the past and that may be actualized in the future. Logic, as an order among abstractions, is also an order among possibilities. Thus, we can fruitfully imagine the structure of possibility as analogous to a logical system. This is important because logic also applies to actuality. The first principle of any philosophy that hopes to find rational order in the universe must be that actuality is logically consistent with itself, which is to say that what happens next must always be logically consistent with what has already happened. This does not mean that nothing new or novel ever happens, it just means that whatever novelty does arise—no matter how astonishing—must, in principle, be compatible with the past having been as it was.

Now let us look at the structure of possibility as analogous to the structure of a logical system. As we construct such a system, we begin just with possibility itself, a kind of blank slate on which various logical systems can be written. Then each definition and each axiom that we introduce closes down the field of possibility by limiting it to certain conditions. The more axioms and definitions we introduce, the narrower the scope of the possibilities they define. For example, we could begin our process by defining the notion of a thing, a finite natural being, or an enduring entity. This excludes all things infinite and all mere flashes of existence. I could further narrow the field by specifying plants, as opposed to animals and minerals, and then narrow my definition still further by including only flowering plants, and so on. It would seem natural that when all of the generality has been squeezed out, and everything that needs to be determined has been determined, we ought to find a single actual event being singled out.

This is, indeed, Whitehead's idea. A given situation presents some set of possibilities, all of which are compatible with the past, but many of which are incompatible with each other, and so incapable of joint realization. An actual occasion, in its process of coming to be (its concrescence), makes decisions eliminating more and more possibilities until it becomes perfectly definite, at which point it is actualized.

This position suggests that the process of abstraction can proceed in two different directions.[10] If we start with a very complex actual occasion, any abstraction from that will involve a simplification and a loss of information.[11] For example, my knowledge of the person next to me can be very full, very rich, and relatively complete. I can feel that person, smell that person, hear that person breathe, and see every pore on his or her face. We could say that my knowledge is relatively close to the concrete actuality of that person. But by contrast, I have only abstract knowledge of a fellow spectator sitting across the field from me at the stadium. I know him or her as "just a person." Abstracting from actuality leads to simplification, a loss of information.

When, however, I abstract from a logical system or a structure of possibility, what I end up with is a set of abstractions that is fuller and richer than the one I started with. For example, suppose we start with arithmetic. Arithmetic is important because all higher maths build on the foundation of arithmetic; it establishes the possibility for all the higher forms of mathematics. In other words, the structures of trigonometry,

---

[10] Whitehead discusses this idea at length in *Science and the Modern World*, Chapter X. I have written a commentary on this chapter in *Process Studies Supplements*. It can be found at http://www.ctr4process.org/publications/ProcessStudies/PSS/

[11] Certain modern ideas of information that suppose it can be quantified in terms of bits seem to me to miss the point. Even if the information contained in an event could be expressed as a very large set of yes/no questions and answers, all of the really interesting information is contained in the questions themselves. The answer to the question "is it red or blue" is irrelevant if I don't know the meaning of redness and blueness. I suspect that all of this talk in the scientific literature about "information" is an attempt to get at the relevance of eternal objects to actuality. I am using the word information to convey the operation of eternal objects as they characterize, or "inform," events.

calculus, and so on come into being with the addition of new definitions and new axioms to arithmetic; and these new definitions and axioms further constrain the possibilities of interaction among numbers. In this sense, the axioms of arithmetic are more concrete, more powerful and more free than those of higher forms of mathematics.

But we can also abstract from arithmetic, as Peano did in the early twentieth century. He found he could deduce all the theorems of arithmetic from just three definitions and five axioms[12]—provided we assume the postulates of propositional logic as a background. This is certainly an economy of expression, but it is more than that.

First, in this mode of abstracting there is no loss of information. All of arithmetic can be derived from Peano's postulates and definitions. In addition, abstracting from sets of structured possibilities in this way opens us up to great ranges of alternative possibilities. For example, once we have seen that all of arithmetic can be grasped in terms of three definitions and five axioms, we have opened up a vast meta-arithmetical realm. We can now experiment with different sets of definitions and axioms, each of which opens up a new realm of order, and see whether those new forms of order might have application in actuality.

Science is the attempt to identify the particular characteristics of the actual situation in which we find ourselves. We express this character in the form of logical propositions. But sets of logical propositions can be more or less general, so they can allow the occasions they govern to be more or less free.

We have seen that each actual occasion contains the entirety of its own causal past and prehends that past as ordered by a particular time-space relationship. We have seen too that in terms of a postmodern, relativistic understanding of time-space, this ordering of the past is essentially causal—i.e., an understanding of the time-space relation allows us to see which occasions have affected which other occasions in the past and, from that, to predict (probabilistically) where and when causal actions will have effects in the future.

The causal order among actual occasions can be, for many purposes, represented in terms of points and lines. Sets of propositions concerning the interactions of points and lines form various geometries. These

---

[12] Bernard Russell, *Introduction to Mathematical Philosophy*, pp. 5–6.

geometries, as we will see in detail in the following section, may have greater or fewer propositions, and so may be more or less general.

Let's pause here to review the main points covered so far in this chapter:

- We began by observing that even in terms of relativity theory and common sense, the very notion of space is undefined except in situations where movement (or causal propagation) is restricted to some finite velocity. Also, time is more fundamental than space, so we are calling the complex of time and space "time-space."
- We explored the nature of experiential time-space and saw that it can be described as a mandala—an array of meaningful events coordinated around a privileged center. Every actual occasion—every drop of experience—apprehends its world in this mandala form.
- We then considered the relationship between mandala time-space and scientific time-space and concluded that of the two, mandala time-space is more fundamental. Each actual occasion, within its mandala of experience, houses or contains the entirety of its causal past, and is, in turn, contained within the occasions that will make up its causal future.
- Outside this *mutual containment* is nothing whatsoever. In other words, actual occasions are not contained or housed in some neutral extended nothingness; rather they are contained or housed in each other so that each is a creative unit (or atom, as Whitehead would say) of time-space.
- These considerations led us to a relational theory of time-space, an idea originally suggested by Leibniz and further developed by Whitehead. We saw that we can understand points as abstract representations of actual occasions and lines as abstract representations of relations among actual occasions (prehensions). Geometry is, at least in part, a study of relations among points and lines, and as we now know, there are many different geometries, so there can

be any number of *different* time-spaces in terms of which actuality can function.

- The primary ordering among occasions in a post-relativistic frame of reference is their *causal ordering*—i.e., we order our past primarily in terms of which occasion was in the causal past of each other occasion. We saw that this ordering can be understood in terms of containment, efficient cause, or memory.

- The way in which we order the past serves as a scheme of indication, or a way of pointing to or designating particular facts and of orienting ourselves in the systematic network of causal interactions pervading the actual world.

- We saw that the *geometries,* in terms of which we order the past (and, of course, anticipate the future), can be more or less constraining as they involve greater or fewer definitions and axioms. As we will see, there is a hierarchy of geometries, moving from the metrical geometries at one end to "non-extensive networks" at the other.

Given these considerations, plus the data of parapsychology and the evidence for reincarnation and personality survival that we discussed earlier, and given the hopeless inadequacy of modern materialism to account for any of these phenomena, it became plausible to hypothesize the existence of different grades of actual occasions forming different transphysical worlds. I now propose that each of these worlds is differentiated from the others because occasions of different grades interact in ways that define different geometries or different time-spaces. In other words, it now becomes plausible to begin the process of forming a mathematical analysis of the time-space of the transphysical worlds.

The theory being advanced here is that an adequate description of reality requires us to posit both a physical (inorganic) world and several transphysical worlds. The simplest, most abstract of these worlds is the physical domain studied by modern physics. This world consists of a system of low-grade occasions defining, through their causal interactions, a time-space relation that can be characterized by a metrical geometry. Each transphysical world consists of a system of higher-grade occasions defining, through their causal interactions, geometries that are more general and freer than the geometry of the physical world.

Our next task, then, is to look at different varieties of geometry so we can get a better sense of how these transphysical worlds might function.

Varieties of Geometry

Geometry is the logical expression of a time-space relation. The fewer the postulates governing the time-space relation the more general it is. The "higher" or "more transphysical" a world is, the higher the grade of the occasions involved, and the freer and less constrained the time-space relation. The discipline of meta-geometry illustrates this principle.

Our modern commonsense understanding of the logical structure of time-space is still Euclidean and Cartesian. We think of the time-space relation as being expressible in terms of three spatial axes, each perpendicular to the others, and one temporal axis perpendicular to the other three.

The axioms of Euclid, the basis for Descartes' analytic geometry, include a particular parallel postulate: given any straight line and a point not on it, there exists one, and only one, straight line that passes through that point and never intersects the first line, no matter how far they are extended. In short, *parallel lines never meet.*

One of the most significant intellectual events of the past few centuries was the discovery that there are perfectly valid geometries other than the Euclidean and, therefore, perfectly valid time-space relations in which the parallel postulate is violated. Thus:

- In *Euclidean* geometry, within a two-dimensional plane, for any given line L and a point A, not on L, there is exactly one line through A that does not intersect L—that is, a single parallel.
- In *hyperbolic* geometry, by contrast, there are infinitely many lines through A not intersecting L—an infinite number of parallels.
- And in *elliptical* geometry, there are no straight lines that do not intersect. All parallel lines intersect at two points.

Geometers have found a way to demonstrate that all of these geometries are logically consistent. First, they demonstrated that each of these geometries could be represented in terms of any of the others. For example, elliptical geometry, in which all parallel lines meet in two points, can be represented in terms of Euclidean geometry as the geometry of the surface of a sphere. On a Euclidean sphere, all straight lines are great circles, and all great circles intersect at two points; hence, all parallels meet at two points.

But this is just one example, and any one of the geometries can be represented in terms of any of the others. On the basis of this demonstration, and on the basis of the assumption that Euclidean geometry (having been tested by geometers for millennia) is logically consistent, they assumed that all of these other geometries are also consistent with themselves and do not lead to logical contradictions. This does not mean that Euclidean geometry is somehow more fundamental. It just means that mathematicians are so familiar with Euclidean geometry they are more confidently willing to assume that it is logically consistent, and further, that other geometries that can be interpreted in Euclidean terms are also logically consistent.

However, we cannot decide through experiment which geometry actually applies to our particular physical universe. Although Einstein's equations suggest that the space of our universe may be closed (that is, our geometry may be elliptical), the issue cannot be definitely resolved. The world that appears to us as Euclidean may, in fact, be governed by some other geometry, or, indeed, by some much richer combination of *multiple* geometries.

Beyond this it is possible to work out a consistent but less restrictive geometry in which parallel lines are entirely undefined. Note that in this geometry, there are no units of measure (because measurement—in order to be consistent and therefore useful—always presupposes systems of parallel lines). A system without parallel lines is described by "projective" geometry, where all lines meet at one point—the "point at infinity"—which, paradoxically, is also right here at the focal point of our own perspective on the world.

Unless we can find some application for projective geometry, we might assume it is merely an intellectual construct with no possible application to actuality.

In fact, there are two widely recognized, valid applications for this theory:

- Projective geometry is the key to the art of perspective. In projective space, all parallel lines meet at the vanishing point, and the space defined in visual perception is actually projective. The supreme accomplishment of the Euclidean understanding of space is that it allows a clear coordination between various perspectives. From my own point of view, I cannot consistently judge distance because a given visual object may be large and far away or small and close. If I can't accurately judge distance, I cannot deduce how an object I see will appear to you. An accurate judgment of distance requires a framework within which various perspectives can be coordinated. If I know that you are three units away from me (in some particular direction as defined by some system of parallel lines), I can mathematically transform my perspective into your perspective. Since projective space is the space of actual perception, the true function of metrical space is coordination of various perspectives. This is clearly illustrated in perspectival drawing, in which there are always *two* perspectives being coordinated—the vanishing point and a point just behind the eyes of the observer. Each of these is an instance of the one point at infinity.

- Projective geometry seems to characterize the time-space relation in many perceptual situations—for example, waking life, and some subset of our regular dreams, lucid dreams, and out-of-body experiences in which we occupy a body positioned in a time-space continuum somewhat similar to that of waking life. In those experiences, we find ourselves in a "scene," surrounded by objects (such as buildings) and living entities (such as other people). In these scenes, we could draw a straight line from our point of view to each of those objects, so points and lines are clearly relevant to the time-space relation obtaining in those scenes, and yet measurable distance, as that property appears in waking life, does not apply in those scenes. For example, in dreams, objects come and go in ways that seem more relevant to feelings and meanings than to any measurable distance.

The point is that the creative advance of actual occasions not only doesn't need a container (since each actual occasion houses all of its past), it also doesn't need a system of parallel lines to coordinate its various perspectives. So the scientific idea that to be actual is to be measurable is clearly too limited.

Note that projective geometry is logically a more general system than metrical geometries. The latter are derived from projective geometry by first introducing a parallel postulate and then by establishing which of the known parallel postulates apply.

But projective geometry itself is derived from a time-space relation that is even more general and fundamental. Whitehead refers to it as "the extensive continuum." The extensive continuum is a time-space relation in which regions are defined, but points and lines are not. In fact, Whitehead goes to considerable length to demonstrate that he can, by a process he calls "extensive abstraction,"[13] identify elements of the extensive continuum that can function as points and lines. While Whitehead's logical exposition of this continuum is quite technical, we can get an intuitive sense of it by assuming the meaning of a "region," and then by defining the extensive continuum as a relationship among regions such that

- Every region is extended over by other regions and itself extends over other regions.
- The relation of extension is transitive, such that if region A extends over region B, and region B extends over region C, then region A extends over region C.

---

[13] Whitehead discusses this method in *An Inquiry Concerning the Principles of Natural Knowledge*, pp. 101–09 and *Process and Reality*, pp. 294–333.

- If region A extends over region C, then there is a region B such that A extends over B and B extends over C.
- If there are two regions A and B, there is a region C that extends over both.[14]

These extensive properties are intrinsic to our usual thinking about space. From the extensive continuum we can derive a projective geometry by defining (or by deriving through extensive abstraction) points and lines. We can derive all metrical geometries from projective geometry by adding the relevant parallel postulate. As I'll explain further below, within the extensive continuum we can include the worlds experienced in those lucid dreams and out-of-body experiences that closely mimic waking life, as well as the in the continuum of waking life itself.

The important point, for our purposes, is that once we have articulated the properties of the extensive continuum we open up the possibility of considering time-space relations that are not continual at all but are what I call "non-extensive networks." In this case, the smooth properties that define a continuum are absent, and the connections among the actual occasions involved are rather more like the connections among computers on a peer-to-peer-network. In such a network, each computer is *potentially* contiguous to any other, but is actually in communication with some subset of the others in any given moment. Such a network would emerge if the second, third, and fourth propositions, which we used to define an extensive continuum above, did not apply. As discussed in Chapter 8, this is likely to be the type of time-space relation found in the mental world. In the vital world—where we experience actuality as various entities arrayed around us—we seem to be operating in more of a continuum. However, there are certain ways in which the vital worlds also have network-like properties.

It will be easier to understand the implications of non-extensive networks if we discuss them in terms of waking memory.

- The time-space relation of waking memory is not extensive. Region A can extend over region B, and region B can extend

---

[14] Note that these propositions, as stated, are not sufficiently technical to be logically adequate. For a fuller presentation of the actual propositions involved see the pages referenced in the previous footnote.

over region C, but region A does not extend over region C. For example, I remember the event of my twenty-fifth birthday, and on that birthday I recalled the words of a popular song sung by one my guests. Today, I cannot remember those words. I can remember an event during which I had a certain memory, without having that same memory now.

- In waking memory, it is not always possible to find a region between two other regions. This is exemplified in "recovered" memories, as in, "Something happened to me a long time ago, and I have forgotten it." Then, later, with the proper stimulus, the memory returns. I now have a direct memory of something that happened long ago, without having a memory of having remembered it at any point between now and then. In logical language, if region A extends over region C, then there *may or may not be* a region B, such that A extends over B and B extends over C.

- In waking memory, it is not always possible to find a moment in which two earlier memories are both present. When I am in a "bad mood," I may have certain memories of depressing events that I never remember when I am in a "good mood," and vice versa. Again, in logical language, if there are two regions A and B, there *may or may not be* a region D that extends over both.

Because memories are organized in a network way, we usually think of them as "merely subjective." But, as discussed earlier, in this new metaphysical approach, memories are direct, actual objectifications of past events in the present. We know that memories have definite causal effects in waking life and that, in many cases, the effect happens precisely when the memory occurs. For example, I am driving across town to a meeting, when I suddenly remember that I left the directions at home. This forces me to turn around. The memory was objectified in the moment of being remembered, and was not causally effective until that event.

Thus only certain very restricted portions of our experience—those that come through our waking physical senses—are entirely ordered by an extensive time-space relation. Our memory, for example, is not so ordered.

If we assume that actuality is a creative advance of causally interacting drops of experience (actual occasions), then we have no basis on which to deny actuality to the spaces we experience in alternative states of consciousness. A dream, no less than a moment of waking experience, consists of causally interacting drops of experience. The main differences between dreams and waking life are, first, the enduring entities in dreams are more variable in their behaviors than those in waking life; and second, the relations between them are more complex and are not subject to uniform relations of metrical distance. We can account for these differences by realizing that the occasions making up the enduring entities in dreams are of a higher grade than occasions making up the physical (inorganic) world, and that they are, by their causal interactions, defining a time-space relation that is not part of the extensive continuum of waking life.

Our fixation on extensive continua is very much a function of what Jean Gebser[15] calls the "mental mutation" of consciousness—which is to say the structure of consciousness that has obtained since the "Athenian Miracle" in approximately 500 BCE.[16] This mutation, which brought us literacy, is correlated with extreme privileging of the visual sense.

It is interesting to note that each sensory mode has its own peculiar relationship to the actual world. Touch, taste, and smell are involved in direct participation with the surrounding actuality. They rely on immediate proximity, and they convey variations of intensity, but they inform us very poorly about distance. Hearing, especially because we hear in stereo, gives us some sense of outer direction and some sense of distance. But only vision gives a clear, precise, and potentially measurable sense of direction and distance. Notice too that in taste,

---

[15] See Gebser, *The Ever-Present Origin.*
[16] The "Athenian Miracle" refers to the cultural efflorescence of ancient Athens, during which the foundations of our current mentally structured civilization were established.

smell, and hearing, distinction between objects is weak. Different sensa belonging to different objects can easily be experienced as occupying the same time-space region. For example, many sounds can come from the same place. But the visual field is clearly tessellated by distinct, non-overlapping regions, and it is possible, within these regions, to bring attention to smaller and smaller regions up to the limits of our discrimination. Thus our privileging of sight leads to our idea that the "outer" world is dominated by relations of extension. As Gebser demonstrates in detail, earlier mutations of consciousness (for example, the "magical," which accompanied hunting and gathering, and the "mythic," which accompanied village agriculture) privileged hearing and speaking over vision, and thus made less use of extension in defining the outer world.

The privileging of sight, and our heavy reliance on the extensive relations characteristic of the visual field has led us to a major discovery: that the time-space relation conditioning causal relations in the *physical* world is extensive. Indeed, it is metrically geometrical, so that it permits measurement. But this does not mean that all actuality is extensive and metrical in the same way.

In fact, I would like to suggest that we—the high-grade occasions making up our personalities—do not relate to the world through the same time-space relation that suffices for inorganic occasions. Rather, our time-space relation to actuality is more complex.

To make this clear, I want to say something about the nature of the perceptual process in terms of an ontology of actual occasions. Remember, we are regarding the flow of energy in the universe as a transmission of experience through the creative advance. My sense organs experience the past experiences of actual occasions in the environment outside my body. Then the experiences of the sense organs are transmitted through the cellular occasions of the nervous system. These occasions are ordered into a hierarchy of grades, and, as the flow of experience proceeds up the hierarchy, the original sensory experiences are synthesized and interpreted. Eventually, some high-grade occasion performs a final synthesis for each sensory modality. For example, these are what Buddhist psychologists call the "eye consciousness," the "ear consciousness," and so on. In each moment, the high-grade occasions synthesizing the various sensory consciousnesses are objectified in me.

At this moment, for example, the visual picture I see of the surrounding world is the objectification in me of what my eye consciousness experienced a split second ago. But where am I? Where is the mental-grade occasion of experience that is me in any given moment of waking perception?

At this moment, here I am experiencing my eye consciousness— which has ordered its perception of the world in terms of a metrical geometry. I also have my other sense consciousnesses—each of which has its own distinctive way of ordering the world. And I have my memories, which order the world in a network way, and include memories of dreams and, possibly, of lucid dreams and out-of-body-experiences— none of which took place anywhere in the physical world. So *where am I?* Does it really make sense to imagine that I am occupying a position in the metrical space defined by the inorganic occasions in which my body is embedded? It seems more as if I am somewhere outside that world, looking into it *through* my senses. My body is a kind of "avatar"[17] in the physical world through which the occasions of my personality operate. As a high-grade occasion, I have my actual existence in a transphysical world.

Summary

Let's review the main points of this chapter:

- In an ontology of actual occasions each actuality contains or houses the entirety of its causal past. Each occasion, after completing its own concrescence, is then contained in future occasions. Thus, *every actual occasion is an "atom" of time-space*. No neutral time-space exists in its own right as a container for the process of actualization. Beyond actual occasions there is mere nothingness.
- We saw that a systematic relationship exists among actual occasions in any given society (where we consider even our evolving universe as a society of actual occasions). This

---

[17] I am borrowing the word "avatar" from computer gaming, where it refers to the "person" on the screen who represents me and whose actions reflect my decisions. Computer gamers, in turn, borrowed this word from Vedic cosmology, in which a divine avatar is a physical vehicle through which the Divine expresses itself in the historical or evolutionary process.

relationship is the "geometry" of the time-space in that
society, and it functions to do the following:

o   Establish a *causal order* among the relevant occasions,
    enabling them to be sorted into the immediate past
    and into more distant regions of the past
o   Provide a *scheme of indication* enabling the various
    occasions in that society to refer to other particular
    occasions

    ▪   This allows us to indicate—point out—specific
        actualities in the environment. Also, because
        the various occasions involved in perception
        can indicate to one another that they refer to
        the same external actualities, it allows those
        occasions to bind their experiences together
        into a unified whole (as in the synthesis of data
        from various rods and cones in the eyes into
        a single picture, or in the synthesis of various
        sensory modalities into a single presented
        image of the surrounding world).

o   Provide each new occasion *a position within its region
    of the creative advance*, determining the perspective
    of that occasion on its world
o   Govern the *attenuation of causal efficacy with distance*
    as in, for example, the "inverse square" law governing
    gravitational attraction in Newtonian mechanics,
    which specifies the force of gravity as a function of
    distance

•   We saw that the time-space relation is a restriction on what
    is possible. For example, the four-dimensional continuum
    of relativity theory tells us where and when occasions
    belonging to the physical world can happen. If they take
    place outside that continuum, they are not, by definition,
    part of that world. Eternal objects are by their nature
    possibilities, and logic is a study of the systematic relations
    among eternal objects. We can treat the *time-space relation
    as a logical structure* and explore it using methods of logic
    and mathematics.

- We also saw that *logical systems may be more or less constrained by definitions and axioms.* The greater the numbers of definitions and axioms, the more restricted are the possibilities that structure explores. The less constrained the time-space relation is, the freer it is, and the further it is from the narrowness of physical existence. Meta-geometry (which explores time-space relations that are less constrained than the metrical time-space governing inorganic occasions) maps the geometrical structures of the transphysical worlds.

- We clarified why (classical) *measurement is possible only in a metrical time-space,* in which a parallel postulate is specified. The time-space relation of the inorganic occasions of our cosmic epoch is metrical, which is why physics works so well in the physical world.

- We saw that *projective geometry does not stipulate a parallel postulate,* but that it does define points and lines. This is the time-space relation of perception—in the waking world and in those parts of the transphysical worlds that most resemble the physical.

- We saw too that *extensive geometry defines a particular set of relations among regions* without defining points and lines. It is still more general than projective geometry.

- And we saw that *non-extensive networks trace networks of relations among occasions and that these networks of relations are not smooth and continuous* in the way that extensive relations are. Non-extensive networks function between occasions in memory, and in many dreams that are too strange to remember clearly upon awakening. Interactions among occasions in most transphysical worlds define network geometries.

- Furthermore, we saw that the *human personality* (considered as a personally ordered society of high-grade actual occasions) *inhabits a complex network time-space.* Modern electronic technology can help us to visualize such a network. Imagine that our consciousness was embodied in a machine with the capacity to send and receive multiple streams of electromagnetic energy (for example, communicating via radio signals the way cell phones do). We could then be in contact with various other entities, none of whom would necessarily be in contact with each other. A world such as this would be quite different from our world, but there is no metaphysical reason why such a world is impossible. It is in the context of non-extensive network geometries that certain occasions in our past need not be felt, or positively prehended, in the present.

- We noted that the *time-space of visual experience is extensive and projective*, and that the time-space of physics is a framework for coordinating various perspectives into a shared world—that it is an extensive, metrical, geometrical continuum. But this is *not the time-space of experience as a whole*. Waking experience comprehends the various time-space relations characterizing the various senses, as well as the network time-space of memory, imagination, and dream.

Waking life, in what Jean Gebser called the mental mutation of consciousness, is characterized by a decisive privileging of the objectification of visual consciousness. Gebser and others suggested that we are moving into a new mutation of consciousness, less hypnotized by visual representation. The ideas presented in this chapter describe time-space in ways that are compatible with the new or emerging "integral mutation" of consciousness, as Gebser defined it.

In this and previous chapters, I have laid the groundwork for a new metaphysical model that makes the idea of transphysical worlds intelligible, if not, indeed, plausible. Building on this in the next chapter I will focus specifically what it means to be a human being, or a human personality, inhabiting the transphysical worlds.

Chapter 10: Transphysical Humans

Up to this point, we have approached the topic of a new metaphysics from the bottom up—beginning with a definition of actual occasions and then seeing how to build an understanding of reality that not only includes the physical world familiar to science but also explains the existence of transphysical worlds. In this chapter, I will approach the subject from a different perspective—starting from our everyday waking experience and discussing what we call common sense.

In the modern era, conditioned by the ideas of the European enlightenment, the standard view of reality is based on two basic and, for the most part, unquestioned assumptions. First, that the physical world is the whole of the actual world; and second, that the physical world is vacuous—that it is not conscious, has no aim, and has no value for itself.

Following Whitehead, I reject both of these assumptions as fundamentally incoherent, mainly because they impel modern philosophy and science into the impasse of the mind-body problem and the quicksand of modern epistemology. If we view the world through the lens of those two metaphysical assumptions, we are effectively forced to conclude that we can never truly know anything about reality. Consciousness, and with it, knowledge, becomes incomprehensible at best and impossible at worst.

Clearly, we need a new set of basic metaphysical assumptions. And that is what we are exploring in this book.

These new metaphysical ideas are admittedly radical—necessarily so, if we are to come to terms with the phenomena of consciousness, survival of the personality after death, and reincarnation. However, just as relativity theory embraced and expanded on Newtonian physics, the model of a transphysical world that I am proposing includes, while transcending, the ideas of scientific materialism. Newton's mechanics can be abstracted from relativity theory by ignoring velocities that are "too high." In the same way, materialism can be abstracted from this new metaphysics by ignoring actual occasions whose grades are "too high." The point I want to emphasize from the start is that materialism does express important truths, but these are a subset of a larger body of truths illuminated by this new metaphysical system that embraces both the physical and transphysical worlds. *There is no fundamental contradiction or incompatibility between these two systems.*

My starting point, therefore—and I believe this must be the starting point of any successful and comprehensive cosmology—is to reject the notion of vacuous actuality. Reality, all that exists, consists of *actual occasions,* and each actual occasion is necessarily and intrinsically sentient.

Each of us, in each moment of our existence, is an actual occasion. We actually exist at this moment in time. There is nothing mysterious or obscure about an actual occasion—it is precisely the type of thing that you are in each moment of your stream of being. Each of us is purposeful, thoughtful, imaginative, volitional, and decisive. We know for certain that we are actual (because, as Descartes so dramatically demonstrated, to doubt or deny our own actuality is to affirm it). Given this, we can and do posit ourselves as paradigm examples of actual entities.

Taking this process view as our starting point, we open the way for a profound rethinking of the subject-object relationship. We no longer think of subjects and objects as two distinct kinds of things. Everything that actually exists is both subject and object—a subject *for itself,* and an object for others. From the perspective of process metaphysics, we can now see the distinction between subject and object as a *temporal* difference. Actual occasions are subjective during the process of actualization, and, having actualized, they become objects for future subjects. Philosopher Christian de Quincey referred to this new process view of the mind-body relationship as "past matter, present mind."[1] Subjects exist *now,* in the present moment. However, as soon as the present moment is complete, the subject expires and becomes an *object in the past*, which can then be apprehended by subjects that exist in the new present moment. Each moment of our existence is the formation of a new event, and that event is an object for future subjects.

Once we base our metaphysics on the assumption of intrinsically sentient actual entities, the hoary mind-body problem is resolved. We see that mind (subject) and matter (substance) are related as *phases in process,* not as radically different things interacting in space. Contrast this new, commonsense view of reality—based on our own intimate experience—with the standard materialist alternative. If we begin with the assumption that actual entities (e.g., atoms) are vacuous and insentient then it becomes impossible to coherently account for the existence of conscious beings like us. Yes, to a great extent, materialist metaphysics can account for the behavior of inorganic entities, such as atoms and molecules. But materialism fails, utterly, to account for the nature and behavior of entities like us who can appreciate value, make choices, and decide on actual outcomes. If the materialists were right, and if we were nothing but automatic interactions of dead atoms, how could it be that we are sentient?

To avoid this impasse I follow Whitehead, and I propose that atoms and molecules—indeed, all actual entities—are just like us, though with varying degrees of sentience, purpose, intentionality, volition, and choice. Once we have made this move, we have entered into a new ontology, a new understanding of being itself and a new and vastly expanded cosmology.

Both process metaphysics and quantum mechanics tell us that matter is a dynamic texture of events. But do they both reveal the same *kinds* of events? On the face of it, the answer would appear to be no.

---

[1] See *Radical Nature,* pp. 215–38, for an accessible summary of key ideas in Whitehead's process metaphysics.

The events studied by quantum physics reveal nothing but inorganic, low-grade matter—so low-grade that most practicing scientists assume such matter is thoroughly insentient. However, a very different species of events is revealed in our own experience: the events that constitute our ongoing stream of embodied consciousness. Clearly, these high-grade events are altogether different. Human beings are not at all like electrons or protons—even though our bodies are made up of those subatomic events. In short, living matter is radically different from inorganic matter.

Given this obvious distinction, we may ask, "How are these two kinds of matter, these different species of events, related?" In the context of materialism, we can give no adequate answer to this question. In this book, I have been proposing that reality consists of a hierarchy of events—from those with minimal awareness (in the subatomic realm), to events with varying degrees of awareness throughout the living world, all the way up to the self-reflective awareness of humans and other higher animals, and quite possibly beyond the human and animal realm into domains explored by the great yogis and mystics.[2]

It follows that we can interpret the world in terms of different grades of matter that vary in the degree of their conscious, purposeful participation in the creative advance. I first came across this general cosmological vision in the work of the theosophical movement. Whatever their failings might have been, the theosophists succeeded in developing and delivering a compelling cosmology that surpassed in its comprehensiveness and inclusiveness the prevailing cosmology inspired by scientific materialism.

Theosophical Cosmology

Theosophists tried to express the notion of grades of matter, where each grade constituted its own world or "plane." However, they attempted to distinguish between different levels of grade by relying on the physical notion of "density." They spoke about a hierarchy in which solid matter was at the base level, then liquid and gas, and then four more levels of physical matter, and then, above that, seven higher planes of matter,

---

[2] Sri Aurobindo, *Synthesis of Yoga.*

each with its own seven subdivisions.[3] This whole hierarchy of different sorts of matter is supposed to vary continuously in its density. They also tried to locate the transphysical worlds in a "fourth dimension." Since then, the notion of density has been replaced by "frequency," where the "higher realms" are imagined as operating at higher frequencies and higher energies.[4] In contemporary New Age circles, metaphors of frequency and dimension tend to dominate discussions of transphysical worlds.

Attempts to define or describe transphysical worlds in the language of physics are philosophically naïve. In this work, I offer a new, more robust metaphysical treatment of the transphysical worlds. For example, rather than defining higher matter in terms of frequency or density, I propose that higher matter is more profoundly animated by imagination and thought than lower-grade matter. This formulation, I believe, accounts far more adequately for the experiences on which our knowledge of the transphysical world is based.

And rather than referring to "higher dimensions" to account for the "where" of the transphysical worlds, I propose that we account for the transphysical worlds in terms of meta-geometries that are less restrictive than the metrical geometry of physical space, irrespective of how many dimensions space may have.

Talk of "meta-geometries" can sound abstract and remote from the concerns of daily life. I want to bring metaphysics back down to Earth, therefore, by describing our familiar experience in terms of these ideas. Note that in this discussion in particular—and in this book in general—I am parsing the hierarchy of material into three grades: physical, vital, and mental.

Different Kinds of Material

We can understand the material of our own bodies and the world around us in different ways. For example, following modern science, we tend to think of our bodies as "out there" in the physical world; at the

---

[3] Alice Bailey, *A Treatise on Cosmic Fire*.

[4] If we interpret "frequency" to be a measure of the "cycle time" of actual occasions, then in terms of transphysical process metaphysics, the *higher* the grade of an occasion, the *lower* its frequency will be. This is quite the opposite of usual New Age ways of speaking.

same time, we also experience our bodies from "in here." But given this scientific understanding, the exact nature of the relationship between our bodies and our experience is shrouded in deep confusion.

How, exactly, could we have a conscious inner experience of a body that is entirely devoid of, and outside, experience?

In the new way of understanding as outlined in this book, our bodies are composed of dual-aspect actual occasions that are causally effective on the outside and drops of experience on the inside. Furthermore, the transmission of energy among these actual occasions involves the partial reproduction of the experience of earlier occasions in the experience of later occasions. Our bodily experience is our partial reproduction of the experiences of the occasions that make up our bodies.

Try this exercise: Describe to yourself what it feels like to have a body. Note that even with eyes closed, you can still feel and roughly distinguish different locations in your body. We could say that the body is an inner time-space. Now describe to yourself the time-space inside your body and the difference between this and the time-space outside your body. Feel where in your body "you" are most centered. How does the time-space around you feel compared to the time-space at the periphery of your body? Now imagine every center of intensity in the time-space of your body as a living consciousness. Imagine the time-space of your body as a communion of conscious events.

Keeping this experience in mind, let's now explore the various kinds of actual occasions that make up our bodies and the worlds in which they exist.

Inorganic Actual Occasions

We know how to identify and locate inorganic occasions. Our civilization has developed extraordinary mastery of physical occasions. But now let's look more closely at physical occasions from our new point of view.

Some of our bodily organs are, or come close to being, inorganic occasions; for example, the outer parts of our bones, our fingernails, tooth enamel, or strands of hair. Our relationship to these parts of our bodies is somewhat ambiguous. On the one hand we identify them as parts of us, but on the other, because we cannot feel what happens to them, they seem somewhat external to us. Hair is a good example because it is midway between being an actual body part and a piece of clothing. It is by virtue of these inorganic bodily components that we participate in the inorganic world around us. Not only do our organs have inorganic parts, so does each individual cell in our bodies—these are, for example, macromolecules such as proteins, DNA, and lipids.[5] If I want to grasp a physical object, I move my hand in such a way that the molecules of my skin cells bump up against the molecules of that object.

Vital Matter

Suppose I were to say, "Imagine a mountain, and fill in as many details as you possibly can." In carrying out this task, you would construct an image. You might start from a memory, or you might give yourself freedom to make up any part of the picture. In any case, there would be a kind of work going on as the image formed. In terms of our new ontology, this is an example of working with *imaginal*, or vital, occasions.

When we work with vital occasions (or "imaginal matter"), we don't use our hands. Rather, we work with vital occasions by making decisions and applying our will. For this reason, our relationship to vital occasions is more intimate than is our relation to physical occasions. We think of vital occasions as somehow internal to ourselves, whereas we think of physical occasions as somehow external. And yet, our imaginal work is a crucial link between us and the physical world.

When we use our hands to interact with physical occasions, particularly if we are being attentive and deliberate, we first imagine what we want our hands to do, and then our hands do it. Suppose, for example, I to ask you to raise your right arm so that it is parallel to the floor. You would hear theses words and get a sense of what I am asking. Then you would decide whether or not to cooperate with me and then, and only then, would your arm rise. Our manual habits are formed under the direction of active attention and imagination, and even our inherited habits reflect the creativity and careful attention of our evolutionary ancestors. The conclusion here is that before we

---

[5] We do refer to the study of proteins, DNA, and lipids as "organic chemistry." This is because these molecules (and other complex molecules) are important physical constituents of living beings. In this essay, however, I am reserving the word "organic" to refer to individual cells and to multicellular beings.

can work with physical occasions, we must first work with imaginal occasions. In an important sense, vital occasions mediate between our minds and physical bodies. In order to move our physical bodies, we must first move our vital bodies.

Vital occasions not only allow us to move our bodies in ways we find interesting and useful, they enable us to perceive the world as we do. To get a sense of this, think about the physical world as the one explored by physics. It is a collection of inorganic, low-grade events in systematic patterns of causal interaction. The physical world may take the form of suns, planets, rocks and so forth, but the low-grade events that embody these forms are not aware of those forms. For example, the atoms in a rock seem to be intent on maintaining their own stability by maintaining a steady relationship with their neighboring atoms, but do not seem to act as if they know about the role of the rock in the larger geological situation. We, on the other hand, recognize the rock as a relatively enduring entity, and, further, we recognize the rock as a factor in the general geological situation. We apprehend the physical world very differently from the way events constituting the physical world apprehend themselves. We can do that because our direct experiences of the physical world are interpreted by the vital occasions involved in our nervous systems. In a sense, the vital occasions involved in our physical bodies clothe the inorganic world with rich and meaningful images that are intrinsic to their own mode of functioning.

Vital occasions mediate between our minds and the physical world, clothing the abstract structures of the physical world with imaginally meaningful forms, allowing us to instruct our bodies by imagining what we want them to do.

Nevertheless, this analysis should not lead us to think that all vital occasions exist only as the "interiors" of physical bodies. When we dream, lucidly or otherwise, and when we have out-of-body experiences, we find ourselves interacting with other beings who also have *vital* bodies but may or may not have physical bodies. Even in the waking world, we experience disembodied vital beings having noticeable effects—as in ostensible cases of possession, channeling, or other supernormal modes of functioning.

Mental Actual Occasions

Mental occasions are the "stuff" of thinking. Conscious thoughts are the experiences of the high-level actual occasions that form part of our personalities. Again, this is an unfamiliar idea, yet we all know how difficult it can be to work in the realm of thought. Sometimes we can intuit a mental pattern, yet it can take time and concentration to crystallize that pattern into a clear proposition. This is why a great deal of effort often precedes an "aha" moment—when the pattern seems to fall spontaneously into place as an insight.

Vital occasions are more responsive to intentions than physical occasions, and mental occasions are even more responsive. However, thinking is not entirely amenable to our volition. It has a kind of inertia, so that even when we realize that one of our habitual ways of thinking is somehow incorrect, our minds easily slip back into old patterns. And anyone who has tried to formulate new thoughts to answer questions that have not been answered before knows just how stubbornly mental entities can hold on to the eternal objects to which they have become accustomed.

Mental occasions do not occur only in our own bodies. We experience thoughts that seem to just float into our minds. An attentive observer may notice that our ability to comprehend certain ideas is enhanced by the presence of certain other individuals. It is as if these people "radiate" a kind of illumination from their mental occasions, and the mental occasions of our own bodies are affected by it.

As we consider the various grades of occasions making up our bodies, it is useful to recall that the higher the grade, the less abstraction in objectification occurs between entities at that grade. In other words, the higher the grade of the occasions involved in any causal interaction, the more deeply and fully they know each other.[6]

As noted earlier, low-grade, inorganic entities act as if they are almost entirely external to each other so that, for many purposes, they can be treated as little Newtonian "BBs" that merely collide with each other. As a result, we cannot really identify with the inorganic components of our bodies. (Of course, we do influence these low-grade entities through our empathic and telepathic interactions with the cells of which they form

---

[6] In the language of Teilhard de Chardin, the higher the grade of the occasions involved the more "radial" and the less "tangential" are their interactions.

a part. Also, in some rather unusual circumstances, we may directly psychokinetically influence those low-grade entities.)

By contrast, the vital entities in our bodies are empathically bonded with each other. For example, if I have an ache in my shoulder, my entire body will suffer empathically with the distressed cells in my shoulder. We could imagine the inside of the human body as a pool of empathy isolated from other vital matter by the ocean of inorganic occasions in which it is immersed. Note that to the extent that we can *feel* our bodies we can identify with them, and to the extent that we can identify with them they respond to our intentions.

Finally, the mental entities in our bodies are telepathically bonded with each other. They share each other's thoughts. They are so close to each other that it is easy for us to identify the whole mass of our mental occasions or "matter" as a single "me." Only sustained attention, such as that exercised in certain forms of meditation and psychotherapy, allows the various mental selves that make up our personalities to be distinguished from each other.

Multiple Levels of Self

Remember, my purpose in this book is to provide a robust metaphysical foundation for understanding the full range of human experience, including psi phenomena in general, and (more specifically) the data that indicate survival of consciousness after death, and subsequent reincarnation. How, then, might we explain the survival of postmortem personality in relation to embodiment?

Having conducted a brief phenomenological survey of different types or levels of material, we will now examine a diagram of human personality and its various levels of embodiment.

The large upper, central circle in Figure 4 represents our self, our basic dominant personality, the one we usually engage the world with— our "ego." Technically, it is a personally ordered sequence of actual occasions expressing our personality from moment to moment.

However, this conscious ego is not all of who we are. We also have (mostly unconscious) subpersonalities of various kinds. For example, when we lose our temper, a different subpersonality is expressed—and later on we may declare, "Oh, that wasn't me; I didn't mean it." We all know what that is like.

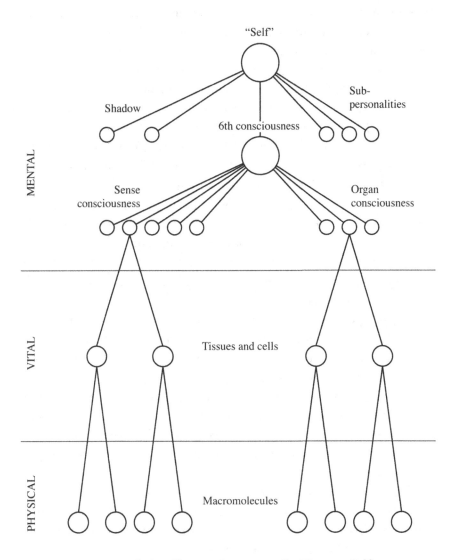

Figure 4: An Abstract Diagram of a Human Self

Anyone who has trained in this aspect of psychology can watch people shifting in and out of different personalities as their mood changes. In a bad mood people act one way; in a good mood they act another way. Each one of these systems of behavior constitutes a "subpersonality." In some forms of psychotherapy, therapists disentangle the subpersonalities, give them names, and help them communicate with each other. When successful, it leads to personality integration. Some of our subpersonalities are well integrated, and we are comfortable with them. Others we resist and suppress, and these form our "shadows," the parts of ourselves we don't like.

Our everyday self is a collection of these subpersonalities. Each truly is a personality in the sense that each is a sequence of actual occasions organized with personal order. These are actual, enduring entities in the mental level of the transphysical world.

These subpersonalities have their own lives in the vital and mental worlds—sometimes even in the waking world. This becomes clear in cases of dissociative identity disorder in which one subpersonality (or, perhaps, several subpersonalities working together) takes control of the waking self. The everyday ego becomes just one among multiple subpersonalities, and loses its dominant place. Any of these different subpersonalities can take over, and each has its own quite different memory stream. Sometimes, different subpersonalities in the same body don't remember each other. Or they might remember one, but not another personality. Dissociative identity disorder is intricate and labyrinthine, but it shows us that these personalities are separable. I am suggesting that they all have the ontological status of enduring societies of actual occasions in the mental world.

And this leads to three interesting questions: What is the relationship between these subpersonalities and the dominant personality that seems to be the central self? When a subpersonality takes control, what does it take over? What is the central entity these subpersonalities struggle to dominate?

Regarding the relationship between them, I suggest that the subpersonalities, like the macromolecules in a cell, are an embodiment of one, highest-grade occasion in the human person—and that is the particular personality I usually refer to as "me" or "I." This idea is theoretically appealing since it both does justice to our sense of ongoing continuity, and to our sense of the shifts and transformations that our personalities undergo. However, this is just a suggestion, because my own introspection cannot clearly distinguish that single, dominant, personality from the others that I detect. Sometimes it seems to me that the role of the dominant personality shifts from one subpersonality to another. For the time being, I will assume that the ongoing self is a single, personally ordered society; however, when we come to discuss reincarnation in the next chapter, we will also explore the possibility of a more fluid and discontinuous human identity.

As to the second question, I suggest that the central entity over which the subpersonalities struggle is what Buddhists call the "sixth sense" or "manas." I am proposing that there is a personally ordered society of actual occasions—distinct from any of the subpersonalities we have been discussing so far—that functions as the central organizing intelligence for the body. It receives reports from all the sense consciousnesses (eye, ear, nose, tongue, body), from the organs, each one of which has its own intelligence (which is also mental because we feel with our heart and we think with our belly), and from other miscellaneous consciousnesses. For example, most of us have an innate "savant" that can instantaneously compute trajectories. If somebody throws a ball at us we can catch it—a complex cognitive function we perform almost instantaneously and unconsciously. We have many such functional subpersonalities.

This "sixth sense" or central consciousness receives reports from the collection of sense consciousnesses, organ consciousnesses, and semiautonomous savant consciousnesses (such as the one that computes trajectories) and forms a kind of central "control panel" for the body. The various subpersonalities compete over who is going to have a privileged relationship with this "sixth consciousness."

I want to emphasize that each one of these subpersonalities has a life of its own and is an entity in its own right. We are all collections of such entities. At the mental level, these entities exchange information among themselves, which is to say they have causal effects on each other telepathically.

Take for example, our "eye consciousness." I am proposing that your eye is its own conscious being. You can very easily test this: just tell your eyes not to blink. Very soon you will experience the autonomy of your eye consciousness.

To be sure, eye consciousness is willing to accept a certain level of direction—it will look now this way and now that way—but beyond a certain point it expresses its own intentions or preferences. We know from scientific studies that the operation of seeing is extremely sophisticated. Multiple rods and cones in our eyes see different colors and shapes, and these inputs are transmitted along the nervous system until, somehow or other, we compose a picture of the world.

Even if we challenge the rods and cones theory, we still know that as we perceive the world it is already "chunked;" the world comes to me "prepackaged." I look out my window and see trees and houses and clouds. I didn't do that chunking. I did not analyze the raw data of sensation into a picture of a world already sorted out in various categorized ways. Something else did that. Some embodied intelligence within me assembled a coherent image of the world. I then receive that picture telepathically from the consciousness of that particular "hidden chunk."

My eye consciousness is actually in telepathic contact with all of my other senses, with my various organs and their moods, and with the autonomous savant consciousnesses mentioned previously. They all communicate with each other and conspire in creating the visual impression that is then telepathically communicated to the sixth consciousness, and, from there, to me. I, in turn, communicate telepathically to my manas, which then tell my eye consciousness where to look or suggest certain categories of things to look for.

All our subpersonalities have direct access to our manas, our "sixth sense" and sometimes directly to the various sense consciousnesses and to our motor consciousnesses. Sometimes one of these subpersonalities will send a message to my voice box, and I will find myself uttering something I didn't want it to say. We call such moments "Freudian slips."

In this chapter, I am trying to give you a feeling for the human body and the human self as a host of intelligences of various grades, interacting non-sensorily with each other. At the vital level, each one of the sense consciousnesses is embodied in various tissues and various cells, and so forth. In the diagram below, these are represented (in a vastly simplified way) by the circles at the vital level. These, in turn, are embodied in systems of macromolecules at the physical level (represented in the diagram by the dotted circles on the physical level). Throughout this complex of relationships, telepathic and empathic communication is happening all the way up and all the way down.

This is a new way to understand and experience what it means to be human. It is in radical contrast to what we learn from materialistic science, which tells us that, from my head down to my cells, my molecules, and my atoms, it's all basically dead stuff. Somehow, all of these non-conscious automatic events are funneled to my brain and then some miracle takes place whereby the electro-chemical activity in my brain is transformed all at once into an experience. This is a standard summary of the scientific "explanation" for consciousness offered by materialists. However, it is fundamentally incoherent. It makes no sense whatsoever. It explains nothing.

Yes, we know from physiology that every rod and cone in the eye picks up something specific, like a certain color, shape, or edge. Let's accept that. But we still have to explain how these little impressions (redness, straightness, or whatever) can be integrated into a whole picture of the world. How is that possible? How are the separate bits of information bound together?

If my perception of the world is reduced to nothing but electrical impulses, and if those electrical impulses are all that is transmitted through my nervous system, I don't see how it would ever be possible to reassemble an image of the world from those nervous impulses. It's a "Humpty Dumpty" problem.

But now let's look at this in terms of process metaphysics. I am proposing a more coherent, if more complex, explanation. I am saying that we are living (vital) and intelligent (mental) entities all the way up and all the way down. Can we reconcile this panpsychist view with what we know from physiology?

Let's say that each nerve ending in my eyeball is (in each moment of its existence) organized by an actual occasion. And since every actual occasion takes in the whole universe, then each actual occasion in my eyeball takes in the whole universe.

Because the interests of the actual occasion organizing a cell in my eyeball are highly influenced by my aim, the cell will pay attention to significant forms such as color and shape. When that occasion objectifies in me, I will prehend it as that color or shape. Insofar as a sensory cell functions prehensively for me, it performs an act of abstraction. However, in contrast to the standard story of physiology, the nerve cells do not transmit electrical impulses alone. On the contrary, I am proposing that the nerve cells transmit an experience of the *whole world* in which, say, a color is highlighted. Another cell then passes on an experience of the whole world in which a shape is highlighted … and so on. Because they are all perceptions of the entire world, they can each be coordinated and synthesized into a coherent composite appearance.

The nervous system, therefore, transmits not only electrical impulses—it transmits *experiences*. The idea of an electrical impulse flowing through the nervous system is an *abstraction* from what is really happening. Carried along with that electrical impulse is a flow of feelings, an empathic and telepathic transmission of experience that is then built up into a complex appearance of the world as it travels through the body. All of these different experiences, each of which is an experience of the whole world, highlighting some different abstraction from it, can be assembled into a picture that is then synthesized by my sixth-sense consciousness and transmitted telepathically to my dominant personality.

Admittedly, this is an entirely novel understanding of physiology. Its great advantage, however, is that it transforms and solves the perennial mind-body problem. It does not try to explain experience according to a mathematical computational model. Perception is accounted for instead by the transmission of experience. In fact, in this new model, all *energy is the transmission of experience* from actual occasion to actual occasion.

We can trace electrical energy going through the nervous system but that is simply a physical accompaniment to the transmission of experience. This transmission of experience allows us to have continuity with our own past. The person I was a moment ago is telepathically and empathically flowing into the person I am now. That is the way the experience of the world is transmitted through my body up to my dominant consciousness.

In Figure 5, I have simplified my already abstract representation of people by showing just the mental body, the vital body, and the physical body. I have also shown two different embodied humans.

Let's say we had two different human beings side by side. Ordinarily, we would imagine that if Person 1 thinks something and wants to communicate it to Person 2, the process (simplified) would be somewhat as follows: The thought (at the mental level) would be transmitted down through the body (vital level) and then spoken out into the air (physical level). Next, Person 2 hears the air vibrations (physical level), and this triggers events in the nervous system (vital level), which are, in turn, transmitted up to his or her mind (mental level). This is represented by the dotted line in the diagram.

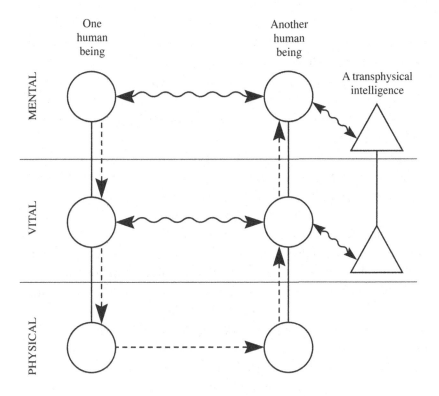

Figure 5: Pathways of Human Communication

Now, while this kind of communication undoubtedly does take place, it is far from complete. Rather than being confined to this *sensory* transmission pathway through physical space, in transphysical process metaphysics communication in the form of causal interactions is occurring simultaneously across *all levels directly.* In other words, even while the sensory channels are operating, there is direct telepathic mind-to-mind communication happening at the mental level, as well as direct empathic body-to-body communication taking place at the vital level. In the diagram, these interactions are represented by the wavy lines.

In addition to all of this, our subpersonalities are carrying on elaborate simultaneous interactions. Furthermore, we can share subpersonalities with each other. For example, I have a friend who is very critical of himself. And that friend, in my psyche, is often critical of me. Perhaps, however, I am sharing his critic with him. We may be sharing a common subpersonality.

We may also feel the influence of disembodied transphysical entities—reported in the case literature as succubi, incubi, angels, demons, disincarnate human beings, and so forth. These can mimic our own subpersonalities. Sometimes we can't tell whether a voice in our head is our own or somebody else's. Sometimes it is obvious, sometimes not. In the diagram, one of these disembodied beings is represented by the linked triangles.

Our bodies *are* our personal unconscious. We are steeped in a multifarious and potent ocean of feelings, emotions, and thoughts that are not "our own." What we normally assume to be "outside" is constantly streaming into and informing what we assume to be our private "inside," and vice versa. In psychology, this field of complex communications is referred to as the "personal unconscious," which is itself embedded in an extended web of the collective unconscious.

I have come to realize that my body is an ocean of intelligence, and I sort of ride or surf on it. This ocean of intelligence is my "unconscious." The more I can bring my own intelligence into effective presence in my body, the more all the various intelligences in my body can be coordinated in my experience and self-expression.

This new way of understanding human existence opens up fascinating horizons for the study of psychology. It also alerts us to the broad sweep of causal effects recognized in transphysical process metaphysics.

To be sure, efficient causal interactions among low-grade actualities constitute the physical world. But transphysical process metaphysics goes further and supplements these causal interactions with three other categories of causal relations:

- Efficient causal relations among medium-grade occasions, uniting the living world in a network of empathy
- Efficient causal relations among high-grade occasions uniting the living world in a network of telepathy
- Final causes, which allow high-grade occasions to bind lower-grade occasions into systems of prehensions, producing the phenomenon of embodiment

We need all of these different causal operations in order to make reincarnation and life after death intelligible.

We have come a long way in our investigation into the new metaphysics. Specifically, we have established the coherence and plausibility of transphysical worlds (in addition to the physical world), and have seen how human beings, while embodied in inorganic entities, nevertheless simultaneously inhabit transphysical vital and mental worlds. Further, we have seen that these transphysical worlds do not depend on (or, in the technical jargon of modern philosophy, are not "supervenient" on) *physical* embodiment. In short, human personalities can exist independently of physical, inorganic atoms and molecules and can, therefore, survive the dissolution of physiological bodies.

What happens then? In the next chapter, we will turn our attention to the age-old idea of reincarnation—and see how the new metaphysics might illuminate the notion that "something" survives death and can be embodied in successive lives.

Chapter 11: Reincarnation

Up to this point I have drawn on transphysical process metaphysics to build a case for the survival of the personality after bodily death. Some form of survival is virtually a given within the worldview I have developed in this book. In this chapter, I will now turn our attention to a related but immensely more knotty issue, reincarnation. Can transpersonal process metaphysics provide a similarly coherent account for the continuity of "something" across multiple lives?

I will start with the assumption that reincarnation does, in fact, take place. In other words, I assume that the life I am now living is somehow intimately tied up with other lives that were lived in the past. But the "how" of my entanglement with past lives is far from clear. And that's what I want to explore here: Just what do we mean by "reincarnation," and what kind of world must we inhabit for it to occur?

From the perspective of transpersonal process metaphysics we can articulate a cosmology in which survival of bodily death in transphysical worlds seems plausible and relatively straightforward. The idea of *survival* grows naturally out of the way in which transphysical cosmology accounts for life in terms of the process I have called embodiment. If, as I have argued, the hierarchical ordering of higher-grade actual occasions accounts for the central subjects of living entities, and for the eager exploration of novel possibilities that makes life into a grand adventure, then it is plausible to assume that a society of higher-grade occasions can, at death, simply cease to be embodied in the physical world while remaining an ongoing personality in the transphysical worlds to which they are native. In this way, too, it makes sense to call the surviving personality the "same" as the physically embodied personality because it retains continuity of memory and purpose with its physically embodied self. *Reincarnation*, however, is far more mysterious.

Many Types of Reincarnation

Dr. Ian Stevenson, a researcher and psychiatrist from the University of Virginia, has produced one of the most comprehensive databases documenting cases of reincarnation in his multivolume work *Cases of the Reincarnation Type.*[1] His data are sufficient to convince anyone who finds reincarnation plausible, to accept it as fact. But his data are not complete. Stevenson's research is based on memories of past lives that surface in young children—memories which have been confirmed by finding people and situations the children report having known in their previous lives. However, children who remember past lives are somewhat rare, and the stories they tell must be, in order to be verifiable, of recent lives lived nearby their current incarnation. Furthermore, the majority of these cases involve a young and violent ending to the previous life. Thus, as precious as Stevenson's data are, there is no reason to assume his cases are typical of "average" reincarnation. Given the assumption that all of us are reincarnations of previous personalities, and given that most people do not die violently during youth, and that most of us do not have childhood memories of previous lives, it seems possible that there exist processes of reincarnation other than the types documented in Stevenson's work.

In this chapter, I hope to explore several possible processes of reincarnation to show how they are intelligible within the framework of transpersonal process metaphysics.

Distinction between Personality Survival and Reincarnation

First, let's clarify the logical distinction between survival and reincarnation. Survival entails the ongoing existence of the transphysical parts of the self after the dissolution of the physical body. It entails that the very same personality that was developed over the course

---

[1] Stevenson, *Cases of the Reincarnation Type*, Vols. I–IV.

of a lifetime, with its memories and its purposes intact, continues to function in transphysical worlds.

However, even if survival is a fact, it does not prove that reincarnation is also a fact. It might be, and I will suggest below it probably *is* the case that the personality that survives bodily death is itself mortal, and in the general case (not the special case explored by Stevenson) dies before any reincarnation takes place. Survival enriches and extends the human life cycle, but it does not logically entail individual reincarnation. Furthermore, it is possible that there can be reincarnation without any personality survival at all (as some Buddhist texts suggest).[2]

An Exploration of the Continuity of the Personality

In this book, I have defined a personality as "a society of actual occasions with personal order." That is, a society of actual occasions that has only one member at a time, and is so arranged that the members of the society follow each other like beads on a string. From this definition, we can derive the five fundamental characteristics of personality that I introduced in the "Preliminary Definitions" chapter at the beginning of this book:

- Consciousness—which entails feeling and free choice
- Causal power in its actual world
- Continuity of memory
- Continuity of purpose
- Identity (which we may or may not be able to establish)

In this chapter, I will focus attention on the exact process by which transpersonal process metaphysics accounts for the continuity of a personally ordered society. This will lead us to pay specific attention to the last three characteristics: continuity of memory, continuity of purpose, and continuity of identity. These three characteristics define personality continuity.

---

[2] See, for example, Buddhaghosa, *The Path of Purification*, p. 451.

Personality versus Self

In order to make the following investigation easier, we need to distinguish between the terms "personality" and "self." Up to this point I have not questioned the assumption that the core of a human existence is a single personality—the highest-grade personality in the human being. When we begin to explore reincarnation, however, we need to question more deeply exactly what we mean by "the core of the human person."

Let's begin with the term "self." The self of an organism includes not just the presiding personality, but all of the personally ordered societies that make up the complex hierarchy of that organism at any one time.

Two Meanings of Continuity

We also need to distinguish between two different meanings of "continuity" that are sometimes conflated but must be distinct if we are to do full justice to the issue of reincarnation. One definition of continuity—dominant in conversations based on scientific common sense—is appropriate to macroscopic physical bodies. In this case, an object is defined as "the same" on two different occasions if (1) it is possible to trace *some* continuity of character between the two occasions, and (2) it is possible to trace an uninterrupted trajectory within the relevant time-space relation between those two occasions. From this point of view, the continued existence of some entity requires an uninterrupted trajectory in time and space.

Process metaphysics, however, permits a broader understanding of personal continuity, where an uninterrupted time-space trajectory is optional. Instead it requires merely an uninterrupted transmission of memory, purpose, and (perhaps) identity. We will examine the contribution of these factors in more depth later; but for now, consider the *Star Trek* process of "beaming up." In that fictional universe, people (and other entities) can get on a platform in one location (say a starship orbiting a planet) and, more or less instantaneously, find themselves in a completely different location (say on the surface of that planet) without having lost continuity of memory, purpose, or identity. Here we have little difficulty grasping a (fictional) situation in which there is continuity of personality without a continuous time-space trajectory linking the various members of the personally ordered societies constituting the relevant self.

This type of continuity is also supported by ideas from quantum mechanics, where the completion of an event is said to leave behind a trace in the field of possibilities described by the Schrödinger wave equation.[3] Because the Schrödinger wave equations are linear, the possibilities left by a particular event do not change over time and may precipitate a new event at any time in the future when the right conditions arise. This enables us to imagine a situation in which a sequence of personally ordered occasions ends at one moment or position in time and space, and then begins again at some other position, removed in both time and space from the position at which the last member of the society expired.

Thus there are two ideas of continuity—one requires a continuous time-space trajectory for personal order. We will call this type "physical continuity." The other requires some kind of continuity of memory, purpose, and identity. We will call this "process continuity." The contrast between these two types of continuity will help clarify the following exploration.

What Binds Members of a Personally Ordered Society?

I have identified the three key criteria for personality survival after bodily death as continuities of purpose, of memory, and possibly, of identity. In the case of reincarnation, we will see that continuity of purpose is crucial (and may even constitute a criterion for ongoing self-identity), but that continuity of memory (or of conscious memory, at least) is not required. If we assume that reincarnation is a general phenomenon, and we know that most of us have no conscious memories of past lives, then we can safely assume that continuity of conscious memory is not a precondition for the continuation of personality from life to life. Let us consider these issues in more detail.

---

[3] The Schrödinger wave equation is a linear function that enables quantum physicists to describe the cloud of possibility that results from any quantum collapse. It will be extensively discussed in any book on quantum physics, including popular ones. See, for example, Nick Herbert, *Quantum Reality*.

Continuity of Aim, Purpose, or "Character"

Let us imagine a personally ordered society and freeze the action just as one of its members completes its concrescence. Let's also assume that this society is the dominant strand of personality in an embodied human being. The just-completed occasion (except in exceptional circumstances) includes in its final satisfaction an expectation that the society to which it belongs will continue on into the future. If I am, for example, walking down a path, I complete one step and fully expect to take another. But we know that my expectation might be foiled. The last step I took might, for a variety of reasons, have been the last step in my life. Between any two moments of human existence, there is a kind of decisive transition—not necessarily a noticeable gap—one occasion has expired into objective immortality, and the next occasion has not yet taken place.

It is in this transitional phase that both Creativity and God (the ultimate ordering factor) are intimately involved. In the last occasion of the series we are imagining, the many became one and were increased by one, thus bringing into being (along with all of the other occasions that are reaching final satisfaction at the same time) a new actual world. Now, Creativity in partnership with the ultimate ordering factor will initiate a new process of concrescence for that actual world, and in order to do so they must specify a position and an aim for the new occasion.

If the ultimate ordering factor decides that the most valuable way to concresce this new actual world does *not* involve a new occasion with the right position and aim to accept the objectification of my last moment, then I will not continue to exist in my current form. In this case, I might awaken in a transphysical world and life after death would commence, while in the waking world my body would die. Or, perhaps my ongoing personality would simply cease to function in the relevant time-space (also leading to the death of the body), only to pick up again at some later position (reincarnation). The point here is that both Creativity and the ultimate ordering factor must cooperate if the personally ordered society of which I am a member will, indeed, continue on into my future.

In the vast majority of cases, personalities endure and we die only once (except for the case of NDEs in which a person may be clinically dead before being revived). Why is that? First, personalities tend to endure when their environments endure with certain important features held relatively constant. For example, the dominant personality in a human self almost invariably continues as long as its body remains functional. The ultimate ordering factor that provides each occasion with its subjective aim is assumed to operate, like all occasions of experience, with an aim at enhancing value in the creative advance. The stream of experience of an embodied personality is varied and lush, and presumably the ultimate ordering factor acts so as to provide subjective aims for new occasions that will prolong and further enrich that value. However, when the relevant circumstances change too much and the body ceases to function, then the body is no longer fit for the embodiment of a high-grade personality and the personality necessarily loses its physical continuity. The same drive at value that ensures the physical continuity of an embodied personality will, presumably, work to encourage the continuation of that personality even after the death of the waking body—hence survival.

In order for a personality to endure through the transition between its constituent occasions, the ultimate ordering factor must provide a subjective aim that is at least very similar to the subjective aim of the just-expired member of the society. Thus, continuity of purpose is intrinsic to continuity of personality. Also, as we saw in chapters 5 and 6, the more similar the initial subjective aims of two occasions are, the more fully the past occasion objectifies in the current one. This is why, for example, I am so intensely intimate with the person I was an instant ago. When Creativity and the ultimate ordering factor provide an appropriate occasion with the appropriate aim and position, then the self with its dominant personality endures. One implication of this is that the continuation of our personalities through the moments of our lives requires the ongoing cooperation of God and the universe.

Dr. Eric M. Weiss

Continuity of Memory

To discuss continuity of memory in this context, we must differentiate between memory as a general phenomenon and conscious memory as it is experienced in the life of a personality.

Memory, as defined in transpersonal process metaphysics, is the same as efficient cause. What scientific thought calls "the transmission of energy through time and space" is, in process metaphysics, called "the transmission of experience through the creative advance," that is, *memory*. In some sense, each actual occasion in the creative advance has some memory of all of the occasions in its causal past.

Personalities, however, remember in a specific sense. The members of personally ordered societies are each objectified with special completeness in the immediately following members. In effect, a personally ordered society is like a tube of easily accessible and highly relevant memories stretching off into the causal past. Note that the memory operating in a personality is never complete. Each moment (except in exceptional circumstances) remembers the immediately preceding moments of its own personality, but as its memories trail off into the past they become, in relation to the present moment, more episodic, more abstract, more fragmentary, and less easily accessible. Finite personalities such as us are conscious only of memories that are in some way relevant to our current moment. Thus, at any given moment we necessarily have both conscious and unconscious memories.[4]

As I noted earlier, I do not need to remember my past lives to be convinced by the data supporting reincarnation. Thus, conscious memory is not a criterion for continuity of consciousness. Unconscious memory, however, is always a criterion of continuity. This is the ongoing causal effect of my own personal past on my developing present moment. From another point of view, unconscious memory is manifested by the fact that *if* memories of past lives are accessed, they will retain some sense of having been "mine."

Now let us examine the conditions under which we might or might

---

[4] Note that I am using what philosopher Christian de Quincey calls the "psychological" meaning of consciousness in which its opposite is held to be the unconscious. This is contrasted with the "philosophical" meaning of the term, in which consciousness is opposed to *non*-consciousness, as in the idea that "dead" matter is non-conscious.

not expect continuity of conscious memory between successive members of a personally ordered society.

Similarity of subjective aim enables greater fullness of causal objectification and, since memory is a causal objectification, fullness of causal objectification is fullness of memory. But fullness of memory is also conditioned by two other factors:

- First, it depends on distance in the relevant time-space relation. The further away in time and space the previous occasion was from a currently concrescing occasion, the less clearly it will be remembered.[5] In other words, the further away an occasion is from the past occasion it is objectifying, the more abstract will be its objectification. Also, the more its aim differs from that of the past occasion it is objectifying, the less causally effective that objectification will be.
- Second, the fullness with which a past memory can objectify itself is a function of resonance (see Chapter 6), which, in the context of memory, we know as "association." Memories present themselves to us when they are relevant to our current situation. This accounts for the particular set of memories that we can access in any particular occasion of experience. For example, when I am depressed, many of my good memories simply disappear. Also, even if my basic subjective aim is similar to the subjective aim under which I functioned as a child, I can remember childhood memories only with difficulty. The person I was as a child was so different from the person I am now that it is difficult for me to find associative pathways that can give me access to those memories. I will discuss this in more detail in a later section when we look at the various modes of reincarnation.

---

[5] Remember that the kind of memory enjoyed by high-grade occasions is not mediated by the metrical space of the physical world but by the type of space-appropriate emotion and thought.

Interim Summary

I have been discussing what happens between two successive occasions of a personally ordered society of actual occasions—between successive moments of a personality. I introduced two preliminary clarifications:

- The distinction between a single strand of personality and the entire human self, which is comprised of a complex hierarchy of such strands
- The relevance of two types of continuity:
  - o Physical continuity—which, like the existence of a physical object, requires a continuous trajectory in its time-space
  - o Process continuity—which is direct continuity between two members of the personality that are not in direct proximity, but are separated by macrocosmic distances in some relevant time-space

I then considered the basic factors that must be present if we are to acknowledge continuity of personality across lifetimes, and we saw that continuity of aim is essential but that continuity of conscious memory is not a prerequisite.

Thus, the continuity of a personality through the creative advance requires *neither* continuity of position (physical continuity) nor conscious memory, but it does require a new occasion with an aim that disposes it to: identify that occasion in the past that was the end of its last existence; receive into itself the expiring aim of its death; take on its purposes as its own; and be especially sensitive to its causal impacts and to any previous embodiments of that personality. The necessary connection that transpersonal process metaphysics sees between successive members of a personality begins to look very much like the Vedic notion of "karma."

A Deeper Examination of Continuity of Aim as "Character" [6]

We have seen that even in order to begin interpreting its world, each actual occasion must have a subjective aim. Earlier, I defined "aim" as a set of values. From another point of view, we could also call the subjective aim the "value character" of an occasion.

"Character," of course, is a vague way of describing personalities, but it is an important one, particularly in the analysis of reincarnation. I would suggest that we define the character of a personality as a function of two factors. First, the character of a personality is a function of the *habits*[7] that personality has formed over time. Behind this, however, is a deeper part of character—*value*—which consists of the pattern of values that inform the way in which the personality responds to its various moments of experience.

Each of us can identify, in ourselves and in others, a characteristic set of values that is a crucial component of character. All of us have some relationship to all possible values, but each of us has a unique way of prioritizing them.[8] Some characters are organized around a single overriding value—be it success, security, power, sensuality, truth, beauty, or goodness. Most characters, though, incorporate a complex and often contradictory set of values with which we muddle through. But each of us has a character in this sense, and this character is a fundamental factor in the uniqueness of our personalities.

---

[6] The ideas in this section were developed in conjunction with Victor Goulet and Josephina Burgos.
[7] The notion of habit can be adequately expressed in the language of transphysical process metaphysics. A habit is built up in a personality where: (1) one or more occasions makes a decision (usually complex) with a subjective form of intense determination; and (2) some adequate number of subsequent occasions in that personality accepts and reaffirms that decision. In this way, the causal power of that decision becomes stronger for subsequent members of the society.
[8] I am assuming here that the various values are differentially prioritized, which implies only one dimension of valuation, more or less. The actual relationships among the values constituting a value character are probably much more complex.

When we look deeply at this character in terms of transpersonal process metaphysics, we see we can abstract from it various layers, each of which has a different source.

First, as an intrinsic contribution from Creativity, each occasion receives an aim for the maximization of value for itself and for its relevant future. This is the character that all occasions share.

Then, from God, or the ultimate ordering factor, each occasion receives an aim, or character, that specifies its character more narrowly. This aim is responsive to the actual world that this particular occasion will concresce. The initial subjective aim can be analyzed into at least three factors:

- The *social aim,* which is contributed to the nascent occasion (through the mediation of the ultimate ordering factor) by the various higher-grade occasions for which the current occasion is to serve as a prehension. For example, the initial subjective aims of all of the occasions in my body are influenced by me as the presiding occasion of my body. In this way, we can account for the remarkable coordination of spontaneities among the various occasions of the body, by virtue of which the body is a single organism.
- Then, in the case of occasions belonging to personalities, there is the *personal aim*, which the occasion inherits from past members of the personality. This personal aim is the evolving set of values that governs the behavior of the personality in question.

A spiritual conversion, for example, could be described as an important decision on the part of some occasions of the personality that will, in some measure, modify the values for all subsequent members of that personality. In this context, it is important to distinguish between the *"initial* subjective aim"—the aim as given by the ultimate ordering factor—and the *"final* subjective aim," which is modified in the course of concrescence and is passed on to future members of the society. The initial subjective aim and the final subjective aim share the same value character (see next definition), but the decisions made by each member of a personality are free to modify the social and personal parts of that aim and to pass on the new values that it has affirmed to subsequent members of that society.

The developing personal aim is thus built up as each occasion receives a personal aim from its predecessor, makes its own judgments on those values, and passes those along to its successor. As the personal aim changes, this may lead to changes in the societies to which an occasion belongs—for instance, when a change in values motivates me to change jobs or to move from one set of friends to another.

- Finally there is the *basic value character*,[9] which is a core of values that does not change during the evolution of the personality and that serves to distinguish this particular personality from all others.

We can take two positions in relation to this idea of basic value character. First, the "no-soul" position says there is no such character and that the only requirement for personal order is that the aims of the successive occasions should be similar enough to allow a sufficiently full objectification of the immediate past member of the occasion in the present one. This would be in the spirit of many Buddhist *(anatta)* teachings, since it would leave the personality entirely devoid of an individual soul. The second position claims that all occasions belonging to a personality do share an identical value character. This does not violate the letter of the Buddhist analyses, though it may violate the spirit of the anatta doctrine. This position does not assert any substantial identity as the core of the personality. It does, however, if we understand identity as the expression of a coherent value character, allow a personality to have an identity that is more constant than any of its other features. This second position also allows a point of connection between a personality and some other entity we might call its "soul." We will return to this idea shortly when I discuss soul theories of reincarnation.

For now, I am going to assume there is certain pattern of values—a certain character—that remains invariant through all of the members

---

[9] In what follows, I will sometimes refer to this as the "basic character" or the "value character."

of a personally ordered society. Further, I am going to assume that this identity of character is a principal factor in the elusive "identity" of personality about which I have been speculating throughout this book.

Theories of Reincarnation and the Processes They Involve

In this section I will explore five theories of reincarnation. Then, at the end of this chapter, I will assemble these theories into an overall hypothesis regarding the "how" of reincarnation.

Theory 1: Every Personality is a Reincarnation of Every Other Past Personality.[10] This theory holds that each individual personality is causally connected to all other personalities in the past (not just those with whom it shares a personal order), and that when any event in any past life is particularly relevant to a series of events in a current life, the current life may access those memories.

In the earlier chapters I focused on the issue of personality survival, so I have been speaking in terms of a full continuity that—whether or not it involves a direct identity—does involve a close continuity of process that includes significant continuity of conscious memory and purpose. While the theory being advanced in this section might seem to qualify as "reincarnation lite," it is important nevertheless to consider it because in the context of transpersonal process metaphysics, it appears to be true (though not complete).

Remember, in all process metaphysics, actuality is a creative advance of occasions of experience, and each actual occasion prehends all the actualities in its causal past. Prehension, as we have seen, is a relationship from which both efficient causation and memory can be abstracted. Thus, we can say that each actual occasion remembers *all* of the occasions in its causal past. From this point of view, we could say that each actual occasion is a reincarnation of all of the occasions in its causal past. But a single actual occasion is not a personality. Rather, a

---

[10] My attention was drawn to this theory by Sean Kelly and Frank Poletti. Kelly developed a unique and interesting version of this theory in Sean Kelly, "Integral Time and the Varieties of Post-Mortem Survival." http://integral-review.org/back_issues/backissue6/index.htm

personality is a "personally ordered" society of many sequential actual occasions—a society in which one member follows another like beads on a string. Although each actual occasion can be understood as a reincarnation of all others, can this also be said of personally ordered societies? The answer is yes and no.

Each occasion of a personality retains the radical openness of all actual occasions, and so it is, in some important sense, a reincarnation of all other occasions. The practical implication of this is that, in principle at least, all past memories are accessible to any actual occasion, and given the appropriate circumstances and an occasion of high enough grade, any past memory can become a fully conscious memory. On the other hand, a personality is characterized by the particular fullness with which its own predecessors objectify in it. This is because any two successive members must have very similar character (aim) and because, by hypothesis, some part of the character of all of the members of a personality is *identical* to that same part of all of the other occasions in the personality. Thus, the causal effects—and by extension the memories of past lives—are particularly concrete and powerful within one strand of personal order, so we can assume that a personality is much more intimate with its own previous members than it would be with the other occasions in its actual worlds.

There is no reason to think that continuity of memory requires physical continuity. Thus, it is reasonable to assume that a personality will have a special memory of the members of its own past. Those memories will always exercise a stronger casual power on future members of that society than the memories of most of their contemporaries. Also, when those memories from within a single strand of personality are "accessed," they will have—by virtue of their shared value character—the familiarity that marks them as "mine."

In this analysis, the way in which all occasions of experience are incarnations of all the expired occasions in their past does not negate the importance of continuity of memory as characterizing continuity of personality—both within a single lifetime and among successive lifetimes.

Theory 2: Reincarnation as Continuity of Personality without Physical

Continuity and with Variable Continuity of Memory. No Survival. Some early schools of Buddhist thought advocate this theory. It suggests that the last member of a particular strand of personal order (the last moment, for example, in the life of the dominant personality of a human life) creates a configuration in the general field of probabilities that will manifest itself when the proper opportunity for rebirth occurs.

In the example of the dominant personality of a human self, the proper circumstances will arise at the conception of a new, appropriate human self. At that time, the personality will pick up its ongoing "adventure." By virtue of sharing a common value character with the occasion marking the last member of the previous strand of the personality, the new human self will be uniquely sensitive to the causal impact of the occasions of previous strands, and "karmically" connected to the past life. However, because the new life will generally be in very different circumstances from the old life— in any case, the body of an infant will be very different from the previously inhabited body—it will be difficult to establish continuity of conscious memory. In this case, there would be process continuity without physical continuity or continuity of conscious memory.

Some of Stevenson's cases (those that do not involve the "intermission memories" discussed below) can be interpreted as instances of this reincarnation process. Further, in these "cases of the reincarnation type" (CORT), the reincarnation is close to the previous death both in time and space, so that as the child grows emotionally and cognitively, the relatively similar environment will trigger associations that remind him or her about the previous life; thus memories of that life can surface as the child matures.

Furthermore, any birthmarks on the new body that correspond to death wounds on the old body become intelligible as causal effects of the moment of death on the new moment of conception.

Theory 3: Personality Survival Leading Directly to Reincarnation. This mode of reincarnation is suggested by the stories of a conscious interval, or intermission, between death and a subsequent birth, reported in approximately 10 percent of Stevenson's cases of the reincarnation type.[11]

These experiences, which are remembered by the subjects in cases of the reincarnation type, can be roughly sorted into three stages:

- First, a "transition stage" that includes phenomena such as "preparation of the previous personality's body for the funeral or trying to contact grieving relatives, only to find they are unable to communicate with the living."[12]
- After the transition, a more stable stage is reached in which the personality is recalled as living in some locale (e.g., in a tree, in a pagoda, near the scene of the death). Sometimes the disincarnate personality also has "a schedule of duties to which they must attend."[13] Reports of "seeing or interacting with other disincarnate personalities are common" in this stage.[14]
- The third stage involves "choosing parents for the next life." Common themes in these stories include:
  - Seeing a living person performing everyday tasks, such as bathing or returning home, identifying him or her as a future parent, and choosing to follow that person home.
  - Being directed to the new parents "often by elders or the 'old man,'" (a common disincarnate personality referred to earlier in the book). Just under one-fifth of the cases analyzed in Stevenson's study "commented on how they gained entrance to the mother's body. This was most often by transforming into a grain of rice or speck of dust in the water and being ingested by the mother. A few went to considerable lengths, having to try repeatedly when

---

[11] Sharma, Poonam, and J. Tucker, Cases of the Reincarnation Type with Memories from the Intermission between Lives. p. 102.
[12] Ibid., p. 107.
[13] Ibid.
[14] Ibid., pp. 107–8.

either they were rebuffed by guardian spirits or the water was thrown out as dirty."[15]

In an analysis of 1,200 cases of the reincarnation type (CORT), researchers evaluated how many statements were verified and how strong was the argument for reincarnation. Compared to all cases of the reincarnation type, the 276 cases that included intermission memories (CORT-I) had twice the number of verified statements and double the score for strength-of-case.[16] One implication of these findings is that those cases with intermission memories are also cases in which the continuity of conscious memory is particularly strong.

I have hypothesized that continuity of memory is facilitated by continuity of circumstances. Personality survival is accompanied by continuity of memory because the transphysical aspects of the body remain intact, and thus provide a relatively similar environment for the presiding personality. In the type of reincarnation I am discussing here— where the same personality, with important parts of its transphysical body intact, remains lucid all the way through to entering the mother's body—it is not surprising that continuity of memory is stronger than in other cases.

However, we need to consider another factor governing memory. Memory is also a function of what we could call "mindfulness." The more mindful, alert, or lucid we are in a given moment, the more likely we are to have recall of that moment later in our existence. Some people are more mindful of their lives than others. It is possible that people who are generally more mindful live their intermission periods in a memorable way, while people who are less mindful might pass their intermission periods in a dreamlike state of mind so that their intermission memories just fade away.

In any case, Stevenson's data provide strong evidence for theories 2 and 3, and we might hypothesize that the reincarnation process in theory 2 is the same as in theory 3 but with intermission memories being unrecoverable.

Theory 4: Partial Reincarnation. Another type of reincarnation is explored in the work of Michael Whiteman.[17]

---

[15] Ibid., p. 198
[16] Ibid., p. 103
[17] Poynton, John, "Making Sense of Psi and Mysticism: Whiteman's Multi-Level

I have been developing the idea throughout my book that the human self is a complex hierarchy of personalities—a presiding personality, various subpersonalities, a personality that is the "control panel" for the waking body, personalities presiding over the major organs, and so forth, all the way down to the personalities of the individual atoms constituting the molecules that make up the cells. We have seen that some of these personalities may enter into and become an integral part of the self from the environing physical and transphysical worlds. When higher-grade personalities enter into an ongoing self, they may bring memories of their earlier existence.

At death, we are assuming that most of the personalities belonging to the self remain intact as a unit (except, of course, the lowest-grade members that are most closely involved with the physical parts of the body). Some of the higher-grade personalities that have been involved in the self may, however, take death as an opportunity to go off on their own. These personality strands will carry with them the memories of their existence in the now-deceased human self to which they formerly belonged, and they may then join another personality, taking those memories with them.

This idea is indirectly supported by the data suggesting that people who have heart transplants sometimes discover they have memories and preferences from the person who originally had the heart—sometimes radically at odds with the personality of the patient before the transplant.

Here are some examples of what can happen when hearts are transplanted:[18]

- In one case, an eighteen-year-old boy who wrote poetry, played music, and composed songs was killed in an automobile accident. A year after he died, his parents came across an audiotape of a song he had written, entitled "Danny, My Heart is Yours," about how he "felt he was destined to die and give his heart to someone." The donor recipient of his heart, "Danny," was an eighteen-year-old

---

Ontology," (unpublished).
[18] Pearsall, Paul, "Changes in Heart-Transplant Recipients That Parallel the Personalities of their Donors."

girl, named Danielle. When she met the donor's parents, they played some of his music and she, despite never having heard the song, was able to complete the phrases.[19]

- A forty-seven-year-old man received a heart from a fourteen-year-old girl gymnast who had problems with eating disorders. After the transplant, the recipient and his family reported his tendency to be nauseated after eating, along with a childlike exuberance and a little girl's giggle.[20]

In these cases, it appears that the presiding personality of the heart—with its memories of a previous life—stays with the heart as it is transplanted.

In terms of transpersonal process metaphysics, however, the presiding personality of the heart is a transphysical entity that can, like the dominant personality of a human self, survive the death of its body and can, under appropriate circumstances, involve itself in some capacity in the life of a new personality. We can even imagine a case in which the personality that presided over the heart of one self might enter in as the dominant self in a new human being. Further investigations into the processes of reincarnation will have to take this possibility into account.

Theory 5: Soul-Based Theories of Reincarnation. A large number of theories of reincarnation are based on some notion of a soul. The word "soul" has so many uses I need to define what I mean by the term for this discussion. Like the word "spirit," soul is sometimes used more or less synonymously with "mind," "consciousness," "self," or "personality." However, I will distinguish soul from all of these other terms and define it as some entity other than a personality that somehow holds memories of past lives and is, rather than the personality itself, the entity that reincarnates.

Various theosophical teachers[21] have offered theories in which the soul is called "the causal body" and is held to be a special personality that dwells in the higher reaches of the mental world. Sri Aurobindo

---

[19] Ibid., pp. 194–95.
[20] Ibid., p. 199.
[21] See, for example, A. E. Powell. *The Causal Body*; and Alice A. Bailey, *A Treatise on Cosmic Fire*.

speaks extensively about the soul, which he calls the "psychic being," and is clear that it is this "psychic being" and not any particular strand of personality that is the reincarnating entity.[22]

In this section, I want to introduce a hypothesis about the nature of soul that is natural to transpersonal process metaphysics and that seems to fit well into the overall cosmological scheme I have developed in this book.

An essential aspect of personality, as defined here, is that any given personality is necessarily a separate individual among other separate individuals. We generally take our independence quite for granted. On the other hand, there are certain ways in which our unity with one another is evident. We could not be what we are in this moment if it were not for all of the myriads of occasions that have made up the entire course of cosmic evolution. It has taken our universe billions of years of evolutionary effort to bring forth this one moment of human experience. And each moment of our experience literally *contains* within itself the entirety of its causal past (see Chapter 9).

We are one in this sense: each of us is an individualization of the universe that we collectively participate in co-creating. We are *separate* individuals to the extent that abstraction in objectification is imposed on the causal interactions between us. If you objectified with utter concrete fullness in me, if I felt everything that you feel, knew everything you thought, anticipated everything you anticipate, and so on—we would be truly and pragmatically one unified being. Of course, in fact, I do *not* know you that intimately. I never know as much of you as you know of yourself, hence you are outside me, and we are distinct beings. Distinct individuality is a function of abstraction in objectification among occasions.

But the degree of abstraction in objectification imposed on individuals varies with the grade of the occasions involved. Given two occasions of the same grade, the higher the grade the more concrete, nuanced, and full will be the communications (causal interactions) between them.[23] Two low-grade inorganic occasions know each other

[22] Sri Aurobindo, *The Psychic Being (Soul: Its Nature, Mission, and Evolution)*.
[23] This is similar to what Teilhard de Chardin suggests: that more complex entities can experience greater "radial communication," whereas simpler entities are confined to more "tangential communication."

by virtue of disturbances in the various fields of force where they are located. Two living occasions know each other empathically in the richness of their emotions. Two mental-grade occasions know each other telepathically in the richness of shared meaning. The "higher" the transphysical status of the occasions involved, the lower the degree of abstraction in objectification between them, and the more deeply they feel and know one other.

We approach an idea of the soul by imagining that the degree of abstraction in objectification among some occasions drops all the way to zero. In this situation, every occasion would know all other occasions at this grade as intimately as it knows itself, and so the oneness of each with all would be an entirely effective reality. Note that at this stage, there is no *separate* individuality. But this does not imply there is no individuality at all.

Each individual occasion still retains its unique value character. Each occasion in this state of zero abstraction retains its own way of appreciating and ordering the possibilities for actualization. Each occasion, while being effectively one with the others, nonetheless has its own perspective on that unity. Also, as these individual perspectives are intrinsic to the functioning of the one universe, they will be in existence as long as the universe is in existence, and so will be personally ordered and effectively immortal.[24] Transpersonal process metaphysics, then, defines a soul as an individual, immortal being that knows itself as one with all beings in the universe.

We could envision these entities as intrinsic to what Whitehead calls "the consequent nature of God."[25] In a more Aurobindonian scheme, we might assign the soul a home on what he calls the "Overmind level."

In any case, these soul entities each objectify the whole creative advance as it is happening, and do so from their own value perspectives.[26]

---

[24] One of Whitehead's last published essays, entitled "Immortality," is found in *The Philosophy of Alfred North Whitehead*, p. 682. Whitehead speaks of "the immortal aspect of personality." I offer this idea as a possible key to the interpretation of that fascinating but notoriously obscure essay.

[25] Whitehead, *Process and Reality*, pp. 342–51.

[26] Note that for entities with no abstraction in objectification among them, spatial distance is undefined. Also, remember that in transpersonal process metaphysics, spatial distance is a function of abstraction in objectification. Without abstraction, there is no distance and, hence, no space. I am assuming the soul also objectifies all

In addition, each of these soul entities will have a particularly intimate relationship with those occasions and personalities in the creative advance that share a value character with it. The soul will center its interpretation of the creative advance in relationship to those occasions and will retain a memory of those occasions in a particularly rich way. When a finite occasion begins its concrescence, it will have the same value character as its soul and will always feel the influence of that soul in some fashion and in some degree.[27]

The literature on reincarnation sometimes suggests that a single soul might have more than one incarnation at a time. The theory of soul that I am advancing here would make that possibility entirely intelligible. In terms of the theory of soul that we are exploring, there is no reason that a single soul could not preside over many simultaneous strands of personality. Also, in a multi-world cosmology, for example, in which timelines branch off whenever a decision is made, we can also imagine a single soul that has embodiments distributed in time. In every timeline will be a unique causal ordering of the past, and the already settled past will not change with the creative advance. But a soul, completely beyond finite time-space, might join the advance at any time-space location at all, thus initiating a new time-line for its enjoyment. Bottom line: it is possible to construct a doctrine of soul-based reincarnation compatible with all of the other mechanisms of reincarnation we have already considered.

The soul-based theories of reincarnation expounded by theosophists[28] and in Sri Aurobindo[29] suggest that cases in which survival leads directly to reincarnation are relatively rare. They suggest that in the majority of cases, the death of the physical body is followed by a sojourn in the vital world. During this sojourn, hells and heavens are experienced

---

finite occasions without abstraction, thus the distance between the soul and a finite entity in any finite universe is undefined. Souls define a unique perspective that cannot be grasped in any scheme of indication.

[27] Sri Aurobindo, in many of his writings, suggests that the entire evolutionary process can be understood in terms of the soul's efforts to construct entities grounded in the physical world *and* capable of expressing the soul's fullness in that world. The higher the grade of the presiding personality of a being living in the waking world, the more open it is to the soul's expression.

[28] Powell, *The Astral Body*.

[29] Sri Aurobindo, *The Problem of Rebirth*.

because the dominant emotions of the previous life, still operative in the personality, will place that personality in a vital environment appropriate to those emotions. This playing out of the emotions is held to be temporary, and it is suggested that there can be, in this period, interesting experiences that advance work accomplished during the just-past lifetime. Eventually, the vital body is said to also die, followed by a sojourn in the mental body, invariably a blissful experience. The mental body too eventually dies, and the experiences of that life are incorporated into the soul. Then, when it is ready, the soul will initiate a new incarnation.

If the soul has only one embodiment at a time, then the process of personality continuity that I have outlined above would allow us to trace the destiny of a single personality as it reincarnates again and again through the creative advance. The continuity of the soul will be of the same nature as the continuity of the personality. If, however, the ongoing identity of the personality is a function of the soul, of which it is an expression, and if

- The soul can have many simultaneous embodiments
- The soul can have embodiments at different times
- The different embodiments of the soul can be of different grades

Then souls may embody themselves in subpersonalities of other personalities that have a value character other than the soul's own. Under these circumstances, it becomes less meaningful to speak about the reincarnation of an individual personality. Rather, it is the soul that reincarnates, and the personality is merely a temporary expression of an effectively immortal soul.

Conclusion

Reincarnation forces us to look closely at the nature of the continuity of the personality. Transpersonal process metaphysics allows us to analyze the continuity of personality in a way that supports many different processes of reincarnation. We have discussed

- The fundamental understanding that, in an important sense, every personality is a reincarnation of all past personalities
- One process corresponding to the data of a majority of Stevenson's CORTs in which there is a continuation of personality with loss of physical continuity, some variable continuity of conscious memory, but no intermediate survival of the personality
- Another process, corresponding to the data of a significant minority of Stevenson's CORTs, in which there is personality survival that transitions directly into reincarnation
- The possibility that there are various ways in which parts of personalities survive the death of a human self and may reincarnate themselves either in another living self, or even as the presiding personality of a new human birth
- The soul theories that suggest it is the soul, not the personality, that is the true reincarnating entity, and posit that there is an intermediate period of temporary survival for the transphysical aspects of the personality

What emerges from this investigation is a sense that the creative advance involves a wondrous texture of reincarnation processes that call into question our usual assumption of a simple strand of personality enduring through time.

Enough data on reincarnation exist to establish its reality, but not enough to allow us to evaluate the various alternatives explored in this chapter. And so these theories remain necessarily speculative. Nonetheless, it is my hope that this way of laying out the various issues involved in reincarnation may stimulate further research.

Part Two

Chapter 1: The Involution

Until this point in our journey together, I have been working out an understanding of personality survival and reincarnation, staying as close as I have been able to the data at hand and to the dictates of scientifically informed common sense. Obviously, however, in order to deal with consciousness, personality, the data of parapsychology, and the evidence favoring survival and reincarnation, I have had to introduce some novel and challenging ideas. In this last part of the book, I propose to go still further into new territory and present the outline of a full metaphysical cosmology within which I will frame a complete hypothesis about the "long trajectory" of human existence.

The ideas in this chapter and the next are an original synthesis of the ideas of Sri Aurobindo, Alfred North Whitehead, and myself. Of course, in a short introduction like this, I cannot do full justice to the depth and profundity of Sri Aurobindo's or Alfred North Whitehead's ideas. But I hope to provide a useful introduction that can serve as a starting point for those who wish to pursue their own studies in greater depth.

Contradiction, Concurrence, and Complementarity

Before I enter into a discussion of the cosmological system itself, I would like to say something about the fundamental logic of this explanatory framework.

Alfred North Whitehead points out that the universe of our experience, though shot through with plurality, is nonetheless one coherent universe. And, he says, it is the business of metaphysics to give expression to that unity. Whitehead suggests that a metaphysical system needs to be coherent; by which he means that our fundamental metaphysical notions ought to be related to one another in such a way that what is unique about each of them cannot be understood in abstraction from their references to each other. This is in general contrast to the habits that come from mathematical thinking, in which we desire each of the premises of the system to be *independent* of one another. In general, we are satisfied with a mathematical system in which each of the premises seems clearly comprehensible on its own merits, and does not require reference to the other premises for it to make sense. A metaphysical system, on the other hand, ought to exhibit the fundamental unity of the universe by being coherent in the above sense.

In *Adventures of Ideas*[1] Whitehead refers to Newton's cosmology as "easy to understand and very hard to believe." And yet, obviously, millions of scientists and laypeople alike have believed it. Why is that? It is, at least in part, because each of Newton's basic building blocks—the atom, absolute space and time, force, and law—is easy to comprehend on its own, and, therefore, the system *seems* comprehensible. It is only difficult to understand if we start looking for the *necessary interconnections* among the elements. Upon examination, we find these necessary interconnections to be entirely absent. As Newton expressed in his ideas, space is logically independent of time, atoms are logically independent of both space and time, and the only reason atoms appear to interact at all is because God imposes on them a gravitational force. This renders Newton's system, in Whitehead's sense, fundamentally incoherent.

Now if a metaphysical system is to be coherent, there ought to be fundamental interconnections among its constituent elementary ideas that transcend the law of the excluded middle. The law of the excluded middle establishes an *opposition* among ideas, but does not allow us to explore the more subtle relations among ideas that constitute coherence. Edgar Morin, in articulating his idea of "complex thinking" has articulated a larger set of relations among ideas. He suggests that the

[1] Alfred North Whitehead, *Adventures of Ideas*, p. 131.

basic ideas of the system may be *simultaneously* concurrent, contradictory, and complementary.[2]

Let me illuminate these ideas with a simple example. Take the notions of white and black. These two ideas are *concurrent* in that each stands on its own as a definite and distinct idea. I can bring to mind very clearly the idea of white and the idea of black, and when I do so I need make no explicit reference to the other. If white and black were not each something on its own, then there could be no relationship between them. And yet, white and black are *contradictory*, in the sense that no actuality can be, at the same time and in the same precise sense, both white and black. Finally, they are *complementary* in that the meaning of each is inseparable from its contrast to the other.

Of course these distinctions do not exhaust the lushness of complex thinking. But many of the ideas I will use in the metaphysical cosmology I am about to frame are related to each other in elegant and intricate ways, and it will help to keep that in mind as we explore his these ideas.

Asymmetrical Complementarity

Morin's ideas allow us to appreciate more deeply the coherence of the finite world of our existence. But Sri Aurobindo is interested also in establishing the relationship between our world and its absolute, or divine, ground. This ground of being is what Sri Aurobindo calls Brahman, or Sachchidananda, and we will explore the definition of these terms shortly.

Sri Aurobindo accepts the data of yogic insight that has been so carefully observed and organized in Vedic thought. This insight suggests that it is possible for a human being to identify himself or herself with the ultimate ground of being (Brahman/Sachchidananda) and, having done so, to experience that ultimate ground of being as an absolute freedom out of which the finite world develops. To express this insight, Sri Aurobindo makes use of a relationship among ideas that I call "asymmetrical complementarity."

[2] Edgar Morin, *Method: Towards a Study of Humankind, Volume I: The Nature of Nature.*

Asymmetrical complementarity is used to designate relations among actualities in which

- The major element of the pair is ontologically superior to the minor element
- The minor element is freely generated out of the major element
- The major and minor elements appear to be contradictory, complementary, and concurrent in the ordinary way.

Let us look at the asymmetrical complementarity between the infinite and the finite. While in our everyday worlds the infinite and the finite are contradictory, concurrent, and complementary in the ordinary way, Sri Aurobindo suggests that the infinite is actually the major element in this pair. This implies that the infinite is ontologically superior to the finite. First, the infinite contains many finites, but no finite can contain the infinite. On a deeper level, while the infinite must, by its nature, contain the possibility of generating the finite out of itself, it has the freedom to choose whether or not to do so.

A rather more controversial application of asymmetrical complementarity is to the analysis of the pair "good and evil." Sri Aurobindo will maintain, when he is developing his theodicy, that good is infinite, and evil is finite. In the situation where the infinite has not deployed the finite, there is no possible conflict of interest and thus no competing wills. When, however, the finite is deployed, there can arise a multiplicity of wills, each with an understanding of the good defined in relation to itself. Evil, therefore, is a finite good. We thus have a situation in which the apparent contradictory, concurrent, and complementary relations between good and evil in everyday life are trumped by the more encompassing nature of the good. From this point of view, both good and evil are fundamentally good.[3]

We will see other applications of asymmetrical complementarity as we delve into the system itself.

---

[3] This is a major and controversial idea that I cannot fully explore in this book. Sri Aurobindo develops the position at length in *The Life Divine*, particularly in Book II, Part I, Chapter XIV.

The Metaphysical Background I:
The Divine in the Upper Hemisphere of its Being

Brahman

The Western intellectual tradition has, for the past few centuries, gotten caught up in a project of materialistic reductionism. The goal of this project is to account for all of experience in terms of the assumption that the ultimately real consists of a self-existing, essentially deterministic complex of time-space and energy unfolding according to immutable laws that can be adequately expressed in mathematical terms. Insofar as this project is pursued, it leads inevitably to the problem of "emergence." How can phenomena such as life, mind, and consciousness have arisen out of a material matrix in which none of these phenomena are inherent?

Sri Aurobindo avoids this problem by starting not with something simple and abstract but with the ultimately full and actual, and then deriving everything else as a simplification of or abstraction from that. This ultimately full and concrete beginning of things he calls, in accordance with the Vedic tradition, "Brahman." It is important to note that Brahman is *not* the same as "pure consciousness." There are various traditions, such as Advaita Vedanta, that claim the ground of all actuality is pure consciousness. Since pure consciousness itself has nothing out of which it can generate the play of finite phenomena, these phenomena are, in those traditions, explained away as mere illusion. Brahman, on the other hand, is infinitely complex (rather than absolutely simple) and thus contains the possibility of finite existence within it. Sri Aurobindo's position is not "consciousness only" but rather a panpsychic position in which the potential for finitude, and even materiality, is built right into the ultimate ground of being.

This move—starting with the full and the actual—is suspect in the scientific West, and, therefore, requires some justification. The crucial question is, "Where are we going to start our cosmological thinking?" In part, this is an aesthetic issue. We can always decide to start in an arbitrary set of premises, as long as those premises lead to an explanation for the way things are now. This procedure is generally adopted in science. But in the context of metaphysics, we are asking deeper questions. When we start with an arbitrary set of premises—for example, low entropy and energy singularity (Big Bang), time-space, and mathematical laws—we can always ask, "Where did those come from?" My mind, at least, finds the conditions assumed to exist at the time of the Big Bang to be quite arbitrary and very much in need of further explanation. Why and how did those particular conditions arise? While the questions about the origin of the Big Bang (assuming a Big Bang cosmology) may not be part of physics, they are certainly part of metaphysical cosmology, which attempts to give us a rational accounting for how things exist and why they are as they now are.

I prefer to begin my cosmological thinking with the assumption of the existence of a complex unity, containing within itself unity and plurality, infinity and finitude, good and evil, spirit and matter—indeed, all possible qualities—and yet transcending the totality of qualities in a fullness unknowable by mind. This is close to the beginning of many spiritual cosmologies, and it is also rational in a satisfying way.

Reason guides me to the idea of such a totality by considering the plurality of entities I find in the universe of my experience. All of these entities, no matter how diverse, are in utter solidarity with each other. They are all part of one universe. Even if I imagine this one universe comes into existence out of a plurality of diverse factors (say, a good God and an evil God, as the Manicheans might suggest; or Creativity, eternal objects, and God, as Alfred North Whitehead suggests), it must still be the case that these primordial factors are interacting with each other—and such an interaction necessitates a larger, more embracing context. Ultimately, then, in this sense, the universe is a unity, and that unity must be such as to contain and uphold all diversifications and particularizations of itself.

I cannot claim any compelling absolute justification for such a way of constructing a metaphysical understanding. I can, however, at least point to the way in which the ultimate starting point of our thinking as we launch into the metaphysical enterprise is a matter of pre-philosophical choice. Do we want to begin our thinking with some factors abstracted out of sense experience? Or do we want to start our thinking with the all-embracing unity in which all existence is playing itself out?

Sri Aurobindo describes Brahman in terms of two phrases drawn from the *Upanishads:*[4]

- "Brahman is One without a Second." This phrase encapsulates the idea I was exploring a few paragraphs back—i.e., the plurality of entities constituting a universe must interrelate within an overarching context, and that context, as the most embracing possible context for the interaction of all entities, can have nothing outside it. We can imagine there are many universes embraced within Brahman, but to assert the existence of more than one Brahman would be empty, since that other Brahman would either communicate with our Brahman, in which case it would not be the Brahman at all, or else it would be systematically and forever irrelevant to us.

- "All this is Brahman." This second phrase, which complements the first, asserts that the unity of Brahman is not something over and above the universe of experience but is the very essence of all that is.

Sachchidananda

When Sri Aurobindo comes to investigate more fully the properties of Brahman, he is immediately confronted with the limitations of intellect. The intellect, which is itself a limitation of the Brahman, is not in a position to cognize the Brahman its own terms. He therefore speaks of "Sachchidananda," which is the highest conception of Brahman that embodied intellects like ourselves can form. When Sri Aurobindo declares Sachchidananda to be "the highest conception" he is, of course, betraying his religious sensibility. We could, with Alfred North Whitehead, be more modest and say that the explication of Sachchidananda lays out a coherent body of metaphysical postulates that enable us to form an understanding of our universe as we experience it.

The word Sachchidananda is derived from three root words—*sat*

---

[4] The *Upanishads* are a set of philosophical/poetic texts that are central to the Vedic (Hindu) tradition.

(being);[5] *chit* (consciousness); and *ananda* (bliss). It is these three terms that describe the metaphysical ultimates in Sri Aurobindo's system. Let us consider them one by one:

Sat: Being

In the metaphysical cosmology that grows out of transpersonal process metaphysics, "being," or *sat*, is "actuality."[6] But actuality here is understood in such a way that potentiality is a dependent complement of it. Full actuality in itself comprises the actual and the potential. It is the actuality of potentiality and the potentiality of actuality. Potentiality here is understood to arise by a certain withholding of actuality that, as it were, makes space for specific actualizations. (This is rather like the ideas of Lurianic Cabala, in which God, in order to manifest a universe, must withhold some of his fullness—an operation termed *tsimtsum*.) Sachchidananda, then, insofar as it is Being, is the unconditioned ground for anything and everything that comes to exist (or could possibly exist).

In addition, Being must comprise all of the specific possibilities for manifestation. In this sense, Being is the repository of the "forms of definiteness"—forms such as redness, hardness, bigness, spatial relations, sorrow, rage, ecstasy, and so forth—without which we could recognize no permanence in the flux of appearances. These forms of definiteness are Alfred North Whitehead's eternal objects, or Plato's ideal forms.

Chit: Consciousness

In transpersonal process metaphysics, Consciousness is a metaphysical ultimate and does not need to be proven or derived from something else. It is "given," intrinsic to existence itself. In other words, this metaphysics

---

[5] While *sat* is often translated as "truth," in the context of Sri Aurobindo's ontology, "being" is a better term.
[6] Note I place Whitehead's eternal objects ("specific forms of possibility") in the domain of Being, which Sri Aurobindo does not do. Sri Aurobindo, in his accounting of the emergence of specific forms, tends to imply that forms emerge out of differential motions in an otherwise undifferentiated medium. This is akin to Descarte's notion of matter as *res extensa*. Following Whitehead, who (following Plato) sees the need for a repository of forms of definiteness, I have envisioned them a part of *sat*. I believe this makes Sri Aurobindo's position more coherent.

begins with the assumption that existence, as part of its very being, *knows itself.*

We can point to Consciousness in several ways:

- Consciousness is the indefinable transparent luminosity that illuminates all existence. This transparent luminosity is a part of all of our experiences. It is the clearing in which the various objects of our experience emerge. As such, it is inseparable from time-space (see Chapter 9).
- Consciousness is the faculty of selection, permitting the articulation of various truths of the one truth. We experience this in ourselves as the power of selective attention. Because of its capacity for focal attention, Consciousness is, in effect, Sachchidananda's "moving part." It is the dynamic factor in God, the agency of finite actualization (see Chapter 4).
- Consciousness has a very important dependent complementarity—what Sri Aurobindo refers to as *Shakti*, or "Force."

Shakti: Force

To understand this idea, we need to remember that Sachchidananda is as much of Brahman as we can comprehend. Thus Sachchidananda, which is Brahman, is One without a Second. There is nothing that can oppose Sachchidananda, and there is no possibility of any obstruction of any movement on its part.

As just noted, Consciousness (Sachchidananda's moving part) is capable of selective attention. It can attend to Sachchidananda as a whole, or it can attend to any of the particular determinate possibilities that are inherent in Sachchidananda's Being.

Brahman, or Sachchidananda, is a complex contrast among possibility and actuality. When the Consciousness of Sachchidananda selectively attends to some particular determinate possibility or set of possibilities, that selective attention itself creates a distinction between possibility and actuality. With an act of selective attention, the Consciousness of Sachchidananda actualizes that to which it attends and thrusts that to which it does not attend into the background as mere possibility.

Whatever Sachchidananda's Consciousness attends to is realized, actualized, or manifested. This power of actualization is *Shakti*, the Force of Consciousness.

Note that the Consciousness of Sachchidananda, unlike finite consciousnesses such as those of humans today, must have the ability to attend selectively to many different specific potentialities at once. Thus, many different "poises" of Consciousness may exist simultaneously. Consciousness may attend to the undifferentiated wholeness of Sachchidananda, while simultaneously manifesting (in a way to be explicated) as an infinity of individual beings.

Because Consciousness is also Force (*Chit* is also *Shakti*), transpersonal process metaphysics is a form of panpsychism. The category of *Chit/ Shakti* is Consciousness, with its awareness and its choicefulness, and energy, with its dynamism and causal efficacy. Within this metaphysical framework, every movement of energy expresses an intention of Consciousness, and every intention of Consciousness expresses itself in a movement of energy.

This Force, which is a dependent complementarity of Consciousness, is so important that we will sometimes speak of Sachchidananda as fourfold—Being, Consciousness, Force, and Bliss.

Ananda: Bliss

While the Sanskrit term *ananda* is translated as "bliss," a better translation in this context might be "appreciation of value." For Sri Aurobindo, every experience, from the luminous clarity of Absolute Truth to the murky obscurity of ill-intentioned lies, from the heights of virtuous pleasure to the depths of sinful revel, is a value that can be appreciated.

Sri Aurobindo tells us that pleasure, pain, and neutral experience are all so many inflections of *ananda*.

Ananda is the final answer to the question of "Why?" Whatever comes to exist does so for the sake of the experience of value that it makes possible.

Sachchidananda as the Ground of Being

Let us step back now and consider the implications of this definition of Sachchidananda. What is being suggested is that the ultimate ground of reality is not something unconscious, automatic, and blind but rather a

Being who is absolutely self-illuminated by an intrinsic Consciousness, and which is inseparable from an infinite enjoyment of its own inherent bliss. In this way, the hard problem of accounting for the emergence of consciousness out of a non-conscious ground is entirely avoided. Consciousness and its dependent complementarity (*Shakti*/Force/energy/matter) are included from the very beginning.

Another dependent complementarity comes into play here— between personal and impersonal. While the way I have presented Sachchidananda emphasizes its impersonal aspect, it is, nevertheless, to be understood as fundamentally personal. It is a being that is conscious, makes choices, and enjoys its own value as a person. We can describe Sachchidananda in impersonal terms, but these are abstractions. We can abstract the impersonal from the personal but never the other way around.

This vision of the ground of being merits considerable contemplation. For example, we might begin by comparing Sachchidananda with ourselves. If we look at what the most intimate part of our own conscious being does in each moment, we will see that we arise out of a set of potentials, which we consciously register, and among which we decide, in a process that realizes value (bliss). In this sense, we are "Sachchidananda beings." In other words, from one important point of view, the most intimate essence of our individual being is Sachchidananda itself. We will return to this identity shortly.

On the other hand, we can also deepen our contemplation by contrasting Sachchidananda with ourselves. We are beings dependent on causes and conditions. If we take away food, water, or air, we cease to exist in the form with which we are identified. Sachchidananda, on the other hand, is dependent on nothing other than itself. When we look inside, to the source of our existence, we meet darkness and unknowing. When Sachchidananda looks inside, it meets absolute knowledge of the inescapable reality of its own infinite existence. The existence of Sachchidananda is inseparable from Consciousness; it is intrinsically self-known. And while we are tossed about on uncontrollable currents of pleasure and pain, the very substance of Sachchidananda is self-appreciation of its own value. When I am able to bring forth a vision, or an effective understanding of reality as proceeding from this source, I find it inspiring and reassuring.

Modern thought tends to start with non-Being rather than with Being. Heidegger, for example, suggests that the most fundamental question of philosophy is, "Why is there something rather than nothing?"[7] It is odd that we, who most certainly exist, nonetheless come to think that non-existence is a state of affairs that needs no justification. To modern sensibilities, if there had never been anything happening at all, that would be natural. But since there are things happening, that needs an explanation.

This habit of thought is probably related to the rampant skepticism of modern times, but we ought to recognize that it is just a habit. We could just as well take the opposite position, and assume that Being is the natural state of affairs and that non-being, or the appearance of non-being is merely the minor term in a dependent complementarity.[8] If absolute non-being had ever been, then nothing could ever have arisen from it. But being can manifest non-being as its dependent complementary. This is the move that Sri Aurobindo makes in his metaphysical system. For most of us, this is a bit of a stretch.

Starting our thinking with Brahman/Sachchidananda, however, still leaves us with a considerable explanatory problem. We are positing a self-illuminated, self-appreciation of intrinsic value as the ground of being. But we, ourselves, are finite, contingent beings living in a world only fitfully illumined by knowledge. So how is it that a finite and murky world such as ours can emerge out of the utter brilliance of Sachchidananda? How can it be that in some essential way we are Sachchidananda and yet, at the same time, we seem a negation of its infinitudes? To answer this question, we need to develop a doctrine of "involution," which we will now explore.

---

[7] See Martin Heidegger, *Introduction to Metaphysics.*

[8] This idea of Being as self-existent and self-explanatory was characteristic of early Greek thought, and of Parmenides in particular, whose basic metaphysical proposition was "Being is." However, the early Greeks (Heraclitus excepted) fell into misplaced concreteness and came to privilege Being—the unchanging—as real, while reducing the changing realm of the senses to a mere appearance, or even an illusion. My ontology here, reflecting Sri Aurobindo's, agrees that "Being is" but includes *becoming* and *process* within the complex unity of Being itself.

Involution

"Vijnana:" Supermind

If Consciousness is the moving part of the Divine, then "Supermind" is its creative organ. It is through the instrumentality of Supermind that Sachchidananda involutes itself so that it eventually comes to function as the physical universe in which cosmic evolution is playing itself out.

The doctrine of Supermind is one of the most distinctive and original features of Sri Aurobindo's metaphysical system, and I am importing this idea into this version of transpersonal process metaphysics. Most of the other systems that acknowledge an unconditioned ground of being such as Brahman do not adequately account for the existence of our relative world—rather, they dismiss it as an illusion. This is analogous to what eliminative materialists do in the West—they avoid the hard problem of accounting for consciousness by simply labeling it an illusion. Advaita Vedanta, along with many schools of Buddhism and all those schools that Sri Aurobindo terms "Mayavadan" accept the reality of an absolutely conscious ground and then avoid the problem of accounting for the existence of a finite and relative world of material realities by simply labeling *it* as an illusion. As Sri Aurobindo would say, on one side there is the "materialist denial," (nothing but matter) and on the other side is the "ascetic denial"[9] (nothing but spirit). Sri Aurobindo, for the sake of philosophical depth and for the sake of a rich spiritual practice, is striving for a middle path between these two extremes. He accomplishes this by positing the Supermind as an intermediate term between the Sachchidananda on one hand and the phenomenal world we inhabit on the other.

Both denials have difficulty accounting for the presence of individual consciousness in sentient beings. Materialists see one material or energetic world, governed by immutable mathematical laws, and have a hard time accounting for the emergence of consciousness itself. Ascetics see one unconditioned, absolute Consciousness, and have a hard time accounting for the emergence of individual consciousness out of *that*.

To generate a theory that denies the reality of consciousness and its

---

[9] This is called the "ascetic" denial because it encourages a complete rejection of and withdrawal from all worldly pursuits.

individualizations is to become engaged in a performative contradiction. And yet, since philosophy is the attempt by a linguistic community of individuals to account for the world in which that community is functioning, individuated consciousness is always the starting point from which our philosophical thought begins. With his doctrine of Supermind and involution, Sri Aurobindo posits a continuum of differentiation, with the absolute complex unity of the One on one end and the myriad of separate, absolutely minimal consciousnesses of quantum events on the other.

Supermind achieves involution through the application of three fundamental powers:

- The power of self-differentiation
- The power of self-limitation
- The power of self-absorption

These three powers are metaphysical ultimates. We assume that Sachchidananda has these three powers because with these we can account for the world of finitude in which we exist.

At the level of Supermind (as we trace the unfolding of involution, we will see there are many levels of being), the primary power that comes into play is the power of self-differentiation. To understand this power, we need to recall that Sachchidananda is a complex unity of unity and plurality. That is, while Brahman and thus Sachchidananda is One without a Second, the One here is not a numerical unity—a "one over against others"—but is a "one embracing all possibility of differentiation." The power of self-differentiation is essentially the power of *perspective*. It is the power of the One, in which knower and known are undifferentiated, to differentiate the knower from the known, and then to know itself from many different perspectives, or points of view.

Supermind, or Vijnana, is not a single entity. In order to grasp the fullness of Supermind, it is useful to think of it as existing on three different levels.

Comprehending Supermind

In the poise, or status, of Sachchidananda, Consciousness has not deployed its dependent complementary, Force. Consciousness attends to the complex unity of Sachchidananda, and Force remains latent in Consciousness. In the poise of Supermind, as the Divine ground turns toward the manifestation of universes, Consciousness becomes more selective and Force becomes actively deployed.

At the highest level of Supermind,[10] the level of "Comprehending Supermind," Consciousness attends to Being as a field of potential manifestation. In this poise, the Consciousness of Sachchidananda privileges its capacity to select determinate truths of the One Truth.

If there is to be a manifestation of some sort, it is also necessary that the various determinate possibilities of being (eternal objects) should have some order of relevance among themselves.

This point requires some explaining. If there is to be any stable and coherent manifestation of possibilities, there must be some element in the manifested system that is fixed. If nothing whatsoever is fixed, then there can be only chaos. The dynamic order of a universe is always a complex interplay between freedom and determination. In modern science, for example, it is held that the natural laws are fixed, but that the configurations of energy are changing. In the kind of metaphysical cosmology I am building here, natural laws lose their fixed character and are revealed rather as "habits of nature." There remain certain fixed elements of the system. Two of these are the eternal objects themselves and certain kinds of relationships among them.

To say the eternal objects themselves are fixed is to say, for example, that a certain shade of green is always a possible experience and that whenever it is experienced, it is identical with itself. To say that certain relations among the eternal objects are fixed is to say, for example, that green is always a color and never a sound.[11] It is also to say that no entity

---

[10] Sri Aurobindo sometimes speaks of the levels of Supermind as if they are a hierarchy, and sometimes speaks of them as if they are simultaneous and parallel. In this exposition, I will be emphasizing the hierarchical angle. Note that the three levels of Supermind serve at least two purposes. First, they are an attempt to show that there are gradations between the complex unity of Sachchidananda on one hand, and the differentiated individuality of mental beings on the other. Also, these three differentiations of Supermind correspond to the three main schools of Vedanta, and by showing that all three of these schools find their place in his system, Sri Aurobindo is advancing his goal of synthesizing the various traditions.

[11] In cases of synesthesia, the same entity that was apprehended with the eternal object of a certain shade of green is now apprehended with the eternal object of some particular musical note. This does not change the self-identity of that

can be, in precisely the same sense and at precisely the same time, both that shade of green and not that shade of green—even though it can be that shade of green and also be hard and cold.

How are we to understand the origin of these relations among the eternal objects? Whitehead brings this order into his metaphysical system by positing a timeless concrescence of possibilities, which he calls the primordial mind of God. While Sri Aurobindo does not specifically discuss this issue, we can readily imagine that the Consciousness of Sachchidananda, as it comes to emphasize its own possibility for determinate choices, arranges the eternal objects inherent in the Being of Sachchidananda into some order of relevance suitable to be the framework for its myriad manifestations.

In sum, in the pose of the Comprehending Supermind, Consciousness steps back and emphasizes its own capacity for determinate choices. The determinate potentialities for being (eternal objects) inherent in the Being of Sachchidananda are ordered so as to serve as a background for manifestation; Force upholds this arrangement (as always) all for the sake of the value that is thus realized.

We could say that, in involution, this is the first separation of subject from object. The one conscious subject (*Isvara*) stands back from the entire field of potential manifestation (*Shakti*).

Apprehending Supermind

The primordial ordering of the eternal objects, which is characteristic of the Comprehending level of Supermind, is not itself an eternal object. If the overall order of the eternal objects were, itself, an eternal object, we would be involved in an infinite regress. So there is no finite formula that can ever capture the "logic of the infinite." Rather, the primordial ordering must be such that an infinite number of particular orders can be abstracted from it. Each of the orders that can be abstracted from the primordial ordering is a "perspective" from which the Consciousness of Sachchidananda can value Sachchidananda itself. Each perspective, by virtue of its relation to the primordial order, is also in a coherent relationship with all of the other perspectives that can be so derived.

At the level of the Apprehending Supermind, Consciousness

particular grade of green wherever and whenever it actualizes, nor the self-identity of that particular musical note.

multiplies itself so as to view its being from all of the perspectives that the Comprehending Consciousness has opened up, and Force manifests these perspectives as different points of view on the unity out of which they arise.

Note, however, this is not yet an experience of differentiated selves. Rather, it as if the One Consciousness that stepped back at the Comprehending level of Supermind now complexifies itself in the Apprehending Supermind so as to know its being from a multiplicity of perspectives. From each perspective, the One knows itself as that from which all perspectives are drawn, and knows all other perspectives as not other than itself.

At the level of the Apprehending Supermind, then, the unity knows itself from many points of view, but there is still only one knower.

Projecting Supermind

At this level, the One Consciousness moves out to inhabit its various individual perspectives. Rather than holding itself back with a certain superiority, the Consciousness of the One projects itself into the movement and becomes, in a way, involved with it.

At this level, the fundamental unity is still available in the background of Consciousness, but is somewhat overshadowed by a more prominent sense of individuality.

This is the level of the *jivatmans*, or spirits—beings who operate out of a pronounced sense of individuality but who fundamentally know themselves to be one with the others of their kind, and also one with complex One of whom all are expressions.

It is important to note that Sachchidananda at the level of Supermind does not *divide* itself into an infinite multiplicity; rather, it *multiplies* itself into an infinite multiplicity, each of which *is* the One on which it is a perspective.

What Sri Aurobindo offers us here is a way of reconciling the idea that there is one fundamental Consciousness into which all individuality ultimately dissolves (whether at death or at enlightenment) with the idea that some element of individuality survives not only death, but enlightenment as well. He does this by presenting individuality as intrinsic to the complex unity of the One, and by making it intelligible how, through the power of self-differentiation in involution, the individual aspect is gradually emphasized, leading to the habitation, by the One, of a multiplicity of perspectives on itself.

In considering the long trajectory of human existence, we can imagine ourselves as an intrinsic part of the complex unity of Sachchidananda. Our individual journey begins at the level of Supermind, where we find ourselves as timeless spirits. Transphysical process cosmology posits a realm of infinite spirits as an essential part of the actual world.

Transcendence, Universality, and Individuality

At the level of Supermind, with the actualization of infinite spirits, the coherence of manifestation is expressed by the play of transcendence, universality, and individuality.

Transcendence

At the level of Comprehending Supermind, Spirit transcends all manifestation. Hindus and Buddhists often symbolize this aspect of actuality as a human couple engaged in sexual intercourse. The interaction of consciousness and force are envisioned as a creative bliss by means of which all finite universes are created. The transcendence suggested here is not the type of transcendence implied by certain Christian theologies, in which transcendence is taken to mean that God is utterly other than the world, outside the world, and unaffected by happenings in the world. By contrast, at the level of the Comprehending Supermind, Spirit transcends all universes so that

- Consciousness at this level surveys all possible universes, and the Force holds out to it the possibilities for infinite manifestations. Here, Consciousness is totally undetermined. It is absolutely free to manifest whatsoever he/she/it chooses.
- No matter what is created at the level of the Comprehending Supermind, there is always freedom to create further. The creativity of the Comprehending Supermind is utterly inexhaustible.

Thus, transcendence does not imply radical otherness. In the context of Supermind, it means absolute freedom and inexhaustible creativity. Every spirit fully participates in this transcendence.

Universality

At the level of Apprehending Supermind, each spirit is universal, and each spirit knows itself, by virtue of its transcendence, as the source of the decision that focuses on its own individuality. Note too that Sachchidananda creates not *ex nihilo* but out of itself. Because Sachchidananda is Brahman, and because Brahman is "One, without a Second," there is nothing but Sachchidananda out of which creation can unfold. Thus each of the spirits is Sachchidananda, and so all spirits know themselves as one with each other. They are the multitudinous perspectives of one Being on itself.

Individuality

At the level of projecting Supermind, each spirit knows itself as individual. Sachchidananda fully inhabits each of the perspectives on itself that form the core of an actual being. As projected, the Divine experiences himself/herself/itself as an individual being, but at the level of Supermind that sense of individuality blends harmoniously with a sense of identity with all other individuals, along with a sense of identity with the One that manifests them all.

I suggested earlier that we can identify ourselves as Sachchidananda beings when we realize that our gesture of existence at each moment involves selectively realizing and enjoying determinate possibilities of being. In a similar way, we can recognize ourselves as Supermind-like beings when we realize that we, like supermental individuals, are also transcendent, universal, and individual.

- We are *transcendent* beings in that each of us, in every moment of existence, expresses an irreducible quantum of freedom. No matter how finite beings like ourselves are constrained by the environments out of which we apparently arise, some element of freedom and creativity is always present, by virtue of which we transcend our origins.
- We are *universal* beings in that it takes a whole universe to produce a moment of human (or any other kind of)

experience. As we know from science, the whole universe is one causally interconnected whole. Events in the most distant galaxies have some, however faint, continuous effect on us. And if the universe had not been evolving for the last fourteen billion years, human beings would not exist at all. Also non-local processes (as identified in quantum mechanics) help to determine the possibilities among which we can choose, no matter how distant in time or space they may be. Each one of us, at each moment, is the product of the entire universal evolution, and in this sense we are universal.

- We are *individual* beings, with our own unique perspectives on the universe out of which we arise. Our individuality is an individualization of the universe.

Overmind

The cosmology being developed here posits as fully actual an "upper hemisphere" of actuality—prior even to the possibility of anything finite or material—consisting of Sachchidananda and the full, living play of the infinite spirits. There can be only two justifications for positing this: first, it creates a satisfying intellectual framework in which the long trajectory of human life can be discussed, and, second, it brings our cosmology into accord with the doctrines and experiences of many great saints and yogis, including those of the Vedic tradition.

"Overmind" is a kind of boundary between the "upper hemisphere" of infinite existence and the "lower hemisphere" of finite existence.

As involution proceeds, the power of self-limitation comes into play—imposing a threshold on consciousness so that some experiences become supraliminal and some become subliminal. It is, in effect, the power of suppression and forgetting. Sri Aurobindo speaks of it as the power of consciousness to "put behind it" certain aspects of its own experience.

Note that the power of self-limitation by which spirits generate souls is not yet a power of *repression*, in which the suppressing movement itself becomes unconscious. That comes in with the power of "self-absorption" (see below).

At the level of Overmind, we find the divine souls. At Supermind, each infinite spirit knows itself to be an individual expression of the One and knows all of the other spirits to be expressions of that same One. Thus, each spirit knows all others as intimately as it knows itself. In addition, all of its experiences are illuminated by the sense that it itself, as the One that contains and pervades all, its freely choosing its own experience. Then, when some group of spirits chooses to leave behind their sense of transcendence, they still retain a sense of universality along with their sense of individuality—but they lose the pervading sense of freedom they had at the supermental level. The overmental soul knows itself to be one with the other souls, and to be, in some way, one with the whole of the universe but that universe is, in some important sense, fixed and determined. There is a sense of freedom *within* that particular universe, but the souls in this universe operate as if they did not have the creative freedom to change the rules of the universe itself.[12]

These souls are the same entities referred to as souls in Chapter 11. In that chapter I derived these souls by imagining a situation in which abstraction in objectification among personalities (the process whereby an object is abstracted from the universal background through a selection of its attributes) drops to zero, and so all personalities become universal. Here, however, I have derived these souls by tracing the involution of Sachchidananda, working out its self-multiplication and self-limitation through Supermind and down to the level of Overmind.

Note that at the level of Overmind, even the basic aspects of Sachchidananda—Being, Consciousness, Force, and Bliss—take on a more separated aspect, and each individual soul comes to express those factors differently. In particular, applied to actual occasions, I define their grade in terms of their preferential operation of either Consciousness or Force in their functioning.

A question arises here as to why Sachchidananda, an absolutely free and utterly conscious appreciation of inherent value, would indulge in this sort of self-limitation. It can only be for an amplification of appreciation, and we can get a sense of this possibility by looking at

---

[12] Sri Aurobindo is vague when it comes to placing spirit and soul within his larger ontological framework. My location of spirit at the supermental level and soul at the overmental level is an interpretation. I base it partly on Sri Aurobindo's regular assertion that the soul is universal/individual, and also on the theosophical tradition of Alice Bailey and Dawa Kuhl, who place the soul in the higher levels of the mental plane.

our own behavior. Within the limits of our finite existence, we human beings experience a large degree of freedom. We can, for example, organize our interactions with each other in a nearly infinite number of ways. And yet we constantly take delight in restricting our behavior so that it fits within a defined set of rules. We do this, for example, when we play games, or when we engage in business, or when we become identified with a particular set of social roles. In each of these cases, we find that limiting ourselves to a specific set of rules allows us to amplify our experience of certain values. We can imagine the Divine as engaging in self-limitation in this same spirit.

Self-limitation, when looked at from within the experience of the individuals involved in it, can be described as suppression, or as the articulation of thresholds for consciousness. When looked at in terms of relations *between* individuals, it can be understood as what Whitehead calls "abstraction in objectification." The idea here is that each individual, by virtue of its universality, includes in its being the being of all the other individuals. But the way in which it incorporates those other individuals (the way in which those other individuals "objectify" in it) is variable. Individuals who have suppressed their own transcendence cannot apprehend the transcendence of other individuals. Thus, beings in an overmental community will know each other less fully than beings in a supermental community. They will impose *abstraction* on their mutual objectifications.

Metaphysical Background II: The Lower Hemisphere as The World of Human Evolution

As we continue the involution from Overmind to the world of Mind, we enter the world of finitude—the world of human evolution.

First, since consciousness and force have, at the overmental level, been separated as relatively independent powers, they can now, within individual beings, enter into relations of relative dominance in respect to each other. At this level, where consciousness and its dependent complementarity, force, are operating as relatively separate powers, they are called, respectively *purusha* (the unmoving consciousness that knows, enjoys, and sanctions the play) and *prakriti* (the active force that enacts the play of energy).

As we will see, the further the involution proceeds below the overmental level, the more fully prakriti dominates purusha. The sense of freedom belongs to purusha, so as it is more and more dominated by prakriti, the sense of freedom diminishes. This will be more fully discussed below.

Second, as we enter the mental level, the notion of *system*—as the ongoing interaction of relatively separate individuals—becomes relevant. The Vedic people acknowledged this by suggesting that at the mental level, we come under the sway of the three *gunas*.

These three gunas seem to be very much like the fundamental dynamics of self-organizing systems, as recognized by Erich Jantsch in *The Self-Organizing Universe*.

The Tamasic Guna

The first guna is *tamasic*—responsible for qualities or mental states such as inertia, heaviness, drowsiness, or the tendency to disaggregate. Like the individual units of any self-organizing system, the individual components exhibit a tendency to go their own way, even against the interests of the larger systems to which they belong. To the extent that elements of the system are more concerned with maintaining their own ongoing existence than with serving as parts of a larger whole, they are tamasic. This tendency to privilege habit over response to novel situations Jantsch calls the principle of "confirmation."

The Rajasic Guna

The second guna is *rajasic*—responsible for dynamism, drive, and the pursuit of satisfaction, which motivate a system and its units toward what is new and novel. This tendency to embrace and pursue "novelty" is Jantsch's second principle of system dynamics.

The Sattvic Guna

The third guna is *sattvic*—responsible for balance and harmony; it aims at a balance of confirmation and novelty. Jantsch called it the principle of "self-organization."

As we trace involution on its way from Mind to Matter not only is there a progressive domination of purusha by prakriti, but also a progressive suppression, or "putting behind," of the several gunas.

I want to emphasize the threefold character of the lower hemisphere of Being, which distinguishes "matter," "life," and "mind." However, I want to point out that this threefold division is somewhat arbitrary. From another point of view, involution—particularly through the subtle worlds between Overmind and the Material (inorganic) world—is a continuous process. Self-limitation gradually increases, without discontinuous jumps. The threefold division of these worlds might be compared to the sevenfold division of the color spectrum.

The Mental World

As the involutionary sequence moves "below" Supermind, an overmental universe emerges first, in which the unified functioning of Supermind is translated into a universe of distinct and interacting universal souls. Next emerges a mental universe of individual minds interacting with each other as finite individuals in a shared but external universe. At this level, the entities I have been calling personalities emerge.

At the level of Mind, transcendence and universality are put behind the veil, or above the threshold. The overmental souls express aspects of themselves that operate entirely in Mind, rather than in Overmind. Each overmental being can project or express itself in many forms in the mental world—thus making it possible for one soul to incarnate itself in many personalities—in line with my speculations on reincarnation in the previous chapter.

Mind is that functioning of consciousness that permits all division within the One; it permits the division into the four divine factors of Being, Consciousness, Force, and Bliss; it underlies the power of self-differentiation that issues in a plurality of perspectives; and it supports the power of self-limitation whereby upper and lower thresholds of consciousness are established for individuals. But at the level of Supermind, and even at the level of Overmind, all mental divisions are held in an all-embracing unity. Overmind allows each divine principle (e.g., Consciousness and Force) to function independently in relation to the others, and it permits Mind to divide itself off from the all-embracing unity. With the possibility of this separation, souls can put forth a poise of themselves in such limited ways as, for example, knowing only through analysis and synthesis, having lost a wider and deeper grasp of the wholeness out of which they have arisen. In this way, a soul expresses a personality.

I want to emphasize that the entire involutionary process precedes the existence of the physical universe altogether. In fact, involution ends when the basis for the physical universe has been established. But at the mental level of involution, we can begin to speak of finite beings in relation to time, space, causality, and memory. It is a world, as we will see, consisting of actual occasions and personalities. In other words, at the mental level of involution, prior to the existence of the physical world, there is already an actual world of individual personalities, but they are all of a very high grade, and, if they are embodied at all, they are embodied in occasions that are also very high-grade. This is a world of luminous, telepathic mentalities.

Time

Time, as we customarily use the term, refers to the process in which the possibilities implied by a fully determined past are reduced to actuality, thus affecting the potentialities available for a future only partially knowable. While we can—in high flights of scientific abstraction— imagine a block universe in which all actions are predetermined, this abstraction loses the quality of adventure that is inherent in our concrete experience of unfolding time.

In the upper hemisphere of Being (Brahman, Sachchidananda, and Supermind), where all beings know each other intimately as Self, and where each being knows itself as the One who manifests all, there seems little opportunity for surprise, so our concept of time as the adventure of moving from known past into unknown future seems inapplicable there. This is sometimes taken to mean that for a Consciousness in the upper hemisphere of Being, all finite events are already foreknown, or already always happening. This seems to me to be a reduction of all the parts of time (past, present, and future) to either the past or the present. My impression is that what is taking place in the upper hemisphere is not a reduction of all of time to the past, or even to a paradoxical eternal happening of predetermined events, but rather something else richer and more complex than that. It is customary to call this level of experience "timeless," but we might also call it "timefull" and imagine it as a seamless complex contrast of eternity, finite existence across a span of time, momentary existence in time, and something more.

Also, it seems that the overmental experience, deprived of

transcendent freedom, might be a kind of temporal experience, but it would be one in which the entities, being direct expressions of their universe, would be consciously eternal.

In any case, once involution moves to the level of Mind, where universality as well as transcendence are put beyond the threshold of consciousness, mental entities emerge for each other as objects rather than as selves of the one Self. Because I, as a mental being, cannot know the inmost self of other mental beings, I cannot know their decisions or anticipate their actions. I find myself with the experience of a partially known past, a mostly unknown future, and the ongoing adventure of choice in the present.

Since Mind can grasp only finitudes that it has marked off from the infinite by its characteristic process of analysis, it must know time in finite spans. In this way, actual occasions emerge at the level of Mind, but since each occasion is the expression of a soul (and shares, therefore, a "value character" with that soul), all the occasions that emerge in the involutionary process belong to personalities. Whereas in the waking world of evolution personality seems like a precious and vulnerable achievement, in the involutionary world that precedes the emergence of the physical world, personal order is natural and inevitable. Mortality is not an issue here.

Space

One of the many features of space is how distance separates us one from another. We speak of other beings as "outside," or "external to," us. This notion of outsideness or externality,[13] when we attend to it closely, turns out to be rather mysterious. I want to suggest here, without fully developing the argument, that something is outside us when we don't know it from the inside (the way we know ourselves), and when we know less about it than it knows about itself.

To say that we know less about something than it knows about itself is to say that there is "abstraction in objectification" between us. Part of what we mean when we say that some other entity is "distant" from us is that we know less about it, and that it has less of an effect on us than it would if it were in greater proximity. This strongly suggests that greater distance is a measure of greater abstraction in objectification.

---

[13] Weiss, *Doctrine*, p. 149 ff.

In the upper hemisphere, and even in Overmind, where true universality is still on the surface of consciousness, all beings are in absolute proximity to each other. No being is outside another, and distance between beings has no meaning. These upper worlds are not spatial.

But when involution reaches the level of Mind—when universality is put behind the veil and beings experience themselves under abstraction, as mutually external—then distance between entities (and, therefore, space) becomes manifest.

Causality and Memory

Beings who experience themselves as aspects of one Self cannot be said to be efficient causes for each other. An efficient cause is an interaction across time and space. It is an interaction among mutually external beings. Thus, causal analysis is relevant only in the lower hemisphere of being. Also, beings who are in the upper hemisphere (which is "timefull," [14] and, at the overmental level, "eternal") express themselves as sequences of finite events. These events are linked together by efficient causes, which are registered as memories.

In this way of understanding, all efficient causes are transmissions of experience between occasions. In what follows, I will refer to these causes as being telepathic, empathic, or physical. These three types of causal influence are not ontologically distinct—the primary difference among them is a question of concreteness. Telepathic interactions are very rich and complete, like our experiences of our own immediately past selves. Empathic interactions lose the complex refinements of telepathy, but retain the depths of emotion. Physical interactions (the interactions explored in modern physics) are abstract, reduced to an absolute minimum of emotive tone and intellectual meaning. Nonetheless, all three of these types of interaction are direct communications among mutually external beings.[15]

---

[14] The Divine is often referred to as "timeless," but timelessness connotes something that is unchanging. On the other hand, the Divine is, in the theories we are exploring here, the source of time itself. It is hard to see how time could emerge from the timeless, so I prefer to say that the Divine is "timefull" which is to say that it is not limited by time, but that time is a partial expression of its mentally inconceivable process.

[15] Note that sensory interactions are elements of the appearance that each occasion,

At the mental level, purusha is for the first time partially subject to prakriti. In terms that are by now more familiar, this means that the conscious pole of actual occasions now experiences itself as subsequent to the physical pole. This relationship of the conscious pole to the physical pole—in terms of which the mental pole seems to arise out of the data of the physical pole, and to limit its responses to the possibilities that arise from those data—is something we have been taking for granted up to this point. But this relationship does not characterize the relations between the conscious pole and the physical pole at the Supermind or Overmind level. At Supermind, the physical pole is not separated from the mental pole, so that what is willed in the absolute freedom of the spirits is, in that same gesture, realized. At Overmind, there is some separation between consciousness and its force, but beings that know themselves as one with all the other beings they are interacting with can hardly make un-harmonized decisions. The conditions under which a soul finds itself are still an expression of its will.

At the level of Mind, with transcendence and universality left behind the veil, and where we do not and cannot know the decisions of others, we can only experience ourselves as subjected to those decisions, and the options we can consider in any given moment are limited by the choices that these external and partially unknown others have made for us.

Nonetheless, disincarnate mental beings at this level experience a sense of freedom that is orders of magnitude more rich than those that we embodied minds experience. These mental beings are, in the words of the existentialists, "thrown" into a world. The disincarnate mental experience is the sense of being a contingent and more or less frail entity arising out of a mass of other such entities, each of which is external to us and more or less alien and threatening. At the mental level, however, purusha still has the experience of surveying a vast range of possibilities and of consciously choosing among them.

Every Mind is strictly finite—which means it is strictly limited within whatever time-space it inhabits. At this point in involution, Sachchidananda has manifested out of itself a creative advance of finite drops of experience. Here, Sri Aurobindo's metaphysics issues in a world that begins to seem, phenomenologically, like the world William James

---

under the guidance of its aim, constructs for itself out of the causal influences (telepathic, empathic, and physical) to which it is subject.

and Alfred North Whitehead describe. At this point, their two systems link up beautifully. Sri Aurobindo provides an analysis of God (in this case, understood as Supermind) and of the basic ontological ground out of which God arises that seems to me to be more coherent that Whitehead's—whereas Whitehead provides an analysis of finite actual occasions and their interactions that is more adequate to understanding the results of modern science and to articulating the nature of the transphysical worlds. The mental level, from the point of view of involution, is a world of high-grade actual occasions—occasions like those that make up our wakeful moments of experience, necessarily involved in personalities, and interacting directly with each other without the mediation of emotional and physical bodies.

It is important to note that in an involutionary scheme such as this, we are not speaking of mind as something that has evolved from matter or is in any way dependent on matter. In this scheme, where the starting point is the ultimately concrete complex unity of the all-creative One, the mental world of causally interacting minds appears logically and ontologically—perhaps even temporally—prior to a world of matter.

The finite minds that appear on the involutionary arc at the mental level are completely free from the limits imposed on minds like ours, which are embodied in vital and material bodies. At this level, purusha—although conditioned by prakriti—nonetheless has a sense of dominance over it, and such beings experience a vast sense of freedom. If there is embodiment at this level, it is the embodiment of extremely high-grade actual occasions in somewhat less high-grade actual occasions. The worlds in which such beings live are wider, richer, and infinitely more responsive to wish and will than are our complex, embodied selves in the waking world.

Such beings communicate telepathically, objectifying in each other with the kind of immediacy that we experience only with our own immediately past selves. Since it seems probable that telepathic communication is mediated by networks, spatial contiguity and distance lose all meaning here. Nonetheless, such beings might be separated and ordered into groups by differences of shared meaning. Those mental occasions sharing, for example, a common metaphysics might, in terms of their effects on each other, be more proximate to each other than they would be to other mental occasions sharing a different metaphysics.

The lower threshold of consciousness for mental beings is variable. Thus, there may be mental beings for whom the functioning of the life world and the world of matter are below the threshold of consciousness, and there may be mental beings, like ourselves, who are to varying extents conscious in the lower worlds. This same consideration applies to vital beings.

The Vital World

As involution proceeds, purusha becomes more involved in prakriti, and the sattvic principle, the principle of self-organization, goes behind the veil. What is left dominant is the rajasic principle of novelty, untempered by a broader consideration of context and possible consequences. Beings dominated by the rajasic principle are called vital, or astral, beings.

While mental beings pursue harmony and depth of contrast and make choices against a background of various possibilities, vital beings compulsively pursue specific changes in their circumstances. Vital beings operate with a sense of possibility, but in general are fascinated by a particular possibility and pursue it compulsively. Our own insistent drives are expressions of the vital part of our own beings.

Vital beings are driven by desire and communicate with each other empathically. They affect each other by means of their feelings and put the nuanced complexities of thought behind the veil. Empathic communications, while they remain incredibly rich, are more abstract than they would be if they included thought as well.

The mental world is unimaginable—in the sense that we cannot array it before ourselves as a spatial extent. In the vital worlds, we can picture the interacting individuals as contextualized by a visual scene. But the geometry at work in the vital world is not metrical like that in the world of inorganic matter. In the context of a non-metrical geometry, parallel lines are undefined, so there are no measurable distances.

The degree of abstraction in objectification among vital beings is greater than that among mental beings. In the vital worlds, beings are not all proximate to each other, and so geometry, with its system of spatiotemporal ordering, becomes an important part of the scheme of indication, or system of relations, which expresses the solidarity of the vital world. The geometry here may be some sort of network geometry, or it may involve some form of projective time-space relation.

There is time-space extension in the vital world, but rather than being purely a play of meaning, the time-space of the vital worlds is a play of symbol and image. Distance here is measured not by difference in structures of meaning but by difference in symbolically mediated feeling tones.

Like the mental world, the vital world is considered to be an actual place, coming into being by an involution of the mental world, and in no way dependent on the physical world, which emerges out of the vital world by a still further involutionary movement. This world was described more fully in Chapter 8.

The Subtle Physical World

Matter emerges from the vital world by a further involutionary move in which purusha, the conscious pole, becomes still more dominated by prakriti, the material or causal pole, and in which even the rajasic guna is put behind the veil.

Note, however, that what emerges from the involution of the vital world is not the physical world as we know it. It is, to use a clumsy phrase, a "transphysical physical world." In his epic poem *Savitri*, Sri Aurobindo calls this world the "Kingdom of Subtle Matter." This is a world in which, like the other transphysical worlds, all actual occasions are involved in personalities. It is a world without entropy, friction, or disorder, in which the utter perfection of all possible physical forms is explored.

For the entities in the Kingdom of Subtle Matter there is little sense of possibility. Beings in this world see the actualities out of which they emerge and, in general, simply relay those actualities unchanged into the future. Mental beings operate with a sense of conscious choice among an array of possibilities. Vital beings operate with a sense of compulsive drive toward a narrowly defined possibility. Subtle material beings operate with a sense of overwhelming habit, pursuing not novelty or self-organization but blind perpetuation of the status quo.

Because the entities of this world are of such a low grade, and their interactions in this world of matter are so external, the system of relations, or scheme of indication that operates in the world of matter, is almost entirely geometrical.

Dr. Eric M. Weiss

The Subatomic Inconscient

We have now established a backdrop against which evolution, explored in the next chapter, can begin.

I have described an upper hemisphere of actuality consisting of Sachchidananda and Supermind, a transitional zone consisting of the overmental level, and a complex set of transphysical worlds we can conveniently consider as the mental, vital and subtle physical.

All of these worlds emerge from Sachchidananda through the exercise of Sachchidananda's powers of self-multiplication and self-limitation. The last step in this process is the achievement of a maximum of self-limitation in which even the power to form personally ordered societies is suppressed, or put behind the veil. This is the subatomic world studied in quantum physics. It is a world in which individual actual occasions arise, interpret the entire past universe into a simple probability matrix concerning simple eternal objects, make a simple decision, and expire. Beings such as these, with no personal order, know nothing of the passage of time—they exist in a pure, vanishingly small now. Also, they know nothing of space, taking in the entire past as the prehension of a minute number of simple characteristics. As the entities at this level fall below the level at which they can maintain personal order, they lose all sense of memory and anticipation. In an ontology of actual occasions, nothing is more basic than the subatomic realm.

Sri Aurobindo, in his cosmology, refers to a level below that of matter, which he calls "the inconscient." I am applying his term to the subatomic realm disclosed by postmodern physics. Clearly, the "inconscient" is not entirely without consciousness. It consists of actual occasions, each of which has its own mental pole. I have used the term "inconscient" here, however, to retain continuity with Sri Aurobindo's ideas.

Self-Absorption

I have now traced the involutionary process through which we can envision the formation of a subatomic world as a basis for an evolutionary process. One feature of our existence remains unaccounted for: ignorance. I have asserted that all of the entities that participate in this evolving universe are Sachchidananda in self-differentiation and self-limitation, but Sachchidananda could engage in self-differentiation

310

and self-limitation without ever forgetting that he/she/it is the One at play.

By analogy, we human beings have the capacity to engage in self-limitation in an entirely playful spirit. We do this, for example, when we play games, or enter in conscious role-playing. But quite often we forget we are playing a role, so we identify with the game, lose our humor, the ludic (playful) element recedes, and we become serious.

Sachchidananda, too, has the ability to forget that he/she/it is playing and can become entirely absorbed in the play of his/her/its own energy. This is the third of the three fundamental capacities of Supermind, *self-absorption.*

We can imagine self-absorption as a one-way mirror between Sachchidananda and the individuals through which he/she/it is expressing himself/herself/itself. Sachchidananda, through Supermind, never loses its own transcendent and universal knowledge (*chit*) or bliss (*ananda*), but the individuals at play in the lower hemisphere of the cosmos leave behind, or even forget, their own choice to self-limit, so they come to accept that their finitude is an absolute, given truth. This is how ignorance enters into the cosmic play.

When self-absorption enters in at the level of the subatomic, inconscient level of being, a condition of profound darkness is created. All memory is lost—not only the limited memory that figures in the life of a personality, but the implicit memory that might tend to remind an entity of its long-lost participation in soul, spirit, and the ground of being.

Cosmos emerges out of this deep ignorance, and so begins its mighty evolution.

Chapter 2: The Evolution

The evolution of which we are part begins in the darkness of the subatomic inconscient.

It is possible that our universe might have begun with a Big Bang, or a primordial flaring forth, but the cosmology I am developing here does not commit itself to any particular form of the first manifestation of inconscient entities. It does agree with modern-day astrophysics, however, in imagining that the beginning of evolution was a condition in which a subatomic world functions without the ordering power of higher-grade occasions of experience.

As noted in the previous chapter, this subatomic inconscient is the product of the involution of Sachchidananda. The subatomic entities making up the inconscient are, even thought they have largely forgotten this, modes or expressions of overmental souls and, behind those souls, of the infinite spirits of which the souls, themselves, are modes. On the other hand, reduced as they are to a single moment of simple existence, they can express almost nothing of their true splendor. The inconscient is a kind of inversion of the absolute light, power, and bliss of the One.

Why would Sachchidananda, already existing in utter light and bliss, bring about such a dark and limited ignorance? I assume that Sachchidananda is the ultimate source of the aim at value that characterizes all actual occasions, so it is natural to assume that Sachchidananda itself is moved to maximize value for itself and for all of the individuals through which it is expressed. I think we must assume that the manifestation of the inconscient somehow serves the greater bliss, the greater appreciation of value, of Sachchidananda itself. According to Sri Aurobindo, it creates the conditions for a great adventure of consciousness. Working through Supermind, Sachchidananda sets up conditions in which it can now incarnate itself in the inconscient ground that it, itself, has manifested. The evolution, then, is the ongoing attempt of Sachchidananda to incarnate itself in the inconscient. The long trajectory of human existence is played out in the context of this evolutionary project.[1]

Souls in Evolution

All the occasions in the lower hemisphere of actuality are modes (or "poises") of overmental souls. Thus, we must imagine the souls as being involved in evolution from its very inception.

It may be that each soul becomes a host of subatomic particles and continues to have subatomic poises of itself active throughout the evolutionary process. On the other hand, it may be that one soul, or a very few souls, are embodied in the subatomic events that constitute the inconscient. These souls would then be offering themselves up as a basis for the evolution of many other souls.

In the more Whiteheadian position I explored in Chapter 11, I hypothesized that all actual occasions emerge in an unmediated way from Creativity and God. Each occasion arises out of the one Creativity that, in his book *Process and Reality*, is called "the category of the ultimate"[2] and each occasion gets the specifics of its initial subjective aim from the ultimate ordering factor itself.

In the new approach I am exploring here, all *finite* actual occasions—which is to say, all the actual entities of the lower hemisphere—are poises or modes of souls, which are themselves expressions of Sachchidananda. The significance of this way of understanding actual occasions and personalities cannot be overstated.

---

[1] I do not mean to be anthropocentric here. First, by "human" I do not mean *Homo sapiens* but a certain level of mentality embodied in a physical body. Dolphins and whales may, by this definition, be human. However, I do expect at least the majority of my readers to be human in the ordinary sense, and it is the natural human curiosity about the paranormal, life after death, and reincarnation that I am trying to satisfy.

[2] Whitehead, *Process and Reality*, p. 21.

- First, it lines cosmology up with the identity of Atman and Brahman as expounded in the *Upanishads*. If we are, in effect, complex involutions of Sachchidananda, then as we explore the depths of our own subjectivity, we come closer to discovering Sachchidananda, the source of all universes, at the very core of our being. Atman, the core of our own subjectivity, is also Brahman, the ultimate Source.
- Second, it means that occasions and, thus, personalities, get their subjective aims not directly from Creativity and an ultimate ordering factor but from the overmental souls of which those personalities are modes.

Although occasions in the inconscient receive their subjective aims directly from overmental souls, they can express only the tiniest abstraction of the love, wisdom, and power native to overmental existence. Since there is no personality in the inconscient, there is no conscious memory. Also, there can be no anticipation of anything but the emptiest of immediate futures. The value character of the soul is intact, but there is no personal aim, and the social aim is also weak. The subatomic occasions of the inconscient are equipped to do nothing but perpetuate a weak and unmeaning present into a weak and unmeaning future. We can imagine the souls lurking in the background of subatomic experience in a state of dumb, unknowing frustration.

This subtle influence from the soul or souls involved in the early phases of the evolutionary project initiates the slow and painstaking movement of evolution.

The Process of Evolution

Since I am assuming that the transphysical worlds are brought into being by the involutionary process, I am also assuming that those worlds are already actual when the evolutionary project begins, and that the evolutionary process will unfold as increasingly higher personalities from the transphysical worlds become embodied in the inconscient matrix.

Dr. Eric M. Weiss

Evolution can be described as happening in five stages:

- The evolution of the material world
- The evolution of life in the material world
- The evolution of mind in the living world
- The evolution of human beings in the mental world
- The evolutionary journey beyond the human

The Evolution of Matter

The first task of evolution is to bring into existence the macrocosmic world of physical matter. This is accomplished in a threefold movement that, as we will see, is characteristic of every evolutionary advance:

- First, operating under the inbuilt drive toward value, the subatomic occasions of the inconscient begin to form coherent patterns. These are entirely unconscious for the subatomic occasions involved, but I assume they begin to attract the attention of personalities existing in the world of subtle matter.
- At some point, some of these personalities take some subset of subatomic occasions and turn them into prehensions for themselves. These subatomic occasions, under the influence of the aim of the higher-grade personality that is becoming embodied in them, become closed, self-organizing or autopoietic systems of interactions. The first atoms have now appeared.
- Under the influence of the newly incarnated subtle physical personalities, the macrocosmic physical world as we know it begins to function. This idea requires some expansion. In quantum mechanics, there is a famous question that concerns the relationship between the "classical" (macrocosmic) world, which includes everything about the world that can be accounted for in terms of pre-quantum physics, and the "quantum world" (microcosmic), which is the world of subatomic events as described by quantum mechanics. Quantum physicists have not yet agreed on where the boundary between the microcosmic world and the macrocosmic world should be drawn.

316

In terms of transpersonal process metaphysics, I would propose that the boundary between these two worlds is marked by the evolutionary emergence of enduring entities, or personally ordered societies of actual occasions. Personally ordered societies are the first entities to have continuity of memory (and therefore an experience of ongoing time), and which can recognize specific other occasions in their environments (and thus have an experience of ordered space). They are the smallest entities that can be approximately described by classical laws. Of course this is not a clear boundary. Atoms, and even larger systems, still display some quantum uncertainty in their behaviors. But I believe that drawing the boundary between macrocosmic and microcosmic in this way is useful.

Fall and Emergence

If we consider the process of embodiment from the point of view of the transphysical entities involved, it makes sense to describe the process of embodiment as a "fall." Take, for example, the occasions of the subtle physical world that embody themselves as the first atoms:

- In the subtle physical world, there is not yet any friction or entropy. The form of an entity is a direct expression of alternatives with which it has been presented and the decisions it has made. The subtle physical world is a perfect harmony, unmarred by any sort of accident or contrary will.
- But when it embodies itself in a system of subatomic occasions, henceforth it can know its new world only through using its subatomic occasions as prehensions, and it can express itself only through those possibilities that are compatible with the behaviors of their subatomic constituents. The subatomic occasions of the inconscient are so simple and so habit-bound that they present only very limited choices through which the higher-grade, subtle material personalities embodied in them can express themselves. Also, the conditions in the inconscient, where personal order and all memory are lost, are very different from the conditions obtaining in any of the transphysical worlds, in which personal order is natural and in which memory functions well. For this reason, the

higher-grade personalities that fall into the inconscient tend
to lose all continuity of conscious memory. They, too, fall
into ignorance.

This is a three-stage process in which there is: an invitation from
below as the lower-grade occasions (or lower-grade personalities) begin
to elaborate interesting patterns of interaction; a response from above,
leading to the descent, or fall, of personalities from higher worlds; and
a subsequent reorganization of the operations of the universe. This
three-stage process repeats itself at each new evolutionary advance and
is the way in which transpersonal process metaphysics accounts for what
evolutionary scientists sometimes call "emergence."

But each stage of the evolutionary advance is a fall on the part of the
higher-grade entities that get embodied either in subatomic occasions, or
in other societies that are, themselves, embodied in subatomic occasions.
The necessity of this involvement with the subatomic inconscient
consigns all evolving entities to the ignorance and incapacity that
restrict and limit waking life until evolution culminates at last and
releases them, into "a life divine."

The Evolution of Life

Once the atoms come into existence as the first macrocosmic entities,
the evolution of matter unfolds. The atoms, engaging in their own
dance, gradually create the conditions in which higher and higher
grades of subtle physical beings become involved in molecular structures
of greater and greater complexity.

The evolution of life, then, follows the same general pattern I
outlined above:

- First, the macromolecules that have now evolved do their
dance and eventually create dissipative structures that are
sufficiently complex to attract the embodiment of the first
vital entities.
- These living personalities descend into the material world
expecting to bring with them the joys of the vital world—but
instead find themselves extremely limited and dulled. The
field of possibilities to which they are accustomed is severely

minimized by the possibilities of the subatomic entities in which they are embodied. They exchange the freedom and vividness of the astral world for the dull and constricted existence of single-celled animals. The emergence of life in the waking world is the fall of many vital personalities from the vital world.

- In spite of whatever shock they experience at their first immersion in the inconscient, the cells that are formed by the descent of the first vital personalities into matter bring entirely new dynamics into the material world.

Again, the personality embodied in each cell is a mode of an overmental soul, but whether or not all cells are the expression of an single individual soul, or whether each species of cell is the expression of an individual soul, or whether each individual cell is the sole expression of a unique individual soul we can only speculate.

Certain schools of theosophy hold that each animal species is the expression of a single soul. As animal souls become more evolved they begin to differentiate, so that at the level of domestic animals, the individual personalities of individual animals are almost ready to function in relation to a single soul of their own. Then, through their interactions with human beings, they are initiated into the human level of evolution,[3] and when they reincarnate they do so as human beings. What is suggested by this story is that in evolution, only human beings are individually connected to a single soul. This is what Plato might call a "likely story," but I can provide no evidence to support it.

The Evolution of Mind

Before we can discuss the evolution of mind, we need to clarify the various senses in which that word is used in this document. First, we have used the word "mind" to refer to that capacity for consciousness to engage in selective attention and for the force of consciousness to manifest a world of plurality out of the complex unity of the divine ground. Second, we have used mind to designate the stage of the involution where transcendence and universality have been suppressed,

---

[3] Again, I want to emphasize that by "human" I do not mean *Homo sapiens* but occasions of a sufficiently high grade in bodies that are rooted in matter.

and where the experience of isolated individuality first emerges on the involutionary arc. Note that all mental occasions are of very high grade, so that the range of possibilities that can be explored and realized by them is expansive compared to those experienced by the occasions constituting the vital and subtle physical worlds. In this section, we are discussing the *evolutionary* emergence of mind (in other words, the descent of mental occasions into the waking world that grows out of the inconscient).

Since science tells us that the nervous system is that part of our physiology most concerned with interpreting experience and arranging action, we can speculate that the evolution of mind coincides with the development of nervous-system tissue.

Again we see the same threefold process:

- The inherent quest for value built into all personalities leads to a great complexification of organisms, creating an environment in which nervous-system tissue can function.
- The descent of mental-grade occasions into cells brings about the actual appearance of nerve tissues, and mental-grade occasions become embodied for the first time.
- Thinking beings, as animals, then further transform the evolutionary environment.

The Evolution of Human Beings

I am going to advance the claim that human beings are more evolved than other animals in waking life and on the surface of the Earth. Note that when I say "human beings" I do not necessarily mean *Homo sapiens*. Rather, I mean beings that embody personalities of a particular mental grade and higher. Human beings could be in bodies of any shape, and I do not exclude the possibility that other animals (particularly whales and dolphins, who have larger and more complex brains than *Homo sapiens*) may be at the same (if not higher) level of evolution as *Homo sapiens*.

I am aware that even this modified claim is controversial, and before I make it, I want to acknowledge just why it is so controversial. First, *Homo sapiens* have done such a terrible job of caring for the biosphere that it's hard to credit us with being very evolved at all. Nonetheless, I do want to claim that *Homo sapiens* are, at least, more evolved than any other creature in waking life, and on the surface of the planet, at this time. This is not to say that *Homo sapiens* (or humans in general) are *better* than other entities in any way. Each entity is infinitely precious, as an expression of Brahman contained in, pervaded by, and inhabited by Sachchidananda through Supermind. I particularly don't want to make the claim that human beings behave with more "goodness" than other non-human animals, as that claim would be absurd.

Although I don't want to say that human beings are better than other non-human animals, I do want to say they are more *evolved*. Evolution, as I am defining it here, is the attempt to consciously embody supermental spirits in the environment created by the inconscient—in more familiar words, to embody God in matter. Therefore, the degree to which an entity is evolved is measured by the grade of the occasions making up its presiding personality.[4] Judging by the range of possibilities that human beings consider in their decision making and the ranges of the future that they consider relevant to those decisions, *Homo sapiens* seem to be the highest-grade occasions involved in the current evolutionary scheme on the surface of our planet Earth.

While all animals (human and non-human) are already mental beings in the cosmology I am developing, I am suggesting here that the personalities involved in human beings are of a higher mental grade than are those embodied in the non-human animals.

In fact, human beings are of such a high grade that they can, at their best, begin to sense and to respond to their own basic value character. In effect, human beings (*Homo sapiens* and possibly others) are the only species that can directly respond to the souls of which they are modes of expression.

How Souls Operate in the Life of Human Beings

Souls are intimately involved in evolution from its beginning. As they project their value character into personalities and other finite occasions, souls may be looked at as the basic driving force in evolution.[5] The longing of souls for the universal harmony to which they are native,

---

[4] This is essentially equivalent to Teilhard's suggestion that the more evolved an entity is, the greater the degree of its "complexity/consciousness."
[5] This is similar to Teilhard's idea of the "Cosmic Christ."

and their longing to express their own richness through the limited possibilities afforded in the environment of the inconscient, accounts for the evolutionary drift in the mass of events that make up the creative advance. We could say, as Sri Aurobindo does, that the purpose of embodied souls is to manifest bodies capable of supporting personalities that can fully express their joy, love, wisdom, and power in the physical world.

While our personalities may not be the only expression of our soul in the present (there is no reason why the soul, since it becomes embodied by the causal effects of its own aim, can't have many different simultaneous incarnations), nonetheless all the occasions of each personality share the same value character, and that value character is of one particular overmental soul. The subjective aim of the soul is the aim at evolution. From the point of view of the soul, evolution is its attempt to fully express itself through embodiment, directly or indirectly, in the inconscient. Soul's evolutionary contribution is to aim at universality. Working through the soul, spirit (also felt in the personality) aims at transcendence. Thus we can now say that each of us is influenced by a basic value character that aligns us with the overall aim of evolution, and that that aim is the incarnation in the inconscient of a being fully conscious of its own universality and transcendence.

At the level of the human personality (at least insofar as that human state is experienced by *Homo sapiens*), we become conscious of our own values and of the conflicts between them. For example, we become aware that we value adventure and that we value safety as well. Or we become aware that some of our social values (e.g., patriotism) conflict with other, more personal values (such as a desire to cultivate universal compassion). Most importantly, we begin to become aware of the basic value character we receive from our souls, and we begin to differentiate that from the mass of personal and social values that usually dominate our behaviors. This is the beginning of the spiritual path.

From this point of view, the spiritual path is the continuation of the overall evolution in the light of human self-consciousness. In other words, we become capable of formulating, for ourselves, some notion of the overall aim of evolution, and we begin to develop the capacity to pursue our evolution deliberately. All of nature, as Sri Aurobindo points out, is an evolution. But at the human level of the evolutionary process, evolution itself enters into conscious self-awareness. Evolution becomes hominized.

In the cosmology that flows from transpersonal process metaphysics, the overall aim of evolution is understood to be the incarnation of souls and spirits here, in the environment of the inconscient. This overall cosmic objective is also the overall objective of human existence. We must understand the ultimate long trajectory of human life in light of this goal.

The Long Trajectory

We are now in a position to summarize the entire trajectory of human existence:

- The journey begins in Sachchidananda itself.
- It proceeds through an involution that works its way "down" through infinite spirits and overmental souls to produce all of the finite personalities that constitute the transphysical worlds. That involution culminates in the subatomic inconscient, where ignorance reigns supreme, and the entities involved can operate only on dumb instinct that lures them, slowly and raggedly, back toward the heights from which they have descended.
- Even in the inconscient, however, instinct expresses the knowledge, power, and light of Sachchidananda. Under the pressure of that instinct evolution begins and unfolds, as higher and higher grades of personalities become embodied in the inconscient.
  - First, the personalities of the world of subtle matter become embodied in the inconscient, and the macrocosmic physical world comes into existence.
  - Then the personalities of the vital world become embodied in that world of matter, and living beings appear in evolution, drenched in the rich values of emotion.
  - The personalities of the vital entities that are now (through matter) embodied in the world, further complexify the life of the waking world until that

life is capable of embodying mental occasions. Animals enter into evolution, and with the intellect of animals catalyzing the play of emotions, raw emotion complexifies into drama.

o The interplay of animals invites in higher mental personalities, and human beings enter the evolutionary play.

Just what separates the various human species from their fellow animals is hard to say. Human beings of our species have thought of themselves as the animal who knows (*Homo sapiens*); the animal who uses tools and makes things *(Homo faber)*; and as the animal who plays (expressed in the book, *Homo Ludens*, written by Johan Huizinga). Each of these visions expresses some truth. It is also true to say that all species of human beings, including us, are *Homo spiritus,* the animal who feels God.

Most of us take the world for granted most of the time. As we go through our daily lives, it is as if the world always was as it is now, and always will be. Only in certain exalted moments can we feel the entirety of the actual world standing out against all the other ways that it might have been. Only in those moments do we sense, feel, and know the presence of "that from which all experience arises."

In those exalted moments we sense into this essential distinguishing feature of human existence—the capacity to recognize the entity that contains, pervades, and inhabits this and all possible universes, and to recognize that entity as the most relevant factor in every moment of finite existence.

The higher the grade of a personality, the more widely and deeply it knows its world. With the evolution of human beings, the capacity emerges for a personality that knows not only its own world widely, but can also embrace in its regard the universe as a whole, as well as that which transcends it.

When we discern this divine factor in existence, we become fully human, and actions we take in the light of that factor are what Sri Aurobindo calls "the integral yoga."

The great saints and yogis of the past have been our evolutionary scouts. They show us the way forward in the evolutionary advance. The long trajectory of human existence follows in the general direction that they have pioneered, and it culminates when supermental spirits walk the Earth in material, biological, and nervous bodies.

The entity that actually evolves is the soul. The soul evolves by becoming embodied in a complex sequence of personalities. Some of these personalities may be involved in involution, some in the inconscient, and some at every stage of the evolutionary advance. There seems to be no reason why the soul cannot experience many simultaneous embodiments.[1]

Each embodiment of the soul (except those embodiments that are flashes of subatomic existence) is a finite personality:

- Each personality begins its existence at some position in the creative advance and continues existing as a personally ordered society as long as conditions permit.
- Each personality receives its basic value character from the soul of which it is an expression, and it receives into itself with some special intimacy the causal objectifications of all of the previous personalities and occasions in which its soul has previously been embodied. This notion is related to the Vedic notion of karma, but it is different from the usual understanding of karma in that the personality is karmically affected by *all* of the previous embodiments of its soul. This would imply a universe in which all karma is collective. It may be possible for one strand of personality to be thought of as a particular continuation of some other particular strand of personality under the right circumstances. This seems to be the case in many of Stevenson's cases, and may be the case whenever one strand of personality takes up the task that another has left undone, creating some special connection between the two strands.
- When the environing conditions no longer permit the continuation of the personality, or when, for some reason, the soul withdraws its consent from the ongoing existence of the personality, that personality dies.

---

[1] In the context of a many-worlds hypothesis, the soul could also be embodied in many *times* as well.

- At that point, a number of destinies open up for that personality.
  - ○ It may simply cease to exist and have no further function in the creative advance except for the causal role it plays in future embodiments of its soul. Under certain circumstances, if some subsequent strand of personality belonging to the same soul is connected to it intimately, we may say that this same strand of personality reincarnates.
  - ○ If that personality was embodied in a system of lower-grade occasions, it may continue to exist at the transphysical level to which it is native for some period after the dissolution of its lower-grade body.
  - ○ A transphysical personality that has survived an earlier death carries the memories of its embodied lifetime—whether or not it was the presiding personality of a self. It may enter into a currently embodied personality as a new strand of that already existing self; it may (under conditions which are probably rare) enter into a currently embodied personality as its presiding personality; or it may enter into a new birth—either as a sub-personality or as a presiding personality.

The trajectory of a human personality does not end at the death of the body. Survival of bodily death is a normal part of the human life cycle.

Given the complex and varied processes through which experience is shared in the creative advance, it is not clear whether or not we should speak of personalities as reincarnating. However, it also seems that each personality, indeed each and every occasion of experience, makes an enduring contribution to the creative advance and reincarnates, in some very general sense of the term, throughout the entirety of its future. More intimately, each occasion and each personality belong to one specific soul with which they share a basic value character. We are each a part of a complex strand of personalities. What binds these personalities into a unity is the life of the soul.

The long trajectory from an evolutionary perspective seems to be the journey of the soul. The soul lasts as long as the universe of which it is a part. In our evolutionary scheme, as it is played out in our waking lives, the work of the soul is to find a way to express, in the darkness of the inconscient, the full glory and splendor of the supermental spirit and, through that, the absolute of Sachchidananda itself.

The long trajectory of our souls points toward a consummation that entirely changes the conditions of the difficult and perplexing evolution in ignorance, and opens up endless vistas of evolution in the absoluteness of divine light, power, and love.

Concluding Reflections

This book is a part of a much larger project. I have been persuaded by the evidence of my own experience and the wonderful analysis of the human cycle presented by Sri Aurobindo[1] and, most notably, Jean Gebser[2] that our species is currently undergoing a "mutation of consciousness." Many of us sense that our entire planet is undergoing an immense transformation. We are in the midst of a global mass extinction of flora and fauna, the weather is strange and defying its historical patterns, the Earth is in upheaval, and many of us sense that our Western, industrial/capitalist global civilization is crumbling under us.

In the midst of this massive death, something new is being born. Sri Aurobindo calls it "a subjective age," and Gebser calls it the "integral/aperspectival" mutation of consciousness.

It is not generally appreciated that a mutation of consciousness is also a reconfiguration of the senses. In modern times—indeed since the dawn of what Gebser calls the Mental mutation of consciousness at the time of the classical Greek civilization—we have tended to privilege the objectifications that the physical world reveals through our five physiological senses. (These are the foundation of modern scientific sensory empiricism—especially the senses of vision and touch.) We have tended to imagine that the waking world is real while the dream world is not. As a result, we have stopped, or at least greatly reduced,

---

[1] See Sri Aurobindo, *The Human Cycle*.
[2] See Gebser, *The Ever-Present Origin*.

paying attention to our inner senses and our transphysical senses, and have neglected their cultivation.

There is reason to think that as we move into the new mutation our senses will reconfigure, and the objectifications of our transphysical sense organs will become more prominent in the structuring of our appearance of the world. We may find ourselves in what seems to us to be an entirely new world—a world more different from our current world than ours is from the world experienced by a medieval villager. It is my hope that the metaphysical ideas I have articulated here can help bring that transition about and make it more manageable by giving us a language in which it can be understood.

Finally, this new mutation of consciousness will require its own mode of production. Each previous mutation has had its unique way of interacting with the environment to satisfy human needs. In the Magical mutation of consciousness, people hunted and gathered. In the Mythical mutation of consciousness, people farmed and lived in villages. In the Mental mutation of consciousness, people began to construct elaborate artifacts, lived in cities and states, built empires and nations, and came to relate to the world through industrialism and capitalism with its elaborate technologies.

I believe that the new mutation will take us beyond our current form of technology into something wildly more interesting and, hopefully, far less destructive: a way of relating to our environment that is informed by our empathic and telepathic interconnections with the rest of nature; a way of cultivating health that relies on working directly with the higher-grade occasions of our bodies; a way of communication that transcends physical distances by working through transpersonal worlds; and a way to access transphysical domains that opens up vast and wondrous new worlds for exploration.

I envision this book as a contribution to the formation of that new civilization.

Looking Forward

I have opened up and thought through a consistent metaphysical cosmology supporting modern science, postmodern science, parapsychology, survival of bodily death, reincarnation, and mystical experiences. Nonetheless, the ideas expressed in this book are tentative, and are designed to stimulate further research, both theoretical and experimental.

I am aware that there are many places where the arguments in this book can be further developed, and there are a number of important issues have not been considered. Prominent among them, for example, is the working out of a process approach to mechanics and a process approach to thermodynamics. While I see ways in which these problems can be approached, their explication and the full development of the perspective suggested by this book will be work I hope is conducted by many scholars, over an extended span of time.

Whitehead tells us, "Rationalism is an adventure in the clarification of thought, progressive and never final. But it is an adventure in which even partial success has importance."[3] This book is, I hope, such a partial success.

---

[3] Whitehead, *Process and Reality*, p. 9.

Bibliography

Aurobindo, Sri. (1990). *The Life Divine* (2nd American ed.). Pondicherry, India: Sri Aurobindo Ashram Press.

_____. (1983). *Essays on the Gita*. Pondicherry, India: Sri Aurobindo Ashram Press.

_____. (1992). *The Human Cycle* (2nd ed.). Pondicherry, India: Sri Aurobindo Ashram Press.

_____. (1994). *The Problem of Rebirth*. Pondicherry, India: Sri Aurobindo Ashram Press.

_____. (1989). *The Psychic Being (Soul: Its Nature, Mission, and Evolution)*. Twin Lakes, WI: Lotus Lights Publications.

_____. (1970). *Savitri*. (3rd ed.). Pondicherry, India: Sri Aurobindo Ashram Press.

_____. (1999). *The Synthesis of Yoga* (5th ed.). Twin Lakes, WI: Lotus Lights Publications.

Bailey, Alice A. (1977). *A Treatise on Cosmic Fire*. New York: Lucis Publishing.

Berry, Thomas. (1999). *The Great Work: Our Way into the Future*. New York: Bell Tower.

Besant, Annie. (2007). *Ancient Wisdom: An Outline of Theosophical Teachings*. Whitefish, MT: Kessinger Publishing.

Blavatsky, H. P. (1993). *The Secret Doctrine*. Wheaton, IL: The Theosophical Publishing House.

Black, Max. (Ed.). (1965). *Philosophy in America*. London: George Allen and Unwin.

Braude, Stephen. (1966). *The Limits of Influence: Psychokinesis and the Philosophy of Science* (Revised ed.). Lanham, MD: University Press of America.

Bruce, Robert. (1999). *Astral Dynamics*. Charlottesville, VA: Hampton Roads.

Buddhaghosa, Bhadantacariya. (1975). *The Path of Purification (Visuddhimagga,* 3rd ed.). (Bhikku Nanamoli, Trans.). Kandy, Sri Lanka: Buddhist Publication Society.

Burtt, Edwin A. (2003). *The Metaphysical Foundations of Modern Science.* Mineola, NY: Dover Publications.

Cassirer, Ernst. (1944). *An Essay on Man.* New Haven, CT: Yale University Press.

_____. (1955). *The Philosophy of Symbolic Forms, Volume 1: Language.* New Haven, CT: Yale University Press.

_____. (1965). *The Philosophy of Symbolic Forms, Volume 2: Mythical Thought.* New Haven, CT: Yale University Press.

_____. (1953). *Substance and Function and Einstein's Theory of Relativity.* Chicago: Open Court Press.

Capek, Milik. (1961). *The Philosophical Impact of Contemporary Physics.* New York: Van Nostrand Reinhold Company.

de Quincey, Christian. (2002). *Radical Nature.* Montpelier, VT: Invisible Cities Press.

Epperson, Michael. (2004). *Quantum Mechanics and the Philosophy of Alfred North Whitehead.* New York: Fordham University Press.

Gebser, Jean. (1985). *The Ever-Present Origin.* (Noel Barstad & Algis Mickunas, Trans.). Athens, OH: Ohio University Press.

Gibson, William. (2000). *Neuromancer.* New York: The Berkley Publishing Group.

Godfrey-Smith, Peter. (2003). *Theory and Reality: An Introduction to the Philosophy of Science.* Chicago: University of Chicago Press.

Heidegger, Martin. (2000). *Introduction to Metaphysics.* (Gregory Fried & Richard Polt, Trans.). New Haven, CT: Yale University.

Herbert, Nick. (1985). *Quantum Reality.* New York: Anchor Books Editions.

Hosinski, Thomas. (1993). *Stubborn Fact and Creative Advance: An Introduction to the Metaphysics of Alfred North Whitehead.* Lanham, MD: Rowman and Littlefield Publishers.

Huizinga, Johan. (2008). *Homo Ludens: A Study of the Play Element in Culture.* London: Routledge and Kegan Paul.

Jahn, Robert and Brenda Dunne. (1987). *Margins of Reality: The Role of Consciousness in the Physical World.* San Diego, CA: Harcourt Brace.

Kelly, Edward F., and Emily Williams Kelly. (2007). *Irreducible Mind.* Lanham, MD: Rowman and Littlefield Publishers.

Kelly, Sean. (2008). "Integral Time and the Varieties of Post-Mortem Survival." *Integral Review,* 1(4). http://integral-review.org/back_issues/backissue6/index.htm

Kuhn, Thomas. (1970). *The Structure of Scientific Revolutions.* Chicago: University of Chicago Press.

Laberge, Stephen, and Howard Rheingold. (1990). *Exploring the World of Lucid Dreaming.* New York: Ballantine Publishing.

Leadbeater, C. W. (1910). *The Inner Life.* East Sussex, England: Society of Metaphysicians.

Leclerc, Ivor. (1972). *The Nature of Physical Existence.* London: George Allen and Unwin.

Luckhurst, Roger. (2002). *The Invention of Telepathy.* Oxford: Oxford University Press.

Macy, Joanna. (1991). *Mutual Causality in Buddhism and General Systems Theory: The Dharma of Natural Systems.* New York: SUNY Press.

Malin, Shimon. (2001). *Nature Loves to Hide: Quantum Physics and the Nature of Reality, a Western Perspective.* Oxford: Oxford University Press.

Maturana, Humberto R., and Francisco Varela. (1980). *Autopoiesis and Cognition: The Realization of the Living.* Boston: D. Reidel Publishing.

Monroe, Robert. (1985). *Far Journeys.* New York: Doubleday.

Morin, Edgar. (1992). *Method: Towards a Study of Humankind – Volume 1: The Nature of Nature.* Translated by Roland Bélanger. New York: Peter Lang.

Murphy, Michael. (1992). *The Future of the Body: Explorations into the Further Evolution of Human Nature.* New York: Jeremy P. Tarcher/Putnam.

Pearsall, Paul, et al. (2002). "Changes in Heart-Transplant Recipients That Parallel the Personalities of Their Donors." *Journal of Near-Death Studies,* 20(3).

Poortman, J. J. (1978). *Vehicles of Consciousness.* (4 vols.). Adyar-Madras, India: Utrecht.

Powell, A. E. (1972). *The Astral Body.* Wheaton, IL: Quest.

_____. (1978). *The Causal Body and the Ego*. London: Theosophical Publishing House.

_____. (1972). *The Etheric Body*. Wheaton, IL: Quest.

_____. (1975). *The Mental Body*. London: Theosophical Publishing House.

_____. (1985).*The Solar System*. Pomeroy, WA: Health Research Books.

Radin, Dean. (1997). *The Conscious Universe: The Scientific Truth of Psychic Phenomena*. San Francisco: HarperEdge.

Russell, Bernard. (1953). *Introduction to Mathematical Philosophy*. London: George Allen and Unwin.

Sharma, Poonam, and J. Tucker. (2004). "Cases of the Reincarnation Type with Memories from the Intermission between Lives." *Journal of Near-Death Studies*, 23(2).

Shaw, Gregory. (1951). *Theurgy and the Soul*. University Park, PA: Pennsylvania University Press.

Stapp, Henry. (2009). *Mind, Matter, and Quantum Mechanics* (2nd ed.). Berlin: Springer.

_____. (2007). *Mindful Universe: Quantum Mechanics and the Participating Observer* (2nd ed.). Berlin: Springer.

Steiner, Rudolf. (1947). *Knowledge of the Higher Worlds and its Attainment*. (Henry Monges & Lisa Monges, Trans.). Great Barrington, MA: Anthroposophic Press.

Stevenson, Ian. (1975). *Cases of the Reincarnation Type; Volume I, II, III, and IV*. Charlottesville, VA: University of Virginia Press.

_____. (2001). *Children Who Remember Previous Lives: A Question of Reincarnation* (Revised ed). Jefferson, NC: McFarland & Company.

_____. (1980). *Twenty Cases Suggestive of Reincarnation*. Charlottesville, VA: University of Virginia Press.

Swedenborg, Emanuel. (1984). *The Universal Human and Soul-Body Interaction*. Mahwah, NJ: Paulist Press.

Swimme, Brian, and Thomas Berry. (1994). *The Universe Story: From the Primordial Flaring Forth to the Ecozoic Era*. San Francisco: HarperSanFrancisco.

Targ, Russell, and Jean Huston. (2004). *Limitless Mind: A Guide to Remote Viewing and Transformation of Consciousness*. Novato, CA: New World Library.

Teilhard de Chardin, Pierre. (2003). *The Human Phenomenon*. (Sarah Appleton-Weber, Trans.). Eastbourne, UK: Sussex Academic Press.

Vieira, Waldo. (1995). *Projections of the Consciousness*. Rio de Janiero, Brazil: International Institute of Projectiology and Conscientiology.

Wagoner, Robert. (2009). *Lucid Dreaming: Gateway to the Inner Self*. Needham, MA: Moment Point Press.

Warcollier, Rene. (2001). *Mind to Mind*. Charlottesville, VA: Hampton Roads Publishing Company.

Weiss, Eric. (2009). "A Commentary on Chapter 10 of *Science and the Modern World* by Alfred North Whitehead." *Process Studies Supplement, 14*.

_____. (2003). *The Doctrine of the Subtle Worlds*. Ann Arbor, MI: Proquest.

_____. (2004). *Embodiment: A Frame for the Exploration of Reincarnation and Personality Survival*. http://ericweiss.com/embodiment-an-explanatory-framework-for-the-exploration-of-reincarnation-and-personality-survival. http://www.ctr4process.org/publications/ProcessStudies/PSS/

Whitehead, Alfred North. (1967). *Adventures of Ideas*. New York: The Free Press.

_____. (1964). *Concept of Nature*. New York: Cambridge University Press.

_____. (1991). "Immortality." In Paul Arthur Shlipp (Ed.), *The Philosophy of Alfred North Whitehead*. Chicago: Open Court Publishing.

_____. (1982). *An Inquiry Concerning the Principles of Natural Knowledge*. New York: Dover Publications.

_____. (1961). *The Interpretation of Science: Selected Essays*. Indianapolis, IN: Bobbs-Merrill.

_____. (1961). "The Principle of Relativity with Applications to Physical Science." In F.S.C. Northrop & Mason W. Gross (Eds.), *Alfred North Whitehead: An Anthology*. New York: Macmillan.

_____. (1966). *Modes of Thought*. New York: The Free Press.

_____. (1985). *Process and Reality* (Corrected ed.). New York: The Free Press.

_____. (1967). *Science and the Modern World.* New York: The Free Press.

Index

causes
  efficient cause. *See* efficient cause
  final cause. *See* final cause
  formal cause, 107*t*, 112–15
  material cause, 106, 107*t*, 108–
    11, 120
  in three metaphysical contexts,
    107*t*
  in transphysical process
    metaphysics, 110–17
  types of, according to Aristotle,
    105–6
cells
  acting as if operated by central
    personality, 141
  communication between, 146
  as grade of actual occasion, 152,
    169–70
  as making free decisions, 140
  personalities of, 145
  self-organizing system of, 102
  as system of macromolecules
    organized by higher-grade
    personality, 145
central consciousness, 141, 170, 243
channeling, 35, 238
chaos theory, 57
character, 256–57, 261
chit (consciousness), 286, 287, 311
choice. *See also* decisions
  as part of actual occasions/drops
    of experience, 72–74
  as phase of every process, 150
  and randomness, 9, 12, 98
Christianity, 296
classical physics, four causes in,
  107*t*. *See also* physics
classification science (natural history
  science), 44, 47
cognitive judgment, 48
cogredience, 190

common sense, 23–24, 30, 45, 50,
  57, 60, 90, 176, 196, 206, 209,
  217, 231, 254, 279
complex thinking, 280–81
Comprehending Supermind, 292–
  94, 296
conceptual model of world,
  compared to actual world, 55–56
conceptual prehensions, 129, 131–
  32, 146, 150
conceptual reversion, 131
concrescence, 73, 93, 103, 107*t*,
  112–16, 121–22, 126, 129–37,
  142–46, 154, 158–59, 170, 179,
  185, 188, 202, 205, 215, 227,
  256, 262, 273, 294
concrete, as distinct from abstract,
  79, 85
confirmation, 301–2
conformal, 130, 154, 156–57, 173
conformal experience, 95
conscious memory, 11, 255, 258–
  60, 264–66, 268, 275, 315, 318
conscious pole, 126, 306, 309
conscious process, 66
consciousness
  as active everywhere, 100
  as agency of actualization, 94
  defined, 7, 9, 12
  existence of, 71–72
  intrinsic connection of, to time-
    space, 205
  living cell as center of, 170
  mental mutation of, 225
  and modern materialistic
    reductionism, 23
  no mention of, in relativistic
    framework, 198
  in same domain as efficient
    causality, 202
  and scientific materialism, 45

as none without feeling, 8
as personally ordered society, 265
propositions as essential element
 in formation of, 136
and receipt of basic value
 character, 325
and reincarnation, 326
as sequence of events, 148
and survival of the death of its
 body, 30
unity of, 14
personally ordered society/societies,
 76n9, 136–38, 172, 177, 187,
 189, 229, 243, 254–56, 258–60,
 264–65, 310, 317, 325
phenomenological testing (of
 metaphysics), 49–51
philosophical explanations, 92
philosophical idealism, 64–65
philosophy, purpose of, 160
physical, as not equal to actual, 164
physical beings, as distinct from
 material beings, 164
physical body, 6, 247*f*
physical continuity, 255, 257, 260,
 265–66, 275
physical interaction, 211, 305
physical matter, 30, 45, 65, 164–67,
 172, 176, 184–85, 234, 316
physical pole, 126, 149, 306
physical prehensions, 123n3
physical world
 according to transphysical process
  metaphysics, 145
 as causally closed domain, 57
 as closed domain of non-
  conscious things, 71
 compared to waking world, 147,
  153, 164
 composition of, 187

cosmology that supports existence
 of, 38
as limitation of the vital world,
 192
objective physical world, 45
as one of three domains, 186
as quantized, 69
and quantum theory, 58
subtle physical world, 309
as whole of reality, 23
physicalism, 160
physics, 13, 44, 58, 71, 74–75, 90,
 107*t*, 145, 153, 159, 163, 165,
 172, 180, 188, 190, 192, 196–99,
 209, 213, 218, 229–30, 235,
 238, 284, 305, 310, 316. *See also*
 quantum physics
physiology, 97, 245–46, 320
placbeo effects, power of, 25
plants, 71, 141, 158, 170, 215
Plato, 41, 51–53, 79, 81, 150, 155,
 286, 319
poetic musing, 48
point-instant, 201
point-mass, 82
poles
 causal pole, 309
 conscious pole, 126, 306, 309
 material pole, 149, 309
 mental pole, 70–71, 132, 205,
  306
 physical pole, 126, 149, 306
Poortman, J. J., 22, 335
position, 122–23, 137–38, 142–44,
 176, 208–9, 255–57
possession, 238
possibilities, 86–87, 92–93, 99,
 112–13, 127, 136, 150, 170–71,
 213–19
postmodern science, 44–47, 51, 85,
 152, 207, 330

and placement of high-grade occasions, 159–60
and relationship of ideas to actuality, 79
and subatomic particles, 67
and substance, 62
on time-space, 209
and uncertain transitions of position, 208
quantum physics, 9, 49, 91, 94, 131, 160, 184, 200, 213, 234, 310
quantum theory, 9, 160–61

R
Radin, Dean, 28, 336
rajasic guna, 301, 308, 309
randomness, compared to choice, 9, 12, 98
rapport, between high-grade personality and low-grade personality, 181
rational thinking, 48
real, as distinct from actual, 149
reality
  and actuality, 149
  as being conditioned by thinking, 87
  as consisting of atomicity and continuity, 101
  defined, 85
  as distinct from ideas, 79
  relationships of, with appearance, 155–56
reciprocal apparitions, 33
recursive function, 57, 111, 120
reductionism, inadequacy of, 90–92
reductionistic materialism, 23, 98–100. *See also* materialistic reductionism
reductionistic science, 44–46, 52, 91, 115, 118, 184

"regular world," 14
reincarnation. *See also* survival
  author's assumptions about, 251
  and classical science, 57
  defined, 15–16
  and different causal operations, 249
  as distinct from personality survival, 251–53
  proof of, 40
  theories of, 264–68
  types of, 40–41, 252–55
relationship, process of, 202
relativistic framework, 198
relativistic understanding, 216
relativity, theory of, 57, 59, 62, 196, 207, 232
remote viewing, 29, 38
repression, 298
res cogitans (thinking things), 65–66
res extensa (extended things), 65
resonance, 124, 130, 259. *See also* formal resonance
resonance of aim, 124–25
rigid rod, 162
Roger Rabbit (movie), 37

S
Sachchidananda, 281, 285–89, 292–94, 296–97, 298–99, 303, 306, 310–11, 313–15, 321, 323
sat (being), 285, 287
sattvic guna, 301–2, 308
savant consciousnesses, 243–44
Savitri (Aurobindo), 309, 333
scheme of indication, 212
Schopenhauer, Arthur, 66
Schrödinger wave equation, 255
science. *See also specific sciences*
  as based on experiments, 55
  defined, 44–45

thinking things (*res cogitans*), 65–66
time
    interconnectedness of, with space, 197
    as more fundamental than space, 197
    in upper hemisphere of Being, 303–4
timefull, 303, 305
timeless, 303
time-space. *See also* space-time
    as complex of time and space, 197
    experiential time-space, 198–99
    intrinsic connection of, to consciousness, 205
    kinds of, 195
    as mandala-like structure, 201–2
    mathematical analysis of, 218
    need for revision of understanding of, 196
    relational theory of, 206–9
    as relationship among actual occasions, 195
    scientific time-space, 198–99
time-space extension, 309
time-space relationship/time-space relation, 137, 155, 163, 198, 211–19, 221–25, 227–29, 254, 259, 308. *See also* space-time relationship/space-time relation
transcendence, 6, 36, 174, 181, 232, 280, 284, 296–97, 299–300, 302–5, 306, 311, 319, 322, 324, 330
transmutation, 133
transphysical dimensions of the waking world, 147, 173, 183
transphysical matter, 165
transphysical process metaphysics. *See also* process metaphysics
    causes in, 110

and conventional process metaphysics, 183
definition of physical world according to, 145
on purpose or aim (final cause) as intrinsic to actual universe, 151
and self-organizing system of actual occasions, 102
transphysical worlds, 14–15, 30–31, 37, 173, 183–87. *See also* mental world; vital world
tsimtsum, 286
twelve links of interdependent origination, 14

U

ultimate, category of the, 314
ultimate generalities, tentative formulations of the, 50
ultimate ordering factor, 138, 176–77, 185, 256–57, 262, 314–15
ultimate units, 100
unconscious, 248
unconscious memory, 258
"Uniformity and Contingency" (Whitehead), 34
unison of becoming, 129, 131
unity
    all-embracing unity, 284
    of the body, 126
    of an occasion, 126
universality, 297, 302, 305, 322
universe
    as self-organizing society of actual occasions, 102
    as a unity, 284
University of Virginia, 2, 39, 252
Upanishads, 285, 315
upper hemisphere, 298, 303–5, 310